T0103663

EXPERIENCING THE LESSONS OF A COURSE IN MIRACLES

Experience the Course Better than Ever!

James R. Laws

Balboa Press books may be ordered through booksellers or by contacting:

Balboa Press
A Division of Hay House
1663 Liberty Drive
Bloomington, IN 47403
www.balboapress.com
1 (877) 407-4847

Printed in the United States of America.

ISBN: 978-1-4525-1677-6 (sc)
ISBN: 978-1-4525-1678-3 (e)

Balboa Press rev. date: 7/28/2014

For my wife Tesha Fortune Laws –
Thank you for all your laughter and your love.

DEDICATION

I dedicate this book to my pen pal, teacher and friend, Ken Wapnick.

Ken was instrumental in helping Helen Schucman and William Thetford get the first edition of *A Course in Miracles* published in 1976. Since then, he has dedicated his life to learning, teaching and living this powerful spiritual teaching. I'm sure there are many other Course students in the world who will agree with what I'll say here to Ken: "Thank you Ken for all your help. You are the best!"

Ken was also instrumental in me writing this book.

Ever since I went to my first workshop with Ken in Temecula, California in the Spring of 2011, I loved this man. He demonstrated to me what an advanced student of ACIM should be – He was one of the happiest people I had ever met. Add to that his ability to teach during those multiple day classes all aspects of the Course and very significantly add to my understanding of it all - I was hooked on this wonderful man.

Personally, he encouraged me to write books pertaining to *A Course in Miracles.* Since that first time I met Ken, we have become pen pals with many letters going back and forth between California and Florida where I live. It's been great fun with underlying spiritual teachings beneath our written words. A while back, Ken gave me a homework assignment to help me with a person in my life who had been publicly ridiculing me in front of my friends. After delving deeper into the text of ACIM as instructed by Ken, I sent my completed homework assignment to him. Ken never told me but I like to think I got an A or an A+ on that homework – Ha! Ha! Ha!

If you like this book, please give Ken a lot of the credit because it's Ken's influence on me which prompted me to write it. If you don't like it, then just practice your forgiveness lessons from the Course.

Editor's note: Ken Wapnick passed on December 27, 2013. He will be missed!

INTRODUCTION

"Any situation must be to you a chance to teach others what you are, and what they are to you. No more than that, but also never less." (M-Introduction.2:10,11) This book is a situation for me, giving me an opportunity to teach those who read it who I am and what they are to me. In a nutshell, we are all travelers and our purpose is to save each other from this crazy dream we think we're in which we call the world. One of the key teachings from *A Course in Miracles* is that "every other person in the world is my savior" so thank you one and all, whether you read this book or not.

This book is not a substitute for the Workbook from *A Course in Miracles*. My general suggestion is that anyone interested in ACIM read the Text and the Manual for Teachers and do the 365 lessons from the Workbook for Students – at least once - before they spend time on this book. On the other hand, individuals who have not yet read the Course and done the lessons may find this book helpful in getting an idea of what the Course is all about.

A primary purpose of this book is to encourage individuals to dedicate study time to this wonderful Course so their happiness level keeps improving. After spending considerable time nearly every day to this study for over 15 years, this has been my own experience.

For all students of the Course, I believe this book will add new insight into the Course and therefore enhance their own study efforts. If you have completed the 3 Course books, I believe you will find this book an easy read and I hope enjoyable as well as useful.

There is no attempt in this book to explain each aspect of each lesson. To do so would require a book far longer than this book. For that type of study, I recommend Ken Wapnick's 7 volume publication entitled

Journey through the Workbook of A Course in Miracles which can be purchased from the Foundation for A Course in Miracles.

One of the fundamental ideas from the Course is that while we are in this world, there are two different voices we can follow with respect to every decision we make in our mind – the ego or the Voice of God. The Voice of God can be from either Jesus or the Holy Spirit. Whether the Voice is from Jesus or the Holy Spirit doesn't matter in that the guidance we receive will be the same. I personally like the idea that the Voice is from Jesus because Jesus, like me, was at one point a person in this world so I can readily identify with him. I've learned that many other Course students think along these same lines. For this reason, you will note that I nearly always combine Jesus and the Holy Spirit as "Jesus/Holy Spirit" or "Holy Spirit/Jesus". This may be confusing to those students who think of Jesus and the Holy Spirit as being two Spirits with two different Voices and perhaps having two different roles to play in our awakening. However, my purpose is not to confuse anyone but to both share my understanding and to simplify.

Naturally within this book I often include quotes from *A Course in Miracles.* I also sometimes include my own comments within these quotes. My comments are always contained within a set of brackets; i.e., [my comments].

The quotations from *A Course in Miracles* are from the combined volume (third edition) copyrighted 2007 by the Foundation for *A Course in Miracles.* They are referenced by the following system:

P – Preface

T- Text

W – Workbook for Students

M – Manual for Teachers (including Clarification of Terms)

Psychotherapy – *Psychotherapy: Purpose, Process and Practice* (24 page supplement to the Course)

Song – *The Song of Prayer* (22 page supplement to the Course)

Examples of this referencing system follow:

"There is no world. This is the central thought the course attempts to teach." (W-132.6:2,3)
Workbook for Students, Lesson 132, paragraph 6, sentences 2 and 3.

"The world I see offers nothing that I want." (W-128.title)
Workbook for Students, Lesson 128, the title of the lesson.

"The 'chosen ones' are merely those who choose right sooner." (T-3.IV.7:14)
Text, Chapter 3, Section IV, paragraph 7, sentence 14.

"Nothing real can be threatened." (T-Introduction.2:2)
Text, Introduction (1st page of the Text), paragraph 2, sentence 2.

"Prayer now must be the means by which God's Son leaves separate goals and separate interests by, and turns in holy gladness to the truth of union in his Father and himself." (Song-1.Introduction.2:4)
The Song of Prayer, Chapter 1, Introduction, paragraph 2, sentence 4.

"God's Son is crucified until you walk the road with me [Jesus]." (W-Review V.Introduction.6:6)
Workbook for Students, Review V, Introduction, paragraph 6, sentence 6.

Note: The Workbook for Students contains 6 sets of Review lessons which review lessons previously studied.

Each of these reviews begins with an Introduction section of one or more pages. These Introduction sections can be found by referencing the following list:

Review I –	Immediately following Workbook Lesson 50.
Review II –	Immediately following Workbook Lesson 80.
Review III –	Immediately following Workbook Lesson 110.
Review IV –	Immediately following Workbook Lesson 140.
Review V –	Immediately following Workbook Lesson 170.
Review VI –	Immediately following Workbook Lesson 200.

"Forgiveness recognizes what you thought your brother did to you has not occurred." (W-Q-1.1:1)
Workbook for Students, Question 1, paragraph 1, sentence 1.

Note: The latter part of the Workbook for Students includes 14 important questions and answers. These 14 questions and answers can be found by referencing the following list:

1. What Is Forgiveness? Located after Lesson 220.
2. What Is Salvation? Located after Lesson 230.
3. What Is the World? Located after Lesson 240.
4. What Is Sin? Located after Lesson 250.
5. What Is the Body? Located after Lesson 260.
6. What Is the Christ? Located after Lesson 270.
7. What Is the Holy Spirit? Located after Lesson 280.
8. What Is the Real World? Located after Lesson 290.

9. What Is the Second Coming? Located after Lesson 300.
10. What Is the Last Judgment? Located after Lesson 310.
11. What Is Creation? Located after Lesson 320.
12. What Is the Ego? Located after Lesson 330.
13. What Is a Miracle? Located after Lesson 340.
14. What Am I? Located after Lesson 350.

"It is His [the Holy Spirit's] way that everyone must travel in the end, because it is this ending God Himself appointed." (W-Final Lessons.Introduction.2:2)
Workbook for Students, Final Lessons text (found after Lesson 360), Introduction, paragraph 2, sentence 2.

* * * * * * * * * * * * *

I hope all who read this book enjoy it at least half as much as I have enjoyed writing it.

Jimmy Laws

CONTENTS

Lesson 1 – Nothing I see in this room [on this street, from this window, in this place] means anything.

Today, I think of the world as follows: The world comes from me, not at me. The world, as I now see it, is just a crazy dream that I made up. It's never been real, is not real now, and it will never be real.

The world is an insane make believe place. Insanity, by definition, cannot be understood and there is no meaning in it. This is why nothing I see in this world means anything.

Lesson 2 – I have given everything I see in this room [on this street, from this window, in this place] all the meaning it has for me.

Everybody born into this world initially believes it is real. It is only through disciplined study of ACIM that my perception of the world has changed dramatically.

The world is simply a dream. Since those of us stuck in this dream have different opinions, different lifestyles, different ideas of what's important, etc., the world is different for every individual here. For example, I'm typing this book on a laptop computer which is quite important to me whereas, for many people, a laptop computer is not important at all. Such differences help to keep the perceived separation intact and the illusionary world going.

Lesson 3 – I do not understand anything I see in this room [on this street, from this window, in this place].

Periodically, in the text of ACIM, Jesus makes reference to our "sleeping dreams" and our "waking dreams." He effectively states that, until we start awakening to the truth, all our time is spent dreaming.

Although I've experienced some crazy times in my life, my own experience has been that my sleeping dreams have been crazier (i.e., more insane) than my life's experiences. The truth is that we are all in Heaven, dreaming up these lives perceiving our bodies as the "hero of our individual dream." The truth (Heaven) is not insane. The world we think we live in is insane. Insanity is not understandable which is why "I do not (and cannot) understand anything I see in this room."

Lesson 4 – These thoughts do not mean anything. They are like the things I see in this room [on this street, from this window, in this place.]

It can be said that God's greatest gift is the place we're at when we have 100% peace of mind. When I'm in this place, my mind is not thinking any specific thoughts. I'm totally at peace with no thinking or concern about anything in the world – past, present or future. The feeling I have is one of deep contentment, peace, and bliss. During such times, I'm not "thinking" as the world defines it – I'm just "being." This is as close as I've come to remembering Heaven which this insane world can never touch.

From the ego's standpoint, the purpose of worldly thoughts is to keep the ego's survival going which also means to keep our thoughts of separation alive. Over the years that I've been studying ACIM, I've been obeying the ego's voice less and less and adhering to God's Voice (i.e., the Voice of the Holy Spirit/Jesus) on an increasing basis. In other words, I've been making spiritual progress.

Once again, the world is an insane illusionary place. Worldly thoughts are therefore insane thoughts. Such thoughts can't mean anything simply because they are insane.

Lesson 5 – I am never upset for the reason I think.

After many years of continuous study of ACIM, I still sometimes get upset, generally at other people. However, such upsets are, over time, decreasing and their intensity is generally much lower than they were even just a couple of years ago.

Despite the common sense of ACIM and my diligent study of the material, it is not easy for me to always remember that this world is simply a dream and should not be taken seriously. I can even hold on to an "upset" for a day or more before I remember that the world is my dream and, when I get angry (which is my most common "upset"), I am getting angry only at myself. This ties in with ACIM's definition of forgiveness which means "there is nothing to forgive" because the world is just an illusion or a dream which I made up.

As I sit here now, it is clear to me that when I become upset at any level it is because I have once again forgotten this simple and logical definition of forgiveness.

Lesson 6 – I am upset because I see something that is not there.

"There is no world! This is the central thought the course [ACIM] attempts to teach." (W-132.6:2,3)

In the above two sentences, Jesus stresses the importance of the fact that the world we think we're living in is not real. It is a dream, an illusion, a grand hallucination.

When I am fully awake in Heaven, I'm convinced that I will never get upset. Eternal joy, bliss and happiness will be my ongoing experience. The dream world I think I'm in now will be either totally forgotten or, if remembered, I'll think "Wow! That was some bizarre nightmare I had. I'm sure glad I'm awake now."

However, I'm not there yet. As of this writing, I'm still at times stuck in my dream. How do I know this? Because I still get upset sometimes though, as I indicated above, my upsets are both less intense and less frequent than they used to be. All my upsets, of course, have something to do with my individual life here in the dream.

If I stop hearing the ego's voice, I can't get disturbed. Jesus tells us in ACIM that it is possible to accomplish this: "The Holy Spirit is in you in a very literal sense. His is the Voice that calls you back to where you were before and will be again [Heaven]. It is possible even in this world to hear only that Voice and no other. It takes effort and great willingness to learn. It is the final lesson that I learned, and God's Sons are as equal as learners as they are as Sons." (T-5.II.3:7-11) It is important to note that Jesus is pointing out here that we are inherently no different than he – If he could hear only the Holy Spirit's Voice then we too can accomplish this. What makes Jesus important is that he was the first individual in history to accomplish this and is therefore in charge of helping all of us to accomplish this same discipline.

Until I totally stop hearing the ego's voice, I'll get disturbed from time to time at something in the world even though it's not real (i.e., it's just a dream).

Lesson 7 – I see only the past.

Certainly, when I believed the world was real, before I started understanding what ACIM was teaching, I saw only the past. Why would one even think to look elsewhere for answers to anything?

Now I have a much better understanding that my goal is to see only the "eternal now". Jesus points out in ACIM that this goal must be accomplished while our bodies are "alive." The religious idea that after I "die" I'll awaken in eternal Heaven is a myth that doesn't work.

Lesson 8 – My mind is preoccupied with past thoughts.

In my discussion for Lesson 7, above, I made reference to the "eternal now". In this Lesson 8, Jesus uses the word "present" to mean the same thing: "Your mind cannot grasp the present, which is the only time there is. It therefore cannot understand time, and cannot, in fact, understand anything." (W-8.1:5,6)

Understanding once again that the whole world is but a dream and is not real is a powerful tool to recognizing that time, too, is simply an illusion which is necessary to make the dream appear real. When we wake up from this dream, we'll be in a joyful state of mind with no concerns whatsoever and know that we will never have to be concerned for the rest of eternity. Time will no longer have any meaning.

Meanwhile, however, the dream world continues to hold some temptations for us and we therefore have some concerns (which is another word for "fears"). This is as it should be because the Holy Spirit gently wakes us up over a period of time. Jesus points out in his Course that if we were to wake up all at once our whole belief system would be shattered and it would frighten us way too much. Therefore, waking up from the dream world does take some time.

Of course, the vast majority of people you know and meet (like 99.9%) all believe their future will be a repetition of the past and, in the end, they'll die. Do not, as a rule, try and teach the people you meet that their lives here are quite meaningless. Of course, if your Inner Voice (my terminology for the Voice of the Holy Spirit/Jesus) suggests you plant seeds of truth in someone's mind by all means do so.

Lesson 9 – I see nothing as it is now.

This is another lesson for learning that time is just an illusion.

To see the "eternal now" means that this world is seen as nothing but a smokescreen with no reality whatsoever regardless of what's happening to your individual self. When one has reached this level of spirituality, ACIM refers to it as attaining the "real world."

A wonderful example is Jesus earthly life. Clearly, in the last years of his life, he had attained this "real world" status and he was the first person ever to have accomplished this. During these years, Jesus saw the world as just a wispy dream so that his execution on the cross, which the world has made so significant, was not important to him. It was just the end of his personal dream.

What was of real importance to those stuck in the dream at the time (and to so many others since then) was when he returned two days after he appeared to have "died". This witness was proof within this dream that there is no death.

Lesson 10 – My thoughts do not mean anything.

Worldly thoughts do not mean anything because the world is insane and, once again, by definition insane thoughts do not have any meaning.

Please note that our Father God has not followed us into this gigantic insane asylum we call the world. However, He created the Great Psychiatrist, the Holy Spirit, to guarantee we would all be returned to sanity. The first patient who was fully returned to sanity we know as Jesus. All the rest of us will follow in time.

Lesson 11 – My meaningless thoughts are showing me a meaningless world.

One of my favorite lessons is: "I am affected only by my thoughts." (W-338.title) Common sense tells me this is 100% true. Everything I say is preceded by my thought of saying it. Everything I do is preceded by my thought of doing it. And, of course, if I'm not doing or saying anything, but just "thinking", my thoughts are affected by my thoughts.

When I "knew" the world was real, naturally I looked for meaning in it and tried different ways to be happy in it.

Now I know the world is just a dream and not real. It was made to keep me from remembering I am "One with God". No meaning can be found in worldly thinking because, once again, it is all insane.

Lesson 12 – I am upset because I see a meaningless world.

In this lesson Jesus states: "The world is meaningless in itself." (W-12.1:4) Once I began to accept this fact, I stopped searching for meaning where none could be found causing my happiness level to increase significantly.

Therefore, if you're still searching for meaning in the world, I suggest you stop trying to accomplish an impossible task. You can't find meaning in a meaningless place. Any attempts to do so will just upset you.

Lesson 13 – A meaningless world engenders fear.

Let's take an example. Joe and Mary are a young married couple with two children who are both in grammar school. Joe's been the sole wage earner and Mary's done a good job of maintaining the home. As a result of increases in gasoline prices and less overtime for Joe, money is tight. As a matter of fact, they've had to cut back on paying some credit card debt and two of their credit card companies have sent them threatening letters. Naturally, Joe's stress and fear levels have increased. His relationship with Mary, which had been very good, is turning sour. Joe's figured out the solution but has not yet shared this with Mary – Mary will have to get a part time job. He's planning to talk to her about it soon but is concerned (fearful) that she's not going to like the idea. In Joe's (fearful) mind, she might even take the children and go live with her parents rather than get a job. Joe's so stressed out over this that he's convinced if she doesn't like his idea he will just blow up in anger.

Note that all of the above fear and anger thoughts are in Joe's mind – He hasn't yet talked to his wife. This is just one little example of how our worldly mind thinks when we believe the world is real.

Thank God the world is only a dream! As we allow God (i.e., Jesus/Holy Spirit) help us to understand this, we stop taking the dream seriously and we become indescribably happy.

Lesson 14 – God did not create a meaningless world.

This, to me, is one of the most important statements in ACIM. Simple logic explains this simple statement. God only creates the eternal just as He is eternal. There is nothing about this world that's eternal – It's all temporary, including the world itself. God only creates the good whereas in this world a lot of bad things happen. God only creates in unity where His creation is One with Him. In this world, with its 7 billion people and trillions of other different things, everyone and everything is separate from the other.

What does this world have to do with God? And the answer is "It has nothing to do with God." He didn't make it or create it. As the title of this lesson states: "God did not create a meaningless world."

The world, once again, is just a dream. It is a figment of our imagination. It is something we will all wake up from and once again know that we're in eternal Heaven and laugh at this crazy world we currently dream we are in.

Jesus states this quite succinctly in the first paragraph of this lesson: "The idea for today is, of course, the reason why a meaningless world is impossible. What God did not create does not exist. And everything that does exist exists as He created it. The world you see has nothing to do with reality. It is of your own making, and it does not exist." (W-14.1:1-5)

Lesson 15 – My thoughts are images I have made.

The world, as I see it, is my dream. It will never be real.

My eyes are a part of the dream and they are not real. Everything my eyes "see" are part of my dream. None of it is real. Before I understood this, my world was one of hope of some happy times but with times of deep despair. And, of course, my life was expected to end in death probably preceded by a period of pain and suffering.

As a result of many years of diligent study of ACIM, my perception of the world has completely changed. Though I have an image here (in the person of Jimmy Laws), I don't believe the world is real at all nor is my body. It is a smokescreen to keep the truth hidden from me. Behind the world's smokescreen is truth or Heaven where we are all One with each other and One with our Father. The ability to see through the world's smokescreen to truth is referred to as vision in ACIM (also often called Christ's vision or the vision of Christ). Naturally, we use our minds for such vision, bypassing anything we "see" with our eyes.

Lesson 16 – I have no neutral thoughts.

The ego's thoughts always brought me to a place of fear and war. They did their best to convince me the world was real and "others were out to get me." They told me to seek out friends and avoid enemies and hold on to the idea that I should "Eat, drink and be merry for tomorrow I may die."

By contrast, the thoughts from the Holy Spirit (or Jesus) always bring me to a place of love and peace. Over time, they have taught me to see through this world of illusions so I can truly see the truth that sets me free (i.e., using Christ's vision). They tell me I have no enemies and there is no death. God created only eternal life so how can death be real?

In a nutshell, the ego's thoughts are bad and God's thoughts are good.

Lesson 17 – I see no neutral things.

This is just a very simple common sense statement. In this world we think we live in, there are no neutral things.

Here's a couple of examples from my own life. When I was 18, my mother died about two months after a terrible car accident. This was certainly not a neutral event for me. When I was 29, my wife, our 1-year old little girl and I moved into a very nice new house in California and we were very happy. This, again, was not a neutral event.

By contrast, today I know that the world is just a dream, or a cloud, that tries to block us from our true Self – We are eternally One with our Creator with joy being the best word to describe our eternal state of mind.

Lesson 18 – I am not alone in experiencing the effects of my seeing.

It is not necessary to complicate this simple lesson. I'll use another example to explain this lesson.

Today, my 3rd wife and I are very happily married and we have a wonderful 6-year old little girl. Our lives are very busy and, as a rule, our house gets cluttered quickly with dirty dishes in the sink most of the time. All 3 of us like this care free living so we are not sticklers for "cleaning up after ourselves."

We often have guests come over and join us for a meal. Before these social occurrences, my wife and I will go about the house and organize and clean-up. However, we don't make a big deal about it. Our reason for organizing the house is we don't want our guests to think that we live in a messy house. Additionally, it's a good feeling for both of us when we get our physical world organized.

You might be asking "What's your point?" Well, the point is if our house looks messy to me then it will look messy to others too so, as this lesson states, "I am not alone in experiencing the effects of my seeing."

Lesson 19 – I am not alone in experiencing the effects of my thoughts.

As I've understood the Course better and better, this lesson takes on a much more powerful meaning and experience. As I use Christ's vision to see someone I'm talking to, I appreciate the person as an eternally innocent spirit, regardless of what their lot in this life is, and I love him or her. My experience, though not shared in words, is felt by them because "I am not alone in experiencing the effects of my thoughts."

Lesson 20 – I am determined to see.

Sometimes the Course is written such that the word see, with no quotes around it, means to see with Christ's vision and the word "see", with quotes, refers to using our eyes to "see".

And so it is in this lesson which can be expanded to "I am determined to see using Christ's vision." Regardless of what I "see" in the world [And since "There is no world!" (W-132.6:2), I am always looking at nothing.], I want to use Christ's vision to see through it to the eternal truth.

You might ask: "Why should I be so determined to accomplish this?" The simple answer from someone who has made significant progress over the years is that you will find yourself getting more and more happy. Giving *A Course in Miracles* ongoing continued and disciplined study time has reduced all my human fears to almost nothing and increased my peace of mind and happiness incredibly.

Lesson 21 – I am determined to see things differently.

This world we think we live in is full of problems. Whether we blame ourselves, other people, Mother Nature, etc., for these problems doesn't matter for purposes of this lesson.

We want peace of mind which is not possible 100% if we're concerned about anything. What this lesson is telling us to do is to simply be determined to see all our problems as well as everything else in the world differently.

Lesson 22 – What I see is a form of vengeance.

If God actually made this world, He certainly wouldn't be a good god. Thank God He didn't make it! Thank God the world isn't real and is just a gigantic dream from which we'll all wake up.

The last part of this lesson makes some valid points regarding this world we "see" with our eyes:

> "I see only the perishable.
> "I see nothing that will last.
> "What I see is not real.
> "What I see is a form of vengeance." (W-22.3:3-6)

Then Jesus tells us to ask ourselves the following question: "Is this the world I really want to see?" (W-22.3:8)

Lesson 23 – I can escape from the world I see by giving up attack thoughts.

As a child, I of course "knew" this world was real as did all of us. The vast majority of people in the world still think this way.

Now, I understand that the ego, which is not real, made up this dream world. In truth, we are all asleep in Heaven dreaming we're in a world separate from each other and separate from God. Once the last of us wakes up, the dream world (the entire realm of time and space and the physical universe) will disappear just as our night time dreams disappear when we wake up in the morning.

Meanwhile, while we're in this dream world, we like to blame almost anything for our lack of 100% happiness. I like to refer to this as the "ego's blame game." In the Course, Jesus often refers to this type of thinking as "attack thoughts." In any event, following are a few examples of such thinking:

> "My parents didn't raise me right."
> "I should have finished college." (This person is attacking himself.)
> "It's God's fault. He made this world and my life." (Which, of course, is a big lie.)
> "My husband expects way too much from me."
> "If my boss paid me what I'm worth, I sure would be happy."
> "Because of alimony to my ex-wife, I can hardly survive."
> [Of course this list could go on and on, ad infinitum.]

Ultimately, as I've experienced the Course better and better over time, I appreciate that (1) When I think I have a problem, I'm wrong – How can I have a problem unless I forget that this world is but a dream? (2) I have only 2 guides in my mind – The ego and the Holy Spirit/Jesus. (I often think of some of the cartoons where the little red devil is telling the cartoon character to do bad things and the white angel is telling him to do good things so my ego guide is the red devil and the Voice of the Holy Spirit/Jesus is the white angel.) In all its simplicity, the Course is teaching me to listen to the Voice of the Holy Spirit/Jesus and not to the ego's voice.

Clearly, to me, this process is not an overnight matter. To not believe in a world which you firmly thought was real most of your life and the vast majority of people in the world still believe is real takes quite a bit of mind training (in my experience). However, it is possible to fully train our minds over time to stop adhering to any worldly thinking whatsoever. As Jesus tells us in the Course, since he did it so can we.

Lesson 24 – I do not perceive my own best interests.

I don't know what's best for me but God certainly does. To me, this is just common sense.

The ego tells me I want money, a loving wife, some good children, a good name, an enjoyable productive job, some good friends, etc. and the list goes on and on.

God tells me "The world I see offers nothing that I want." (W-128.title) This, intellectually, is easy to understand because the world is nothing but a dream. It is nothing so it has nothing to offer.

Temptations are here, however, and they're not that easy to overcome. A simple definition for a "temptation" is the idea that the world has something that I really want.

As I've worked to hear God's Voice more, and therefore the ego's voice less, I appreciate that the gift's of God for me can be summed up as "peace of mind", "happiness" and the "ability to help carry God's true message to other people."

Lesson 25 – I do not know what anything is for.

Let's keep in mind that the entire world and physical universe was made up by our ego minds to try and maintain our separation from each other and our separation from God. This thing we believe is our life and all its surroundings is one massive insane asylum. Everything about it is insane. So simply accept this lesson as written: "I do not know what anything is for." The reason is that insanity is not understandable.

Now for the good news. As Jesus states numerous times in ACIM, the Holy Spirit will take everything the ego made and use it to help us unremember this world and remember our Source, our Home, Heaven, or whatever term you prefer for who we are… eternal, joyful extensions of God, our Creator.

Here's a little side note. God truly has no favorites. The Holy Spirit speaks to all of us all the time. To be blessed by God means simply to listen for the Holy Spirit's Voice, not necessarily an easy task in this insane, chaotic world. Those who choose to listen, and this does take a lot of mind training, do become happier and happier …. They are blessed. Jesus sums these thoughts up at one point in ACIM by stating: "All are called but only a few choose to listen." (T-3.IV.7:12) He follows this up with: "The 'chosen ones' are merely those who choose right sooner." (T-3.IV.7:14) Eventually, we'll all choose right and wake up at Home in Heaven.

Lesson 26 – My attack thoughts are attacking my invulnerability.

There are a number of ways to consider the honesty of this statement.

"I am as God created me." (W-94.title, W-110.title, W-162.title) He created me eternally innocent with ongoing peace and happiness now and forever. This is who I am still and so are you. We are invulnerable forever. When I have attack thoughts, it's because there's something in the world that I believe is real, I want it and I'm not getting it. So I've made a mistake and I need to forgive myself for forgetting the world is just a dream and should not be taken seriously. The world has nothing to do with who I am.

As Jesus states in this lesson: "The idea for today introduces the thought that you always attack yourself first." (W-26.3:1) Jesus tells us this often throughout ACIM. One simple way to understand this is to once again believe and understand that the world I think I'm in is "my dream", coming from my mind and is not at all real. Therefore, when I attack anything in the world, I'm always attacking me first since it's all coming from my mind. (Your world, or your dream, may be similar to mine in many respects but we'll have different opinions about many aspects of our dreams.)

Lesson 27 – Above all else I want to see.

As for me, I'm hooked on A Course in Miracles. Although I'm not yet home free in that sometimes I get disturbed by people or events in this world, my level of happiness has increased incredibly since I started studying the Course about 15 years ago.

What this lesson is asking us is to have a desire, above everything else, to see using Christ's vision and not giving any credence to what we "see" with our eyes in the world. As we students move in this direction, we get more and more happy. For instance, the unhappy thought of death has become meaningless to me since I know that death doesn't exist.

Sacrifice, which is an unhappy thought, is not from God and is not really a part of my life today. When I do something for me or anyone else here in my dream, nobody loses; everybody is a winner. Jesus makes this point periodically in the Text of ACIM that if, within the dream we think we're in, we're being God directed then there are no losers, only winners. Sacrifice is never a God idea; it comes from our insane ego directed minds.

It is only through my study of ACIM that I'm learning how to see with Christ's vision and experiencing the benefits (blessings) of a spiritual life. So, if the Course hasn't accomplished for you what it has for me, I suggest you keep at it and perhaps put more individual time and effort into it.

Lesson 28 – Above all else I want to see things differently.

This lesson could be written: "Above all else I want to see all things differently. What Jesus is saying here is that what we see with our eyes we want to start seeing using Christ's vision.

The world is an illusion and everything in the world is an illusion. An illusion is an illusion is an illusion, etc. No illusion is real and so every illusion is the same. They are all nothing. Everything I see with my eyes is nothing.

In this lesson, Jesus uses the example of a table as what we want to see differently. As the mind training of ACIM helps me to overcome the ego's hold on me which takes time, I should be able to think: "Beyond this table there is a world I want." This thought comes from Lesson 129 which reads: "Beyond this world there is a world I want."

Although I still use my body like everyone else, as I use Christ's vision on an increasing basis, this dream world becomes a real happy place for me to be in and help others as I'm guided to do by Jesus.

Lesson 29 – God is in everything I see.

In paragraph 5 of this lesson, Jesus gives us some examples for practicing this lesson: "Your list of subjects should therefore be as free of self-selection as possible. For example, a suitable list might include:

> "God is in this coat hanger.
> "God is in this magazine.
> "God is in this finger.
> "God is in this lamp.
> "God is in that body.
> "God is in that door.
> "God is in that waste basket."
> (W-29.5:1-9)

This lesson should not be taken literally. Why? Because as Jesus tells us repeatedly that everything we see with our eyes is an illusion, is not real, and does not exist at all. How can God be in something that doesn't even exist?

Using the coat hanger as an example, one way I think of this is: "God is on the other side of this coat hanger." Another way is: "Beyond this coat hanger there is a world I want." (This idea is from Lesson 129: "Beyond this world there is a world I want.")

I really like the promise Jesus gives us in this lesson: "When [Christ's] vision has shown you the holiness that lights up the world, you will understand today's idea perfectly. And you will not understand how you could ever have found it difficult." (W-29.3:6,7)

Lesson 30 – God is in everything I see because God is in my mind.

To clarify this lesson, I'll expand it a little as follows: "God is in everything I see and think because God is in my mind." You can note that Jesus tells us to do exactly this in our practicing of this lesson: "To help you begin to get used to this idea, try to think of things beyond your present range as well as those you can actually see, as you apply today's idea." (W-30.4:2)

This is a very important lesson. As Jesus tells us in the first paragraph: "The idea for today is the springboard for vision. From this idea will the world open up before you, and you will look upon it and see in it what you have never seen before. Nor will what you saw before be even faintly visible to you." (W-30.1:1-3)

One of the fundamental ideas of ACIM is that the world I've been living in here on earth is a world that was made up by me in my mind 100%. The world always comes from me and never at me. With this understanding, what this lesson tells us to do as best we can is join with everything we see (and think) rather than treating everything as separate from us which, of course, is how the world sees and thinks. This is described by Jesus in the second paragraph of this lesson: "Today we are trying to use a new kind of 'projection.' We are not attempting to get rid of what we do not like by seeing it outside. Instead, we are trying to see in the world what is in our minds, and what we want to recognize is there. Thus, we are trying to join with what we see [or think], rather than keeping it apart from us. That is the fundamental difference between vision and the way you see." (W-30.2:1-5)

The idea that Heaven is the One Mindedness of God and His Creation is not a difficult concept. There are no things, no forms, and no individuals in Heaven because all is One and all is pure Spirit (or Mind) and all is Love, eternal and extending outward forever. Jesus tells us this many times in ACIM. If this makes sense to you, then you can see how important this lesson is because it asks us to mentally join with everything that we always thought (or "knew") was separate. It totally turns around worldly thinking.

Lesson 31 – I am not the victim of the world I see.

"There is no world." (W-132.6:2) How can I be the victim of something that doesn't even exist?

To the extent I still sometimes get caught up in the world (i.e., I forget it's my dream) and so I get irritated or angry, I can reflect on the following thoughts. The world is a dream coming from my mind and, though I know it's not real today, for many years I "knew" it was real. Since I'm the sole maker of my world, when I get angry at any aspect of it, I'm obviously getting angry at myself. Therefore, the cliché which goes "I'm my own worst enemy" can be accurately stated as "I'm my only enemy."

In all its ultimate simplicity, Jesus points out in ACIM that it's all an inside job for each of us. All our problems or issues come from our ego minds and within our minds is also the solution – God's Voice (the Holy Spirit/Jesus). We must simply stop listening to the voice of the ego and listen only to God's Voice. This is simple but not easy. It takes time but, as Jesus points out, it will happen for all of us. Thank God!

Lesson 32 – I have invented the world I see.

The world I see is coming from my mind. It is a figment of my imagination. Or, as Jesus states here: "I have invented the world I see." God did not make or create it so let's not be blaming Him for anything bad that happens in the world.

It is clear, by the way, that when Jesus was young, he thought the world was real. However, sometime prior to his execution on the cross (and I expect before he asked John to baptize him) he stopped listening to the ego voice in his mind and only listened to the Voice of the Holy Spirit. He was the first person in the world to accomplish this. What he's done for us now is to give us this ACIM book which is an instructional manual wherein we can accomplish this also. Thank you Jesus!

Following is the first paragraph from this lesson: "Today we are continuing to develop the theme of cause and effect. You are not the victim of the world you see because you invented it. You can give it up as easily as you made it up. You will see it or not see it, as you wish. While you want it you will see it; when you no longer want it, it will not be there for you to see." (W-32.1:1-5) Although the world offers many temptations which can remain very attractive, Jesus makes it clear that there is nothing in the world that remotely compares to Heaven. To help us appreciate this fact and eliminate any worldly temptations, he includes another lesson which reads: "The world I see holds nothing that I want." (W-128.title; underscore mine)

Lesson 33 – There is another way of looking at the world.

One of the most enjoyable ways I look at the world today is like a massive cartoon. There are about 7 billion characters in this cartoon and all of us have our own "issues."

Some of us are grumpy and some of us are happy; many of us are grumpy some of the time and happy some of the time.

Some are old and some are young. Some of the old ones act young and some of the young ones act old (i.e., they are serious).

Some are ugly and some are pretty or handsome. Some are fat and some are skinny. Some are real tall and some are real short.

Some dye their hair in weird colors. Some have tattoos on their skin and some have earrings on parts of their body other than their ears.

Some are male and some are female. Those who have passed puberty all have sex issues.

In my mind today, the world is a very funny place and taken way too seriously by most persons in this gigantic cartoon.

Especially when we're getting serious, we can say thank God it's not real! "There is no world!" (W-132.6:2) There never was except in our dreams. We all just have to be open minded and wake up to this fact. And we all will because our eternal peaceful and joyous life is what God gave us when He created us and "We are as God created us." (As Lessons 94, 110 and 162 state: "I am as God created me.")

Lesson 34 – I could see peace instead of this.

This is a simple enough exercise. All Jesus asks us to do is review our minds for any disturbing thoughts and then say to ourselves: "I could see peace instead of this."

The best thing I can say to someone new to the disciplined study of ACIM is: "You <u>will</u> see peace instead of what you're seeing now." My own experience has been a miraculous increase in my peace of mind since I started studying this wonderful book. Most things that used to upset me or cause me worry generally have no effect on my peace of mind anymore. Sometimes I still get upset at someone or something. These are mistakes and with the help of my Inner Voice (Holy Spirit/ Jesus), I'm able to see where my thinking went awry (i.e., where the ego caught me in one of his traps). Occasionally, I'll ask for help from one or more spiritually minded friends which has proved a powerful tool to my continued spiritual progress.

Lesson 35 – My mind is part of God's. I am very holy.

As a rule, when we first start out in ACIM, our minds are filled with all sorts of worldly thoughts. As Jesus points out in this lesson, it doesn't matter whether our thoughts about ourselves are good or bad. This is because all worldly thoughts are meaningless because the world doesn't exist.

Consider two different people – One is a professional thief who has killed a number of people in his life and he's very mean spirited. The other is a missionary who has devoted his life to helping persons in impoverished lands to learn about Jesus and he's got a wonderful happy spirit. The truth of this lesson holds for both these individuals. In both cases, their minds are part of God's and they are very holy.

This example may not make any sense to you but remember what Jesus continues to tell us in his Course which is that this world is but a dream.

It never happened and it's not happening now. God created all of us as an extension of Him – eternal, joyous, and peaceful and this is who we are now. We are simply asleep in Heaven dreaming up these different lives which most people believe they were born into and must die some day.

As this lesson, over time, makes more sense to you, you can of course think about anyone and say: "Your mind is part of God's. You are very holy." This might help you concerning individuals you have resentments against. (Note: In ACIM, Jesus uses the term grievances rather than resentments. In this book, they mean the same thing.)

Lesson 36 – My holiness envelops everything I see.

It's been my experience as I've studied ACIM that over time Christ's vision has become clearer to me. My eyesight, however, has not been reduced. As a matter of fact, my observation skills in the world have generally increased.

Jesus clearly states many times in ACIM that when we're fully awake in Heaven, God and His Creations have only one Mind or, if you prefer, there is only one Love. This is because when He created us, God gave us everything He had without exception so we effectively became part of Him. As Jesus states in the Course, the only difference between God and us is that He created us and we did not create Him.

In Heaven, there are no bodies nor forms but only wonderful eternal content which is Love. God is Love and we are part of Him.

My holiness is linked to my ability to think of this world as filled with shadow figures (a term Jesus uses in ACIM) and shadow forms, none of which are real, and see through them to Heaven, using Christ's vision, while listening for God's Voice especially if I'm getting disturbed by anything. God and His Creations, which are one Mind, is all there is so it must envelop everything we see.

Lesson 37 – My holiness blesses the world.

I often sincerely thank Jesus for his ACIM book. Often in his book, Jesus points out that he is available to us all the time and I find tremendous comfort in this fact.

As with all successful ACIM students I've become a much happier person as a result of the changes in my mind linked directly to my ACIM studies. Most persons in my life see me as a very happy person.

With respect to this lesson, I have modified it slightly for me as follows: "Our happy holiness blesses the world." The "Our" means "Jesus and me". You can note I've also added the adjective "happy" to holiness. Since one of God's greatest gifts is our happiness, when I'm not happy, I can't be very holy. (There are quite a few religious people who consider themselves very holy but they're virtually never happy. I'm glad I'm not in their boat.)

Lesson 38 – There is nothing my holiness cannot do.

As author of this book, I must admit to you again that I still fall into some of the ego traps sometimes. Although I have made significant spiritual progress, I have not as yet attained what I refer to as the "Jesus level of spirituality". As Jesus points out in the Course, he was able to stop hearing the ego altogether and listened only to God's Voice, the Voice of the Holy Spirit.

In this lesson, Jesus points out that: "Your holiness, then, can remove all pain, can end all sorrow, and can solve all problems. It can do so in connection with yourself and with anyone else. It is equal in its power to help anyone because it is equal in its power to save anyone." (W-38.2:4-6) The Bible includes a number of examples where Jesus healed individuals of physical and emotional ailments and raised persons from the dead (Lazarus being the most famous). In other words, Jesus actually accomplished what he says we can accomplish.

My understanding is that there have been very few individuals since Jesus who have been able to stop listening to the ego altogether. There have been a few, however. With his ACIM book now available, I'm sure the number will increase in the future.

Please don't believe that you will be able to manifest money or a new car or... God knows what other earthly things people pray for. Remember the world and all things in it don't exist; it is foolish to ask God for something that doesn't exist. In this regard, it is my understanding that the story about Jesus feeding the multitudes with fish and bread (out of thin air) never happened. It is a Biblical myth.

Lesson 39 – My holiness is my salvation.

Jesus, in this lesson, helps me to learn that I am forgiven. I can't be holy, after all, if I'm guilty at any level. My holiness can't bless the world (Lesson 37) if I think of myself as a sinner.

How simple is ACIM once it is understood? The answer is it is very simple. As a matter of fact, the entire Course is summed up on the first page of the Text (in the Introduction) where Jesus States:

> "Nothing real can be threatened.
> "Nothing unreal exists." (T-introduction.2:2,3)

"There is no world! This is the central thought the course attempts to teach." (W-132.6:2,3)

When I "knew" the world was real, there were some things I did in this world that would be considered unforgiveable. I was a miserable sinner at times in this life. Many persons appeared to be much less sinful than me but there were also a lot who were more sinful than me.

After many years of studying the Course, I fully appreciate that the world doesn't exist today (it's just a dream), it didn't exist in the past and it won't exist in the future. So my sins of the past never happened except as a bad part of my overall dream; a nightmare part. Dreams, however, are not real so I need not be concerned about them. In other words, "Nothing unreal exists." (T-introduction.2:3)

Meanwhile, my holiness has continued unabated even though I've forgotten it because of this dream I've been in. As Jesus often points out in his Course, just because we can't remember something doesn't mean it's lost. As a matter of fact, he assures us in ACIM that everyone will eventually wake up from their dreams and remember again who they are, an eternal innocent spirit and one with our wonderful Heavenly Father. This reality can't change nor even be threatened. "Nothing real can be threatened." (T-introduction.2:2)

Lesson 40 – I am blessed as a Son of God.

When I first read through the text of ACIM many years ago, I knew that this book was for me. I read through it quite quickly and did not get bogged down in the many parts which I didn't understand.

Since then, I've learned that ACIM's approach to salvation is definitely for me. I have been blessed by this book and my study of it. My happiness has increased beyond words and I have every reason to believe that ever increasing happiness will be my future in this lifetime. Therefore, I can truly say "I am blessed as a Son of God."

It is very important for all students of ACIM to appreciate that the study of this book is not the answer for all people. It is one avenue, among thousands, for individuals to fully awaken from their dream world and be wide awake once again in Heaven. While I sometimes encourage other persons to take a look at ACIM, I don't preach to them about it. Jesus says this specifically in the Manual for Teachers: "This is a manual for a special curriculum, intended for teachers of a special form of the universal course. There are many thousands of other forms, all with the same outcome." (M-1.4:1,2)

Lesson 41 – God goes with me wherever I go.

"Depression is an inevitable consequence of separation. So are anxiety, worry, a deep sense of helplessness, misery, suffering and intense fear of loss." (W-41.1:2,3) During my lifetime, I have known all of these negative feelings as well as anger and rage. However, it's been quite a few years since I've experienced any of these at any significant level. I attribute this to my experiencing ACIM at ever deeper levels.

"Deep within you is everything that is perfect, ready to radiate through you and out into the world. It will cure all sorrow and pain and fear and loss because it will heal the mind that thought these things were real, and suffered out of its allegiance to them." (W-41.3:1,2) The "everything that is perfect" which is deep within me is God. Hence, "God goes with me wherever I go."

Therefore, the solution to my problems, God, is with me all the time. What Jesus tells us in ACIM is that the problems I think I have which can cause me all sorts of negative feelings are not coming from an outside world. The world I think is causing me all my problems was actually made up by my mind. For instance, in Lesson 32, Jesus tells me: "I have invented the world I see."

So all my worldly problems were invented by my mind and the solution to my problems, God, is also within my mind. The Great Psychiatrist, the Holy Spirit, is that part of God Who is within our minds to make sure we all start thinking properly again and ultimately wake up at Home in Heaven.

Lesson 42 – God is my strength. Vision is His gift.

God created me like Himself and as an extension of Himself, giving me everything He has – eternal peace and happiness. So naturally He is my strength. This all happened long before this world appeared when we were all at Home in Heaven. However, sometime after our wonderful beginning, like everyone here, I grabbed hold of a tiny mad idea and took it seriously which effectively said: "Let's separate from God and try life on our own."

Well, God never left us and, in truth, we never left Him. What God had joined together forever, Himself and His Creation, could not possibly be separated. However, in the sick part of our mind (the ego part) we thought we separated and went into a deep sleep (a coma like state). God, seeing what happened immediately created the Holy Spirit to gently wake us up from our deep sleep. We're in that deep sleep now or we wouldn't think we're still here.

A major part of this dream, of course, is that we think we are a body which was born here and will die here. We strive for happy days but our lives are punctured with sadness and sometimes tragedy. We always, of course, end up dying in our dream life.

Vision is seeing through the eyes of God. It has nothing to do with our physical eyes or any of our other four sensory organs. It's seeing right through worldly appearances to the truth. When I look at my best friend and my worst enemy with vision, they are exactly the same – they are eternal innocent joyous spiritual beings. There is no judgment here, only truth which really sets me (and them) free.

Lesson 43 – God is my source. I cannot see apart from Him.

We start out in this world in a body and we, of course, think the world is real. This happened because we had made a decision to separate from God although we have no recollection of this.

What we learn from ACIM is that the world is not real and our "all important" individual bodies are also not real nor any apart of them. Our eyes, ears, tongue, etc. are all a part of a dream that we made up after we decided to do the impossible which was to separate ourselves from God.

The truth is that God created us and clearly "He is our source." Although I think I "see" with my eyes, this is not seeing but "image making" which is a term Jesus uses as what we do with our physical eyes. We made up this dream world from the ego part of our minds but we all initially believe the world made us; that is, that our lives began when we were physically conceived or the day we were born into the world. The power of our minds is truly incredible. The ego (i.e., the insane) part of our mind has made up all of time and the physical universe (including the billions of stars in the sky). My perception of all this is coming from my mind and doesn't really exist. Wow! What a powerful mind I have! And so do you because your mind has been doing the same thing.

Now the things this incredibly powerful mind has accomplished, which I've touched on in the previous paragraph, has all been done by the deluded part of our mind. Obviously, our God (or spirit) part of our mind is even more powerful.

The second sentence in this lesson is "I cannot see apart from Him (God)." The word "see", here, of course has nothing to do with the use of the physical eyes. With the help of the Holy Spirit, we will all eventually see right through all our dreams (fully knowing they're all just a smokescreen) into the Mind of God of which we are all a part. The term Jesus uses for this ability to see truly is "Christ's vision."

Lesson 44 – God is the light in which I see.

It is important to know that the ego made the world so that we would not be able to see God's light. Not that the ego understands anything about God's light. As Jesus describes it, the ego is aware of some presence outside itself and believes correctly that this presence can put the ego out of business. The ego's days were numbered the instant we started believing it because that was when God created the Holy Spirit to ensure we would all wake up from our dreams here in the world.

In effect, then, "The world is the darkness in which I can't see." With the help of the Holy Spirit (and Jesus), we are all wakened from our worldly dreams over a period of time until we're fully awake again in God (Heaven).

Lesson 45 – God is the Mind with which I think.

There is another lesson which states: "I am affected only by my thoughts." (W-338.title) Even in this world, this is simple common sense. Everything I think, say or do is based on my thinking. Therefore, my thinking is all important.

Within our minds, we can follow one of two guides, the voice of the ego or the Voice of the Holy Spirit/Jesus. What Jesus effectively says many times in ACIM is that when we follow the ego's voice, we are not really thinking. We're hallucinating and allowing our dream to dictate even more hallucinations. We stay stuck in this insane world that we made with the ego part of our mind.

When we follow the Voice of the Holy Spirit/Jesus, on the other hand, we are gently led to the eternal truth where we are a part of God and become ever more happy, joyous and free as we listen to this Voice on an increasing basis.

It appears very common for us to bounce back and forth for a while wherein we listen to the Holy Spirit/Jesus for a while but then we make a mistake and let the ego's voice guide us for a time. Then we realize our mistake and return to the Voice of truth again, etc., etc. However, as we make spiritual progress, the ego's voice slips in less and less and the world's temptations become less attractive. What I've described in this paragraph has certainly been my experience.

Jesus frequently points out in ACIM that we should only listen to God's Voice. In the Bible, it indicates that Jesus taught: "You can't serve two masters." This, of course, summarizes the essence of what ACIM says in this regard – Listen only to God's Voice, the Voice of love and unity, and stop listening to the ego's voice, the voice of fear and separation.

Lesson 46 – God is the Love in which I forgive.

The concept of forgiveness, as explained in ACIM, is not difficult to understand. This whole world is a dream that I made up. It's never been real, it's not real now and it never will be real. Given the unreality of the world, there is nothing to forgive. To me, following is about the best definition of forgiveness: the realization that there is nothing to forgive.

Although it's been happening on a decreasing basis, I often forget that this world is a dream and I get angry or sad or tired or try and do too much, etc., etc. At these times, the ego wants me to "beat myself up" over such mistakes. However, when I get centered with the Holy Spirit/Jesus, He helps me to simply forgive myself for such mistakes, learn from them, and move on.

The ongoing result for me is spiritual progress, fewer mistakes and an ever increasing happiness for me and those around me. This spiritual life, linked to my continuing study of ACIM, is wonderful so if you haven't yet really tried it, I suggest you do so.

Lesson 47 – God is the strength in which I trust.

One of God's greatest gifts is peace of mind which "passes all understanding" by a world whose original purpose was to establish chaos and separation in our minds. The continued study of ACIM, in my experience, is ever increasing peace of mind. This is consistent with the last sentence of this lesson which reads: "Remember that peace is your right, because you are giving your trust to the strength of God." (W-47.8:3)

As I've learned to get my mind to that "inner peace" where I'm not thinking of any worldly concerns, I've found that at some point in time, I'll get inspirational thoughts on how any worldly concerns should be handled by me. Such thoughts are clearly coming from my Inner Voice (Holy Spirit/Jesus).

It is perfectly clear that God wants us all to have peace of mind because this is necessary for both our happiness and our continued communion with Him.

Lesson 48 – There is nothing to fear.

"The idea for today simply states a fact. It is not a fact to those who believe in illusions, but illusions are not facts. In truth there is nothing to fear. It is very easy to recognize this. But it is very difficult to recognize it for those who want illusions to be true." (W-48.1:1-5)

As stated, in truth (or in Heaven) there is no fear. Also, in Heaven there is no form; there is only content and that content is Love. Everything in this physical universe of form is an illusion.

So long as I have some belief in the reality of the physical universe, I will have some fear. In this regard, one of the most important lessons for me is: "The world I see holds nothing that I want." (W-128.title) I've found this is easy to say but not accomplished over night. My continued study of ACIM helps me to accomplish this. It also helps when I parlay this Lesson 128 with the subsequent Lesson 129: "Beyond this world there is a world I want." (W-129.title) The world beyond this world is, of course, Heaven, where there's no past and no future but only the "eternal now" where we feel ever extending joy and bliss with no disturbances whatsoever.

One of the best descriptions of Heaven is contained in Lesson 107. Following are paragraphs 2 and 3 from this lesson. Please note that Jesus uses the term truth and Heaven interchangeably throughout ACIM and in the following passages the word truth is used:

> "Can you imagine what a state of mind without illusions is? How it would feel? Try to remember when there was a time, - perhaps a minute, maybe even less – when nothing came to interrupt your peace; when you were certain you were loved and safe. Then try to picture what it would be like to have that moment be extended to the end of time and to eternity. Then let the sense of quiet that you felt be multiplied a hundred times, and then be multiplied a hundred more.
>
> "And now you have a hint, not more than just the faintest intimation of the state your mind will rest in when the truth has come. Without illusions there could be no fear, no doubt and no attack. When truth has come all pain is over, for there is no room for transitory thoughts and dead ideas to linger in your mind. Truth occupies your mind completely, liberating you from all beliefs in the ephemeral. They have no place because the truth has come, and they are nowhere. They can not be found, for truth is everywhere forever, now." (W-107.2,3)

Lesson 49 – God's Voice speaks to me all through the day.

This lesson is really a no brainer. The problem has been that the ego's voice also speaks to me all through the day. And whereas God's Voice tells me "The world I see offers nothing that I want.", the ego's voice tells me "The world I see offers everything I want." For many years, I fully believed the ego's voice because I fully believed the world was real.

Through the mind training of ACIM, I am learning to ignore the ego's voice and listen to God's Voice, the Voice of the Holy Spirit or Jesus.

Lesson 50 – I am sustained by the Love of God.

We all ended up here on planet earth because we thought we had separated from God. We made up this illusionary physical realm to hide the truth from ourselves. As children, we all had faith in and fully believed that this world was real.

Thank God "There is no world!" (W-132.6:2) We all continue to be sustained by our original Source, our Father, our Creator, Allah, the Highest Power, or whatever other term you would like to use to refer to God. And, as Jesus states repeatedly throughout ACIM, it is 100% guaranteed by God that we will all wake up from our dreams and be together in our only real Home with Him. That Home is Heaven.

Lessons 51-60 – Review I (review of Lessons 1-50)

Each of these lessons, 51 through 60, reviews 5 previous lessons so, at the end of these 10 days, the student has reviewed the first 50 lessons.

Lesson 61 – I am the light of the world.

Jesus was the first "light of the world" because he was the first person in the world to totally stop listening to the voice of the ego and was 100% guided by the Voice of the Holy Spirit.

For me, the first time I did this lesson, I would not say that I was then the light of the world by any stretch of the imagination. However, with time, and continued study of ACIM, today I am much closer to being the "light of the world" on a permanent basis.

Even today, however, there are times when certain things in the world don't go my way and I become a little intolerant or impatient. At these times, what I've allowed myself to do is to once again make the world real and lose sight of the fact it's only a dream. There is some part of my ego mind which I have not yet replaced with God's Voice, the Voice of the Holy Spirit/Jesus. As these disturbances are becoming less and less over time, I know I'm making spiritual progress. I like this saying: "I'm a work in progress. God's not done with me yet."

So today, while I'm the "light of the world" most of the time, occasionally my light is off. So "I am a blinking light of the world." (smile)

Lesson 62 – Forgiveness is my function as the light of the world.

It's only been through repetitious diligent study of ACIM that I've made the spiritual progress that I have. And I will assure you that it's been miraculous progress.

Despite my progress, there have been times during the past 15 years that I've had significant resentments against other individuals. One individual, I'll call Kyle, likes to embarrass me at certain public meetings and social gatherings. In other words, any chance he gets. I've had significant resentments against him. Knowing that this world is my dream didn't seem to help me much.

As it turns out, Kyle has probably been my best teacher over the 10 years I've known him. In truth, Kyle is the same as me and you, an eternal innocent child of God, a spirit brother to me, to Jesus and to everyone else in the world.

So what's been my problem? When I let Kyle bother me, and it of course doesn't matter whether it's at the time he embarrasses me or when I'm thinking about it later, I've fallen into the trap of making the physical world a real place. Another way to put it is I haven't fully allowed God's Voice (the Holy Spirit/Jesus) to replace the ego's voice in my mind. I'm getting there, however. It's just a matter of time.

As Jesus says in the course: "There is no world!" (W-132.6:2) The world is but a dream from which we'll all wake up. If there's no world, there's no sin, no death, no pain, no suffering, etc.

And, of course, since there is no world, there is nothing to forgive. My "function as the light of the world is to forgive, whose definition is that there is nothing to forgive." Another way to define my function is to remain aware at all times that this whole world is but a dream.

Lesson 63 – The light of the world brings peace to every mind through my forgiveness.

So long as I'm here, perceived as a body, I will have some individual identity.

In truth, or in Heaven, there are no individuals. As Jesus states repeatedly in ACIM, God only has One Son. We (God's Son) have split ourselves up into these billions of individuals as part of the separation delusion. The point is that God's Son has only one mind in truth, referred to as

Christ's Mind in ACIM. Since my mind is part of this Christ Mind, as my mind gets healed through my forgiveness it has a positive effect on the total Christ Mind.

One of the positive effects of being healed is "peace of mind" beyond anything the world could possibly offer or comprehend. As I noted in Lesson 61, "I am the light of the world" when I'm thinking properly. As the light of the world, I bring peace to every mind through the great spiritual tool of forgiveness which is the ongoing recognition that the world is a dream so there is nothing to forgive.

Lesson 64 – Let me not forget my function.

As stated in the first sentence of this lesson, this has the same meaning as: "Let me not wander into temptation." (see W-64.1:1) The entire world and physical universe was made by the ego to keep our minds so occupied that "We would not wander into truth." The idea that the entire world, which we believed was real, is just a figment of our imagination does not happen in the blink of the eyes. That is why Jesus has 365 lessons in his book rather than just one.

My own experience is that continued study of ACIM over many years has made the world unreal and Heaven real in my mind. This has also made my life here in my dream a happy, wonderful life so I encourage others to follow my path. One mistake I see some people make is that they try and mix ACIM with one or more other religious or spiritual programs. I see these people not really benefitting from ACIM. ACIM is a standalone spiritual program given to us by Jesus, the greatest teacher who ever lived and, of course, who continues to live in spirit. While I appreciate it is not for everyone, and there are thousands of other ways to wake from the dream, I encourage those who are using ACIM to only use ACIM if they want to become enlightened sooner. I do know of a few people who successfully use one of the 12-step spiritual programs to overcome some addictive personality trait and, in addition, study and apply the teachings of ACIM. These people effectively treat their 12-step program as their undergraduate degree in spirituality with ACIM as their graduate program.

Now back to this lesson. My function is to forgive and to forgive is to remember that this world is but my dream. I should not take it seriously. As I've embedded forgiveness into my mind on an increasing basis over the years I've been studying the Course, I have certainly gotten happier. (This is a perfectly valid reason for studying ACIM – to increase your happiness.) Jesus links forgiveness and happiness in this lesson as follows: *"Let me forgive and be happy."* (W-64.6:4)

Lesson 65 – My only function is the one God gave me.

"Salvation and forgiveness are the same." (W-99.1:1) When we wake up in Heaven from this dream world, we will understand we didn't need to be saved from anything real, we just needed to awaken; we didn't need to be forgiven for anything real, we just needed to awaken. I hope this helps explain why salvation and forgiveness are the same.

Let's suppose when we're all again awake in Heaven and this dream world has disappeared that we'll be able to remember this life we think we're in now. We won't say "I'm glad I was saved from all my sins." Nor will we say "I'm glad God forgave me for all those sins I committed." Instead, we'll say something like: "That was the craziest, most bizarre and scariest dream. I was sure it was real but now I know none of it ever happened. I'm so glad it's over and I'm awake at Home (in Heaven) where I can enjoy happiness and peace for the rest of eternity."

As I've been able to incorporate the spiritual principles of ACIM into my life, I can say in the present tense: "I'm really glad this world is just a grand fictional movie and none of it is real. As I increasingly use the Holy Spirit/Jesus to guide me, I'm truly enjoying my movie. Life is truly a lot of fun. One of the greatest benefits is I'm not at all concerned about dying because death, of course, is not at all real. I hope to live to a ripe old age before I leave my movie because, in addition to it being fun for me, I help quite a few other people also."

Lesson 66 – My happiness and my function are one.

For the many students of ACIM who don't yet understand this simple statement, please consider what Heaven must be like. There is no sorrow, no unhappiness whatsoever, only joy and happiness with no possible end for all eternity.

Now, throw away the religious idea that when you die, you thank God that you can leave this miserable sinful world behind and you'll wake up in Heaven for all eternity. Many religious persons also believe that many sinful persons will spend eternity in hell to suffer forever. (This thinking is so preposterous yet held by many persons. How could a good loving God allow any children He created be condemned to this?) Jesus points out in his Course that we must awaken to our eternal Self while we are still in our dream just as he did; it doesn't happen after our bodies die. In chapter 3 of the Text of ACIM, he says: "The world is not left by death but by truth, and truth can be known by all those for whom the Kingdom was created, and for whom it waits." (T-3.VII.6:11)

My function is forgiveness which, once again, means I know the world is not real but is just a dream. It never happened and is not happening now. Using Christ's vision, my mind sees right through this dream to reality, which is Heaven. So, although I'm still in the dream, I'm also moving closer to being fully awake and I am very happy. How did I get to this state of mind? I've been studying and applying the principles of ACIM quite intensely for over 15 years.

I'll add that my wife and I have a wonderful 6-year old little girl and we have another baby on the way so I'm in no hurry to leave the world anytime soon. It's a real happy place for me today.

Lesson 67 – Love created me like itself.

As you read this lesson, I think you will agree that this lesson could have also been written: "God created me like Himself." A few of the attributes of God which Jesus points out in this lesson is that God is holy, kind, helpful and perfect. (See W-67.2:3-6) What this lesson says is that in truth we are no different than God.

Consistent with ACIM, this paragraph describes how my mind pictures our original creation. God is, of course, not a body but a Spirit. Before He created us, God was this large Spiritual Light, ever shining and ever extending or increasing. He was happy, free and forever and He was everything since nothing else existed. He decided He wanted a Child (ACIM uses the term Son) to share Himself with. So instantaneously the large Spiritual Light which was God increased by, say, 50% which represented His new Creation (which, of course, includes all of us). God and His Creation were totally One because everything God had He shared with His Son and everything His Son had He shared with His Father or His God. From that point on, Father and Son continued as One, happy and free, ever shining and ever extending or increasing forever.

Later on, God's Creation (i.e., Us) thought we would separate from Him and that's why we think we are here in this insane world of separate bodies and unhappy endings. Thank God this whole deal we think of as life is nothing but a dream and the Holy Spirit guarantees we will all wake up and be happy, joyous and free forever just as we were when God created us. So all those children's books and fairy tales where "everyone lives happily ever after" is in fact consistent with God's plan for all of us.

Lesson 68 – Love holds no grievances.

A grievance is a resentment. It is holding in your mind angry thinking against another person. You can also be holding angry thoughts against such things as the IRS or a law that only allows you to have one wife or ... the list can go on and on.

It is an ego tool to maintain the separation in place. It can only come from the thinking of this insane world, a world which, thank God, is only a dream.

As I indicated in the previous lesson, the truth is that God and His Creation are One. There is only One Will in truth or in Heaven. My will and your will and God's Will are the same. Another term for truth or Heaven is Love. Of course there are no grievances in Heaven or in God's Love.

In my own personal situation, though I still carry a few small grievances – in other words, I'm still a "work in progress" – my grievance or resentment level is a fraction of what it was a few years ago and still declining. Thus, my happiness level is on the rise. This is a direct result of my work in ACIM.

Lesson 69 – My grievances hide the light of the world in me.

As noted in the previous lesson, grievances (resentments) are an ego device for maintaining the separation in place. When I've had deep resentments against another person, the last thing I wanted was to be near them, never mind thinking that they are One with me which, of course, is the essence of "the truth that sets me free."

Additionally, deep resentments against just one individual can make me a miserable person to be around for everyone else in my life. There are probably very few people in the world who have not shared my grievance experience. Therefore, it should be clear that "Your grievances hide the light of the world in you."

Lesson 70 – My salvation comes from me.

Salvation is, of course, from God but God and I are one so it is also from me. Since God's Will for all of us is happiness, salvation means happiness.

One very simple way to understand this lesson is as follows: "Happiness is an inside job" because the Voice for God (the Holy Spirit/Jesus) is within me. The other side of the coin is equally applicable – "Unhappiness is an inside job" because the ego's voice is within me. As I learn to listen to God's Voice and not to the ego's voice I get happier. I also learn that I am saved; I've always been saved but I was listening to the ego's voice which was lying to me and telling me otherwise.

This lesson points out that all our attempts to get happy from outside sources or from other people are futile. Being in spiritual places or around spiritual people might make you feel good for a while but your solution comes from within your own mind. About 2,000 years ago, Jesus said "The kingdom of God is within you." This is still true. In the text of ACIM, Jesus modifies this slightly to read: "The kingdom of God is you." This is because each of us is effectively God since, in Heaven (or in truth), our Father shares everything He is with Us. This type of sharing, of course, makes no sense in the physical world of illusions. However, it makes full sense in Heaven or in the real world. The concept of two lights joining together (God and His Son) to make one larger light (the Unity of God and His Son) is a good analogy of what happened when God created Us, His Son.

Lesson 71 – Only God's plan for salvation will work.

Most, if not all, of us are absolutely convinced what's necessary for our lives to improve. Such ideas as "if I only had more money", "if my spouse appreciated me more", "if I didn't have to work", and the list goes on and on and on.

What Jesus tells us many times in ACIM is to forget all these worldly ideas, leastwise for attaining happiness. All we are doing is substituting another worldly illusion for one we're in. And, no matter how good they might seem, illusions will never bring any kind of lasting happiness.

As I discussed in the previous lesson, real happiness is always an inside job. You cannot possibly get it from the world.

And don't be discouraged for, as this lesson specifically states, God does have a plan for your salvation and it works. Just as I have been doing, you must learn to hear His Voice (the Voice of the Holy Spirit/Jesus) and stop paying attention to all the worldly ways to get happy.

Jesus points out many times in ACIM that your end is certain. You will wake up in Heaven where you were before you fell asleep. The "means" for you to wake up has also been provided and is available to you right now – it is the Voice of the Holy Spirit (or, our good friend Jesus who speaks with the same Voice).

Lesson 72 – Holding grievances is an attack on God's plan for salvation.

You don't have to be a rocket scientist to understand this simple lesson.

God and His Creation share One Unified Mind. Other terms within ACIM to define this place are Heaven, Truth and Love. Of course, God's individual salvation plan for each of us is to return to this Place, our eternal Home.

When I hold a grievance against another Son of God I am establishing a separation between us. Any separation thought is an attack on God's plan for salvation.

Another way of saying the same thing is that I can't honestly say I love God but I'm angry at one or more of his other children. God is love and anger and love are mutually exclusive.

However, don't be discouraged because you have some resentments against others. With all the work I've done, I still carry some minor resentments against a few individuals. The ego really wants me to beat myself up for these. God tells me to forgive myself and keep working on my mind. My resentments against others will disappear when they're supposed to in accordance with His salvation plan for me.

Lesson 73 – I will there be light.

Clearly, as you review this lesson, Jesus is continuing to help us get rid of all our grievances or resentments.

In this lesson, Jesus makes a significant distinction between our "will" (the same as God's Will) which is from our sane mind and "wishes" which are things we hope for in the world and our ego wants us to want. In this regard, note that many children's fairy tales end with: "And they lived happily ever after." As the children get older, they realize that no one lives happily ever after because, if for no other reason, everyone dies. The world doesn't seem as bright a place as we "mature."

Now, through ACIM, we learn that everyone, in fact, will live happily ever after....not on earth, of course, but in our Heavenly Home once we wake up from our insane dreams. I assure you this is a real good thing to know and be happy about. And all I did to get to this mindset was to become a devoted student of Jesus' study guide, *A Course in Miracles.*

Lesson 74 – There is no will but God's.

"The idea for today can be regarded as the central thought toward which all our exercises are directed." (W-74.1:1)

What the Holy Spirit and Jesus have been doing for me for the past 15 years is gently waking me up from these crazy dreams I've been having my whole life. They've been the divine Babysitter, sent by God, helping me appreciate I'm still at Home with Him. I can picture myself in bed with the Holy Spirit and Jesus gently shaking my body and saying "Wake up Jimmy Boy. You've simply been having some crazy dreams but don't worry because we're all still here with Dad (i.e., God, our Father)."

What Jesus repeatedly tells us in ACIM is that the ego never happened, the world never happened and the past never happened. This has all been a figment of our imagination.

I assure you that I didn't believe everything I was reading right away. I doubt any student of ACIM could do that. When I started studying ACIM, nobody could have told me this world wasn't real. I had been through a lot of good times and bad times in my life and I had some real emotional scars to prove this world was real.

For someone to suggest, say, 16 years ago that my whole life was just a dream coming from my mind, I'd say "Hogwash! Go back to whatever planet you came from!" However, today I know this to be true.

There is no will but God's because only Heaven exists where God and His Creation share One Will and extend joyously forever. As Jesus states repeatedly in ACIM, it is 100% certain that we'll all wake up to this truth some day.

Lesson 75 – The light has come.

Throughout ACIM Jesus emphasizes forgiveness as the key ingredient to understanding his Course. As I've indicated in many other lessons, all forgiveness means is that this entire world is but a bad dream. It is not real now, it wasn't real yesterday and it won't be real tomorrow.

On the two pages of this lesson, Jesus uses the word forgiveness or forgiven 10 times. The reason is simple. Once we have mentally taken away that which obscures the light (i.e., the dream world), then we can clearly see the light. In other words, once we forgive the world, "The light will come."

In practice, it is likely that the principle of forgiveness will be clear as possible at times especially as you're studying ACIM or practicing one of its lessons. Then, before you know it, you'll get upset at someone or something that's happening in your dream world. When this happens, please don't feel guilty which the ego loves. (Or, when you feel a little guilty, with the help of the Holy Spirit/Jesus, simply forgive yourself.) The Course is a combination of study and practice so that you're future life's experiences will let you know how well you're really doing.

Lesson 76 – I am under no laws but God's.

In my case, I find it's a good idea to generally abide by worldly laws also. For instance, I used to get drunk a lot and get arrested for disturbing the peace or for drunk driving. The consequences were a life of chaos and inner loneliness. Therefore, I don't do these things anymore. I want my dream life to be at a peaceful level so that I can then have time to continue working on my inner world and remove the remaining obstacles which are blocking me from God. The point here is that if you are a professional car thief and are breaking man made laws, Jesus is not suggesting to you that, as far as he's concerned, you should keep doing what you're doing. He does say in ACIM that if you're in God's Will, then everyone benefits and no one loses so stealing cars would seem to be outside of God's Will.

The laws of God are way beyond the world's thinking. For instance, we are all innocent forever. We always feel joyful and loving and we extend these feelings. The idea of loss or sacrifice of any kind never crosses our mind. "We are as God created us."

By contrast, the world is a place of winning and losing, of pain and suffering offset by searching for some happy times. The world guarantees you will die. A valid way to think of the world is that it's a massive insane asylum with the patients running the organization. The world's laws are here to maintain the continuation of the asylum so hopefully all hell won't break loose.

So God sent the good Doctor, the Holy Spirit, into the asylum so we can all recover from this seemingly closed system, become healed and return to our eternal Home in Heaven. Thank God for this solution!

Lesson 77 – I am entitled to miracles.

I am convinced that Jesus performed many physical miracles, including healing of illnesses and raising a few persons from the dead, most important his own resurrection on that first Easter morning. For about the first 10 years of studying the Course, I thought of all miracles as physical in nature even though I was never able to accomplish any. Often, I would see if I could move a coin on the table in front of me by just a few inches but I've never accomplished this. I laugh at this today. Although I had read the "Principles of Miracles" portion of the Text of ACIM many times, I didn't necessarily understand it all. About 4 years ago, I read and understood the 10th principle for the first time. It reads: "10. The use of miracles as spectacles to induce belief is a misunderstanding of their purpose." (T-1.I.10) This means the purpose of miracles is not physical phenomena to help people believe in God.

In Jesus case, the first person to become enlightened (i.e., to listen solely to the Holy Spirit and disregard the ego's voice altogether), the many physical miracles he performed did become an important part of his witness. In order to help people believe his spiritual teachings were from God, he often pointed out the many physical miracles he had performed.

One of the best definitions of a miracle is: "The miracle establishes you dream a dream, and its content is not true. [The world you think you're in is but your own dream and it's a lie.] This is a crucial step in dealing with illusions. No one is afraid of them when he perceives he made them up. The fear was held in place because he did not see that he was author of the dream, and not a figure in the dream." (T-28.II.7:1-4)

Lesson 78 – Let miracles replace all grievances.

Here's what I said in this book in Lesson 42: "When I look at my best friend and my worst enemy with vision, they are exactly the same – they are eternal innocent joyous spiritual beings. There is no judgment here, only truth which really sets me (and them) free."

Clearly, I must hold grievances against my worst enemy or I wouldn't consider him an enemy. I may or may not have certain grievances against my best friend.

In any event, in this Lesson 78, Jesus asks us to use who I've defined as our worst enemy. In effect, Jesus asks us to look at this person using Christ's vision, as an eternal innocent joyous spiritual being, the same as you and me. Jesus points out that this person is our savior. Jesus often points out in ACIM that every person we meet is our savior but it seems that the persons who really appear to cause us grievances are our best teachers. The logic to me is that if I can overcome all my grievances against persons who have given me the most problems in my life then I should easily forgive everyone else.

Of course, as I am able on an increasing basis to remain aware that this world is but a dream (coming solely from my mind), I appreciate that any grievances I have are against me alone and ultimately I will no longer have any grievances whatsoever because I will stop listening to the ego altogether.

Lesson 79 – Let me recognize the problem so it can be solved.

Like everyone else in this world, I have worldly problems but these were never my real problem. My real problem is that I thought I was separate from everyone else on the planet and, of course, I thought God was somewhere out there watching over me but certainly separate from me. My real problem, therefore, was my fixed belief in separation.

As I've incorporated the teachings of ACIM into my mindset, I now understand that this world is but my dream and I never really separated from God. However, I'm still in my dream.

Like everyone else, I encounter worldly problems. The solution to my worldly problems has been to continue my ACIM studies and to spend a certain amount of time each day in meditative thought and total peace wherein the world is totally left behind. As I encounter worldly problems or issues, simple solutions generally come to mind quite quickly.

Also, when I get disturbed for any reason, I know I have a problem. I can usually find out what I did wrong (really where my thinking was wrong) which caused me to get disturbed. Even if I can't fully figure it out, I can regain my composure and get undisturbed once again. Over time, as I've listened to the Holy Spirit/Jesus more and the ego less, my disturbances are less extreme and less often. I am making spiritual progress.

Worldly problems, as I said, naturally occur in my life. Whether they be issues with other individuals, financial, future plans, etc., I usually discuss them with my wife. If the answer is not clear to me, I do my best not to worry about it or get stressed about it. Sometimes the solution to an unresolved problem will come to my mind "in a flash" when I haven't even been thinking about the problem. As I understand it, such solutions are coming from the Holy Spirit.

The Song of Prayer pamphlet (it's only 22 pages) was also authored by Jesus and is a supplement to ACIM. This pamphlet does an excellent job of describing how true prayer resolves all worldly issues without actually asking God for specific solutions. If you haven't studied it yet, I urge you to do so. (To date, Jesus has authored only one other supplement to ACIM, called *Psychotherapy: Purpose, Process and Practice.* Whether you're in the psychotherapy field or not, I urge you to study this supplement also.)

Lesson 80 – Let me recognize my problems have been solved.

"If you are willing to recognize your problems, you will recognize that you have no problems." (W-80.1:1) "Your only problem has been solved." (W-80.2:1)

These two sentences from the first two paragraphs of this lesson make it all so simple. While it is simple, it's not easy. The simplicity of it, as I've stated before in this book is that we have not actually separated from God but we are dreaming that we have and we have to wake up. The world, being only a dream, has no real problems. So can't we at this point just snap our fingers and wake up in Heaven? Apparently it's not that easy or Jesus wouldn't have 285 more lessons following this one.

Understanding the concepts underlying ACIM is one thing. Being in this dream and practicing and experiencing ACIM principles in our daily lives takes, in my experience, a lot of time and disciplined self-study but it's well worth it. If ever increasing happiness for you and those about you is your goal and if you're willing to abandon all your preconceived notions on how happiness is obtained, then ACIM is a wonderful study course for you. It really works!

Lessons 81-90 – Review II (review of Lessons 61-80)

Each of these lessons, 81 through 90, reviews two previous lessons so, at the end of these 10 days, the student has reviewed the 20 lessons, 61 through 80.

Lesson 91 – Miracles are seen in light.

In this lesson, Jesus makes the important point that miracles and vision necessarily go together. (see W-91.1:1) When it comes to another individual, my vision is my ability to see the individual as perfectly innocent regardless of how evil he or she might appear in this world. After all, like me, "He or she is as God created him or her."

I often think of miracles as raindrops in time which reveal the truth to me. As I make spiritual progress, the number of miracle raindrops increase and these raindrops truly make me happy as well as those about me.

Light can also be thought of as truth or Heaven. The world that we all believed in so whole heartedly is the darkness whose purpose was to block us off from the light. To the extent I still make the world real or think there is something the world can offer me of value, I am in the dark. Remember this lesson: "The world I see holds <u>nothing</u> that I want." (W-128.title; underscore mine) Thank God "There is no world!" (W-132.6:2) Or, in my own words, "Thank God the world is a big fat zero (-0-)!"

Lesson 92 – Miracles are seen in light, and light and strength are one.

The world thinks of strength as able bodied and strong. The world thinks of the United States as being the strongest nation in the world. We have strong plastic bags, strong ropes, strong glues and even strong odors.

Spiritual strength or strength from God has <u>nothing</u> to do with worldly strength. A person with spiritual strength will stay calm in the midst of chaos. Why and how does he do this? This person is using Christ's vision.

It is the body's eyes (an illusion) that allow us to "see" the apparent chaos and tragedies in this world. As Jesus states in this lesson: "It is your weakness that sees through the body's eyes, peering about in darkness to behold the likeness of itself; the small, the weak, the sickly and the dying, those in need, the helpless and afraid, the sad, the poor, the starving and the joyless. These are seen through eyes that cannot see and cannot bless." (W-92.3:3,4)

In the next few sentences, Jesus defines (God's) strength which you can note is also a definition of Christ's vision: "Strength overlooks these things by seeing past appearances. It keeps its steady gaze upon the light that lies beyond them. It unites with light, of which it is a part. It sees itself." (W-92.4:1-4)

Lesson 93 – Light and joy and peace abide in me.

I am innocent! You are innocent! Everyone on earth is innocent! We are as God created us – innocent, happy, joyous and free .... Forever!

The preceding paragraph is a good summary of ACIM. If you still believe the world is real, there is no way you can believe these truths. For ACIM to help you, you must believe at some level that this world is just an insane dream. Simple logic should help you at least believe that God didn't create this world, what with its wars, crime, rape, pain and suffering, death for everyone, natural disasters, etc. How could a loving God have anything to do with this place? Common sense will tell you He can't.

The first time I did this lesson years ago, it didn't make much sense to me. However, as the instructions preceding the lessons indicated I should, I did this lesson anyway. Today, when I review this lesson, it is a simple promise from God which I know to be true.

Lesson 94 – I am as God created me.

The importance of this lesson is evidenced by the fact that Jesus repeats this lesson two more times, in lessons 110 and 162.

The simplicity of this lesson is unmistakable which adds to its power. I am an eternal, peaceful, joyful and free extension of God because this is how He created me. And so are you because He created us the same.

All my thoughts different from this represent a mad dream that has <u>nothing</u> to do with God or reality. This world with its chaos, pain, suffering, certain death, arguing and fighting, happy times mixed with sad times, etc., is just a crazy dream. Thank God it's not real.

Lesson 95 – I am one Self, united with my Creator.

"I am one Self" and, in the terminology of ACIM, that Self is generally referred to as Christ, God's One Son. In the Christian religion, Christ is used as a reference to Jesus whereas, in ACIM, Christ means all of us which, of course, includes Jesus. Within ACIM, Jesus points out that we are no different than him in truth. What sets Jesus apart from the rest of humanity is that he was the first in the human race to understand and maintain that this world is but a dream. Also, very significantly, he continues to make himself 100% available until the last one of us wakes up from this worldly dream. Thank you very much for this, Jesus.

There are no individuals in Heaven. Clearly, while here in the dream we must maintain our individuality, just as Jesus did, so we can be "the light of the world" to others and help them wake up from this insane and often very painful dream.

This lesson also says we are "united with our Creator." This means literally that we have everything God has, including all His power as well as His creative ability. He withholds nothing from His children who, in combination, are His one Son. It helps me to know I can give up my individuality because in its place I will have all the power of God Himself. Think about it – Would you rather be an individual or God? As Jesus states in ACIM, the <u>only</u> difference between us and God is that God created us and we didn't create Him.

Lesson 96 – Salvation comes from my one Self.

The only individual in this (dream) world I need in order to be saved is Jimmy Laws; i.e., my one self. As I've talked about previously in this book, within me is the ego, who always wants the worst for me, and the Holy Spirit/Jesus, Who always wants the best for me. When I'm listening to the Holy Spirit/Jesus, I'm moving in the direction of getting myself saved. However, when I'm listening to the ego, I'm moving back into the closed prison yard of the world.

Within this lesson, Jesus effectively defines "Self" as the "One Mind" of "God and His Creation." As I discussed in the previous lesson, this is Who we are in truth. The Voice of the Holy Spirit/Jesus naturally comes from this "one Self" and not from the ego. Therefore, our solution which is listening only to the Voice of the Holy Spirit/Jesus comes from our "one Self." In summary, as this lesson states: "Salvation comes from my one Self."

Lesson 97 – I am spirit.

This lesson is very simple and, in its simplicity, very powerful.

In the physical world, something can't be both liquid and solid. It must be one or the other. In truth, we are spirit and there is absolutely nothing physical about us. The body that we think of as so important here is just part of the overall dream we are in.

This lesson also points out that we share with God His function as Creator. We are, in truth, Co-Creators with God. We have all the attributes of God because He shares all of Himself with us. We are effectively God, the only difference is He created us and we didn't create Him.

Lesson 98 – I will accept my part in God's plan for salvation.

Over the past 15 years, I have spent a full day on this lesson approximately 10 times and studied it another 6 times or so. It has never been as obvious as it is now as I study it again for purposes of this book. I make this point to encourage other students of ACIM to continue the disciplined study of the basic material.

Why would I not "accept my part in God's plan for salvation?" My part means an ever increasing happier life for me and those about me. And it means so much more for me.

Whereas so called "normal" people are concerned at times about their own death or the death of loved ones, I am not. I love life and I find myself making new friends wherever I go.

One of the greatest benefits to me of the mind training of ACIM is not that I can quote a good part of it from memory (which I very seldom do except to myself) but that I can practice its spiritual principles in all my earthly comings and goings. Life here in my dream has become more fun than "a barrel full of monkeys."

It is clear to me that "I am accepting my part in God's plan for salvation" and it is wonderful.

For other students of ACIM, please recognize that ACIM is not the path for everyone. Jesus effectively says that there are thousands of pathways to "awaken from the dream", ACIM being but one. So please don't get stuck, like I did for a while, thinking that the study of ACIM must be preached to anyone who "really wants to get spiritual." There are many other paths for many people.

Lesson 99 – Salvation is my only function here.

"Salvation and forgiveness are the same." (W-99.1:1) This is how Jesus starts out explaining this lesson. Thus, this lesson could just as easily be read: "Forgiveness is my only function here."

You see both salvation and forgiveness both effectively mean we wake up from this world of dreams and awaken in Heaven which we never left. Therefore, there was never anything real to be saved from and the "sins" we thought we and others had committed were not real either.

So both salvation and forgiveness is a process whereby we awaken from this world of dreams and do our best to stay aware that this world is a dream as we go about our daily affairs within the dream. In my experience, this gets easier over time as a direct result of the ongoing study time I give to ACIM.

Let me emphasize that my ACIM study time is simply me sitting alone studying the book called *A Course in Miracles.* Although I've attended quite a few ACIM study groups over the years, I personally have not benefitted very much in these group discussions about the Course. However, other Course students might find such study groups very beneficial.

Lesson 100 – My part is essential to God's plan for salvation.

Your part is also essential to God's plan for salvation. There is nothing special about me in God's eyes. The fact is God's plan for salvation is not complete until all persons are saved so everyone's part is essential.

I really like this lesson because it also includes reasons why I wanted to study the Course and why I want to continue to study it, experience it, and apply it in all my comings and goings in this life. The reason is it truly makes me happy. Following are a couple of examples of the "happiness" promises in this lesson.

"Then realize your part is to be happy. Only this is asked of you or anyone who wants to take his place among God's messengers." (W-100.7:3,4)

"Now let us try to find that joy that proves to us and all the world God's Will for us. It is your function that you find it here, and that you find it now." (W-100.8:1,2)

Lesson 101 – God's Will for me is perfect happiness.

This lesson makes explicit what was discussed in the previous lesson. When I am not perfectly happy, I am not in God's Will. This is true for every one of us. Like any good father, God's Will for all His children is that we all be perfectly happy all the time.

The beauty of ACIM is that we learn that it will happen for all of us once we fully awaken from this dream we call "the world."

In this lesson, Jesus talks as he often does about "sin." Holding on to the essential idea that the world is nothing but a dream, simply realize our so called sins only occurred in a dream. They never happened, they're not happening now and they can't happen in the future. While nearly all of the human race can believe sin is real, you don't have to. I know this because, as a solid ACIM student, I no longer believe in sin because my entire life here is but a dream as it is with everyone. By the way, guilt and sacrifice and blame have also disappeared from my mindset. While nearly everyone else in my life is stuck at different levels to these egotistical feelings, I'm leaving them behind me. I expect some of my readers can identify with my spiritual progress. Everyone will eventually identify because, as Jesus tells us in ACIM, everyone will eventually awaken from their dreams.

Lesson 102 – I share God's Will for happiness for me.

This is a no brainer. Who doesn't want to be happy all the time? Happiness at this level not only means that I am happy within myself but I see, using Christ's vision, happiness all around me.

After many years of mind training using ACIM as my training book, I'm experiencing this type of happiness on an increasing basis. Naturally, I plan on continuing my ACIM disciplined study for the rest of my life. Based on past experience, I expect to get happier in the future and I know that my happiness is not conditional on anything but an ever increasing use of God's Voice (the Voice of the Holy Spirit/Jesus) and an ever decreasing use of the ego's voice within my mind.

To the many people in the world who think happiness at this level can only be obtained in the afterlife, Jesus tells us in ACIM that this is not so. As a good student of his manuscript and an ever increasing happiness level in this life, I can assure you that Jesus is right. Thank you so much Jesus for giving us this book! You're the best!

Lesson 103 – God being Love, is also happiness.

In this lesson, Jesus continues the theme of happiness. When I am in God's Will, I am happy and I am full of joy.

This lesson also moves us away from the ego's myth that we should fear God. Of course, if God did punish us for our "sins" then we would have something to be frightened of. Once we start learning that this world and its sins are all just a bad dream, which God knew all along, we start appreciating that to fear God is simply ridiculous.

We also learn that God and we are One in truth. Therefore, if God were to punish us, He would in fact be punishing Himself also. This, too, is an absurd idea which never happened.

Within this dream, of course, we all feel bad at times and some of us get to feel "hell on earth" at deeper levels than others. In my case, in the years before I quit drinking alcohol in 1997, I really got the opportunity to be in hell. Today, I recognize that God had nothing to do with my near self-destruction. In fact, whenever we're not happy, it is because we are not in God's Will. The wonderful thing is we can be in God's Will while we're still in this dream because God sent His Great Doctor into this dream, the Holy Spirit, to give us the directions for doing so. Jesus is, of course, also here to help us.

Though I'm not perfectly happy all the time, I'm moving in that direction. This is a direct result of my ongoing study of ACIM.

Lesson 104 – I seek but what belongs to me in truth.

At one point in ACIM, Jesus asks us to consider what Heaven must be like and gives us a few ideas to let us know it is a most wonderful place. He then tells us to multiply this "wonderfulness" by 100 and multiply it by 100 again. This, he says, will give us a segment of an idea of what Heaven is like.

It is this that "belongs to us in truth." This is our inheritance from God. Everything outside of this is but a mad dream that doesn't exist at all. This is why, as we approach Heaven through the study of and experience of ACIM, we can honestly say: "The world I see holds nothing that I want." (W-128.title)

Lesson 105 – God's peace and joy are mine.

In Lesson 103, Jesus tells us that "God, being Love, is also happiness." He tells us happiness is an attribute of Love. In this lesson, he effectively points out that peace and joy are also attributes of Love and are therefore part of our inheritance from God since we are "One with God" in truth.

In this lesson, Jesus has us work on our grievances by telling us to pray for our "enemies" as follows:

> "*My brother, peace and joy I offer you,*
> *That I may have peace and joy as mine.*" (W-105.7:2)

Jesus is very realistic in his ACIM. Throughout the Text and many of the earlier lessons, Jesus explains that our grievances are a problem and how we shouldn't have them. He knows, however, that despite our knowledge of the "truth that sets us free", we seem to have at least a few individuals in our lives who seem to keep us from accomplishing this. Leastwise, this has been my own experience. Of course, we learn fairly early that the problem is never that of our enemy but our own faulty perception.

So long as we hold on to any grievance, we can't have the total peace and joy which are our inheritance.

Lesson 106 – Let me be still and listen to the truth.

This is how Jesus begins the second paragraph of this lesson: "Listen, and hear your Father speak to you through His appointed Voice, which silences the thunder of the meaningless, and shows the way to peace to those who cannot see." (W-106.2:1) What is "the thunder of the meaningless" which God's appointed Voice (i.e., the Holy Spirit) silences for us. The answer is any worldly thoughts whatsoever. Why are these thoughts meaningless? Because the world is nothing but a meaningless dream and has nothing to do with who we are in truth.

The third paragraph of this lesson confirms what I have stated above: "Be not afraid today to circumvent the voices of the world. Walk lightly past their meaningless persuasion. Hear them not. Be still today and listen to the truth." (W-106.3:1-4) And the truth is we are all eternal innocent parts of God Himself, ever happy, joyous and free, which is not something the world can ever possibly teach us.

In this lesson, Jesus asks us to ask the Holy Spirit: "What does it mean to give and to receive?" (W-106.7:6) The dominant one word answer when I ask this question of my Inner Voice (the Holy Spirit/Jesus) is "happiness." While the messages I give to the many people I talk to every day naturally vary, there is an overriding extension of happiness in virtually all my conversations.

Lesson 107 – Truth will correct all errors in my mind.

As Jesus makes clear in this lesson, errors are simply illusions which still appear real. In my experience, continuing progress in ACIM allows me to of course continue to "see" the world with my eyes but know that every aspect of it is but a dream. None of it is real. It is like one huge cartoon with billions of characters, each with our own little episodes, some funny and some tragic.

How can I laugh at the world? The answer is that the world is not real and never will be. The billions of characters will all wake up in Heaven. In fact, none of us has ever left Heaven. We just fell asleep for a time and we've dreamed up this bizarre place called the world. Some of you might say this is ridiculous. However, Jesus specifically says this many times in ACIM and, through my own positive experiences, I know he is right.

In this lesson, Jesus asks us to recognize that we are One with the Holy Spirit. Specifically, Jesus tells us to say:

> "*Truth will correct all errors in my mind,*
> *And I will rest in Him* [the Holy Spirit] *Who is my Self.*" (W-107.9:5)

As Jesus tells us many times throughout ACIM, in truth or in Heaven there is only One Mind. There is no separation at all between God and His Creation. Therefore, we and the Holy Spirit, both created by God, are One. Also, we are One with our Father and Christ (Who is all of us, God's One Son), as well as with the Holy Spirit. In truth, nothing exists outside Heaven's Oneness.

Lesson 108 – To give and to receive are one in truth.

When someone asks me for money (a common occurrence) and I give it to them, I have fewer dollars and they have more dollars. This is not the type of giving Jesus is referring to in this lesson or in ACIM.

As reviewed in the previous lesson, in truth there is only One Self, or One Mind, which represents God and all His Creation. Therefore, in truth, when I give to our One Self I also receive what I give since I'm naturally a part of the One Self. In this lesson, Jesus uses the following simple sentence to define our One Self: "One thought, completely unified, will serve to unify all thought." (W-108.5:1)

In this lesson, Jesus offers a few examples of the types of giving he is referring to:

> *"To everyone I offer quietness.*
> *"To everyone I offer peace of mind.*
> *"To everyone I offer gentleness."* (W-108.8:6-8)

In a recent study of this lesson for myself, I added kindness and happiness as gifts I try to offer everyone.

Lesson 109 – I rest in God.

In this lesson, Jesus asks us to simply leave the world (of illusions) and allow our minds to settle in to truth as best we can. In other words, he wants us to be in the peace of God that the world can't possibly understand because it is beyond the world.

While not one of the 365 lessons, I often mentally say "Above the battleground I am determined to see." The battleground, of course, is planet earth. In my mind's eye, while I'm floating above the earth, I have two choices – (1) I can look down at this huge dream with all its craziness, or (2) I can look the other way and simply feel the peace of God or, as this lesson suggests we do, "I rest in God." [The Text of ACIM includes a full section to the idea of remaining above the battleground (T-23.IV)]

Lesson 110 – I am as God created me.

This is the second time that Jesus gives us this same lesson. Please review my comments under Lesson 94, the first time Jesus gives us this lesson.

Personally, I like to combine this lesson with Lesson 199 which states: "I am not a body. I am free." Multiple times a day, I say to myself: "I am not a body. I am free for I am still as God created me."

Lessons 111-120 – Review III (review of Lessons 91-110)

Each of these lessons, 111 through 120, reviews two previous lessons so, at the end of these 10 days, the student has reviewed the 20 lessons, 91 through 110.

Lesson 121 – Forgiveness is the key to happiness.

Once again, forgiveness taught by ACIM knows this world is but a mad dream from which we shall all wake up. Since this world never happened, forgiveness means "there is nothing to forgive."

This can't be accomplished by our unaided mind. An insane mind can't fix itself. We require help from God's great Teacher, the Holy Spirit. Following is paragraph six from this lesson:

> "Forgiveness is acquired. It is not inherent in the mind, which cannot sin. As sin is an idea you taught yourself, forgiveness must be learned by you as well, but from a Teacher [the Holy Spirit] other than yourself, Who represents the other Self in you. Through Him you learn how to forgive the self you think you made, and let it disappear. Thus you return your mind as one to Him Who is your Self [Christ], and Who can never sin." (W-121.6:1-5)

In order to "let the self you think you made disappear", we simply stop listening to the ego just as we probably wouldn't listen to a raving lunatic in a mental asylum. A major problem is that, at least for most of us and certainly for me, until I started the mind training of ACIM, I never doubted what this raving lunatic (the ego) was telling me.

For me, it is clear that the many years of disciplined study of ACIM has allowed me to make steady progress so, while the ego still has some influence on my thinking, it is a whole lot less than it used to be. My life continues to get happier and this also helps many other people I associate with.

Lesson 122 – Forgiveness offers everything I want.

"Forgiveness", as defined by the world, has <u>nothing</u> to do with forgiveness as Jesus defines it in ACIM. As I've indicated many times in this book, forgiveness as Jesus defines it simply means that this world is but a dream that never happened so there is nothing to forgive. It is not easy to hold onto this idea at all times even for advanced students of ACIM. It's also important to recognize that all people born into this world "know" without a doubt that this world is real even though this turns out to be a lie. It generally takes a lot of mind training to begin to learn and remember the world is not real.

It will be helpful to define the different ways the world defines "forgiveness". In Section II of Chapter 2 of the supplement to ACIM called *The Song of Prayer* Jesus gives a few examples of the world's definition of "forgiveness." The title of this Section is "II. Forgiveness-to-Destroy." Following is a brief summary of Jesus' discussion of these examples:

1. The first type is where the so-called righteous person forgives his lesser brother. "In this group, first, there are the forms in which a 'better' person deigns to stoop to save a 'baser' one from what he truly is." (Song-2.II.2:1)
2. This next type is much less obvious than the first and can appear to be a good thing but, I assure you, it's not. This is where the person doing the forgiving knows he's done some real bad things in his life so he can forgive this other "sinner" for what he did. He's effectively saying we're both lesser persons and deserving of punishment. "The one who would forgive the other does not claim to be the better. Now he says instead that here is one whose sinfulness he shares, since both have been unworthy and deserve the retribution of the wrath of God." (Song-2.II.3:2,3)
3. Another type of worldly forgiveness goes as follows: If you do such and such, then I'll forgive you. "Forgiveness-to-destroy can also take the form of bargaining and compromise. 'I will forgive you if you meet my needs, for in your slavery is my release.' Say this to anyone and you are slave." (Song-2.II.6:1-3)

By contrast, forgiveness as defined by ACIM, offers everything you want. Here are the promises Jesus offers in the first paragraph of Lesson 122:

> "What could you want forgiveness cannot give? Do you want peace? Forgiveness offers it. Do you want happiness, a quiet mind, a certainty of purpose, and a sense of worth and beauty that transcends the world? Do you want care and safety, and the warmth of sure protection always? Do you want a quietness that cannot be disturbed, a gentleness that never can be hurt, a deep abiding comfort, and a rest so perfect it can never be upset?" (W-122.1:1-6)

Lesson 123 – I thank my Father for His gifts to me.

Please note, as you read through the 1-1/2 pages of text accompanying this lesson, that the gifts Jesus refers to have nothing to do with anything the world can offer. Whether the ACIM student is materially well-to-do or poor makes no difference whatsoever.

As we learn on an increasing basis as we study ACIM: "The world I see holds nothing that I want." (W-128.title) Jesus does point out in the Course that the Holy Spirit does, of course, know that we have certain physical needs while we're still in our dream and He will make sure those needs are met so we, of course, shouldn't worry about them.

Lesson 124 – Let me remember I am one with God.

Jesus was the first person to understand this lesson. That is why he said some 2,000 years ago: "I and the Father are one." Throughout ACIM, Jesus tells everyone that "You and God are one." This lesson is just another example of this simple truth.

Today, we have this ACIM book which, if diligently studied, allows us to at least move in the direction of this simple truth. By the time any of us get to start studying ACIM, we have thousands and thousands of bits of information about this world we think we live in. None of it is really meaningful in that its intent is to block us from the simple truth stated in this lesson and it does a great job of doing just that. As we come to understand and experience ACIM, this lesson and all the others become ever more meaningful.

For instance, consider the first lesson which reads "Nothing I see in this room [on this street, from this window, in this place] means anything." The entire dream world means nothing because (a) It's a dream, and (b) It gives us no clue whatsoever who we are. And who are we? We are an eternal part of God's Mind, one with Him because He gave us everything He had when He created us, and this has never changed just because we fell asleep. It's nice for me to know, as Jesus states in ACIM, that everyone will eventually wake up in Heaven. God created the Holy Spirit to make sure His separated Sons would all wake up and this was accomplished the instant we fell asleep .... at the beginning of time.

Lesson 125 – In quiet I receive God's Word today.

In the context of this lesson, God's Word means the Holy Spirit. So this lesson simply asks us to listen for the Voice of the Holy Spirit.

In the early years of my ACIM studies, this was difficult but it has gotten much easier in recent years. It's generally difficult for the new student because of all the attention we think we must give to the world which is simply another name for the voice of the ego. The ego, of course, wants us to stay stuck in the world because if we don't (i.e., if we stop listening to the ego) then the ego disappears into the nothingness from which he came.

Jesus sometimes uses the term "above the battleground" to mean mentally leave planet earth. There is even a section within the Text which defines in detail what this means and is entitled "Above the Battleground." (see T-23.IV)

Within my mind today, I can get off planet earth and be "above the battleground." Even here, however, I have two choices: (a) I can look at the happenings on planet earth without being a part of it, knowing it's not real because it's all just an insane dream, or (b) I can look away from everything going on here and be facing the peace of Heaven where all the crazy goings on here on earth are given no thought whatsoever. This second choice is naturally where I best find God's peace and where I can best hear God's Word, the Voice of the Holy Spirit.

Lesson 126 – All that I give is given to myself.

In Heaven, where we all are in truth, there is only one Mind – It is the Mind of God which encompasses God and all His Creation. In other words, there is only One of Us, or there is just Me. This is why "All that I give is given to myself." As Jesus states in this lesson: "Today we try to understand the truth that giver and receiver are the same." (W-126.8:1)

Although we're all dreaming our earthly dreams now, we will all eventually wake up in Heaven, our Home. In this lesson, Jesus once again tells us how important forgiveness is to us which is simply the ongoing remembrance that this whole life we think we are in is but a dream. He also points out how important our Teacher, the Holy Spirit, is to us in recognizing this fact. If we did not have this Teacher and learn to listen to Him, we would never learn how to wake up from our dreams. "Repeat today's idea, and ask for help in understanding what it really means. Be willing to be taught. Be glad to hear the Voice of truth and healing speak to you, and you will understand the words He speaks, and recognize He speaks your words to you." (W-126.10:2-4)

Lesson 127 – There is no love but God's.

This is a very important lesson. As Jesus states within its text: "Today we take the largest single step this course requests in your advance towards its established goal." (W-127.6:5)

As we advance as students in ACIM, my experience is it gets much easier. This lesson could also be stated as: "There is no love but God's and we all are part of that love." We can also say: "God is Love and so are we." Alternatively, "One Love is real which we all share with God. Nothing else is real." Understanding this is our goal and knowing its truth intellectually, for me, was not that difficult. The difficult part had been trying to maintain the happy spirituality taught by the Course when I've run into difficult people or difficult circumstances within my own individual dream life.

Such challenges have become easier as I've advanced in my ACIM studies which, for me, has included the ongoing study of the Course for over 15 years. Jesus does tell us in the Course that God does establish the end for all of us (Heaven) and also the means to get there (the Holy Spirit). As my life gets easier, I know that I'm effectively allowing the Holy Spirit to guide my mind more and, therefore, the ego has much less influence on me than he used to.

Lesson 128 – The world I see holds nothing that I want.

When I was 30 years old and living in our brand new 4-bedroom house in California with my first wife and our little girl and our son was about to be born, I already had everything I ever dreamed of. I remember thinking: "What else can the world offer me? I am so very happy." So I followed what I call the American dream. I knew, without a doubt, that more money meant more happiness and that was my primary goal for many years.

Well, as it turns out, I was wrong. The pursuit of money cannot bring lasting happiness. The pursuit of God can. What this lesson says quite clearly is that if I think that anything in the world, such as relationships, money, fame, travel, living in a special place, etc., is where I'll find happiness and contentment, then I'm barking up the wrong tree. For me, the pursuit of God, Who has nothing to do with this physical world, is where my happiness and joy lie.

Jesus said: "We can't serve two masters." In the same sense, I can't pursue worldly dreams and God at the same time.

"The world I see holds nothing that I want" because I want lasting happiness and joy and nothing in the world lasts – everything here, by definition, is temporary.

By the way, there's a significant and wonderful paradox when one starts incorporating the mind training of ACIM into their life. It's that the world becomes a much happier place to be in as we understand that it has nothing to offer us. As I've said before in this book, a wonderful reason to study ACIM in my experience is that you will become happier.

Lesson 129 – Beyond this world there is a world I want.

As Jesus clearly states, this lesson is a necessary adjunct to the previous lesson – yes, we must give up the world's thinking that the world offers something we want but we must replace it with the eternal promises of Heaven which is the world we want (it is also our natural inheritance from God). Without these eternal promises and experience, the giving up of the world's promises can only lead to depression.

Here are a few things Jesus says in this lesson about Heaven which is the world we want: "Is it a loss to find a world instead where losing is impossible; where love endures forever, hate cannot exist and vengeance has no meaning? Is it loss to find all things you really want, and know they have no ending and they will remain exactly as you want them throughout time?" (W-129.3:1,2)

I can really identify with the following sentences contained in this lesson which basically tell me to keep exchanging my worldly thoughts for eternal thoughts: "Now is the last step certain; now you stand an instant's space away from timelessness. Here can you but look forward, never back to see again the world you do not want. Here is the world that comes to take its place, as you unbind your mind from little things the world sets forth to keep you prisoner. Value them not, and they will disappear. Esteem them, and they will seem real to you." (W-129.5:1-5)

Try to remember, as I've emphasized in this book, "there is no world" so to want anything the world has to offer is to want nothing. Beyond this dream world, however, is Heaven which is the world you want.

Lesson 130 – It is impossible to see two worlds.

Lesson 128 tells us that earth (the world we see) has nothing that we want. Lesson 129 tells us that we want Heaven (the world beyond this one).

What this Lesson 130 tells us is that it is impossible be in both worlds at the same time and asks us to do our best to stay in Heaven's world for 5 minutes. When you realize that your mind makes many decisions every second and there are 300 seconds in a 5-minute period of time, you should appreciate that to stick with only eternal Heavenly thoughts for a full 5 minutes is not an easy task. However, Jesus only asks that we do the lesson as best we can and to ask for God's help in accomplishing it knowing that we can't do this on our own.

Lesson 131 – No one can fail who seeks to reach the truth.

This is one of my favorite lessons. I say it privately in my mind at least four times a day and I follow it with the following: "I will step back and let you lead the way, Jesus."

Within the text of this lesson, Jesus tells us that everyone on earth will reach Heaven – "Be glad as well to learn you search for Heaven, and must find the goal you really want. No one can fail to want this goal and reach it in the end." (W-131.4:2,3; underscore mine)

Jesus also points out in this lesson that Heaven is available to us in this physical life we think we're in – "Why wait for Heaven? It is here today. Time is the great illusion it is past or in the future. Yet this cannot be, if it is where God wills His Son to be. How could the Will of God be in the past, or yet to happen? What He wills is now, without a past and wholly futureless. It is as far removed from time as is a tiny candle from a distant star, or what you chose from what you really want." (W-131.6:1-7)

The essence of this lesson's practice sessions is, with the help of God, to mentally rise above all your worldly thoughts, all of which block us from remembering God, to our eternal Heavenly mind which is one with God and all His Creation.

Lesson 132 – I loose the world from all I thought it was.

This is a wonderful and very comprehensive lesson. Within the text of this lesson, Jesus states: "There is no world! This is the central thought the course [ACIM] attempts to teach." (W-132.6:2,3)

He acknowledges that accepting this fact (that the world is but a dream and not real) is not necessarily easy. For example, following are the two sentences immediately following the two I just quoted: "Not everyone is ready to accept it, and each one must go as far as he can let himself be led along the road to truth. He will return and go still farther, or perhaps step back a while and then return again." (W-132.6:4,5)

Jesus ties the truth of this lesson with the lessons which read "*I am as God created me.*" (Lessons 94, 110 and 162) Specifically, in this Lesson 132, he says "A lesson earlier repeated once must now be stressed again, for it contains the firm foundation for today's idea. You are as God created you." (W-132.9:1,2) And how did He create us? Before we made up this physical existence, God created us as an eternal, innocent, and joyous extension of Himself, one with Him and all His Creation. When we wake up from this physical dream, we'll know that "We are as God created us."

Lesson 133 – I will not value what is valueless.

In essence, this lesson combines lessons 128 and 129: "The world I see holds nothing that I want" and "Beyond this world there is a world I want." In other words, the world is valueless. Heaven, as we can all imagine, is very valuable.

How do we make this choice between worldly thinking and Heavenly thinking? Before attempting to give an answer to this question, please note that our minds are very active, making many choices every second, so we can be choosing right for a while and then revert to choosing wrong within a couple of seconds. We cannot make the right choice without God's help; that is, we need the help of the Holy Spirit/Jesus. Without His help, we could never possibly learn the simple fact that this world is but a dream. Once we appreciate this simple fact, we need a lot more help from the Holy Spirit/Jesus as we make many more choices while we continue to be in this dream world.

Our minds have two guides – the ego and the Holy Spirit/Jesus. We must train our minds to ignore the ego's voice and only obey the guidance we receive from the Holy Spirit/Jesus. When the ego is our guide, we've chosen worldly thinking and when the Holy Spirit is our guide, we've chosen Heavenly thinking. ACIM is a mind training course whose primary purpose, it can be said, is to teach us to obey God's voice and ignore the ego's voice. In this regard, a meditative thought I use every day is: "I hear the Voice that You (God) have given me and it is only this my mind obeys." This is the perfect goal yet to be fully accomplished by me. Personally, the ego still influences my choices today but a lot less than ever before. I am still a "Work in Progress."

Lesson 134 – Let me perceive forgiveness as it is.

What is forgiveness? This lesson digs into this question. This is also a major theme throughout the curriculum of ACIM.

Once again, let's go back to the two important statements contained in Lesson 132: "There is no world! This is the central thought the course [ACIM] attempts to teach." (W-132.6.2,3) Being only a dream, the world is not real. Once this starts being realized by the student, it should be easy to understand and accept that there is nothing to forgive. If I blamed a friend for stealing my wallet and subsequently realized I had simply misplaced it, I would of course have no trouble forgiving him (though he might have a real problem with me for accusing him). The same thinking can be applied with respect to every injury I ever thought was done to me in the world – It never happened! It was but my dream. So forgiveness, as taught by Jesus through his ACIM, truly means "there is nothing to forgive."

Beyond this world is Heaven which consists of God and His Creation. This is where we are in truth but dreaming this earthly dream. Heaven is what we want and, once we fully awake from this insane dream world, we will appreciate that we have always been in Heaven. Heaven is our only reality. This world we think we live in does not really exist, being a figment of our imagination. This is why the Introduction to the text of ACIM includes the following great summary:

> "*This course can therefore be summed up very simply in this way:*
> "*Nothing real can be threatened.*
> "*Nothing unreal exists.*
> "*Herein lies the peace of God.*" (T-Introduction.2:1-4)

Lesson 135 – If I defend myself I am attacked.

Our reality, which cannot be changed because this is how God created us, is that we are an eternal and innocent part of God's Creation and are One with Him. This reality needs no defense because it can't be threatened. Obviously, if something can't be threatened, it does not require any defense and, as I pointed out in the previous lesson: "Nothing real can be threatened." (T-Introduction.2:2)

By contrast, the world's thinking sees potential threats around every turn and with nearly everyone encountered during the day. Jesus describes the so-called normal person in this world in the second paragraph of this section: "You operate from the belief you must protect yourself from what is happening because it must contain what threatens you. A sense of threat is an acknowledgement of an inherent weakness; a belief that there is danger which has power to call on you to make appropriate defense. The world is based on this insane belief. And all its structures, all its thoughts and doubts, its penalties and heavy armaments, its legal definitions and its codes, its ethics and its leaders and its gods, all serve but to preserve its sense of threat. For no one walks the world in armature but must have terror striking at his heart." (W-135.2:1-5) Naturally, for the large majority of people in the world who "know" it as a real place, such threats and fears are reasonable. One of the many treasures I've received as a result of studying the Course is I can smile at everything in the world and say to myself: "Thank God that all this is but a dream and is not at all real."

Jesus, at the end of this lesson, asks the student who is tempted to get defensive and weave plans for his own safety to remind himself to stop doing so by using the following words: "*This is my Eastertime. And I would keep it holy. I will not defend myself, because the Son of God needs no defense against the truth of his reality.*" (W-135.26:6-8)

Lesson 136 – Sickness is a defense against the truth.

Consider the following fact Jesus tells us in this lesson: "Truth [God] merely wants to give you happiness, for such its [His] purpose is." (W-136.12:4) Sickness, by definition, brings unhappiness and therefore does not come from God. It is clear that in Heaven there is no such thing as sickness.

This lesson answers the question: "Where did sickness come from?" During my life, I've had very bad colds that have lasted for over a month and, at times, I've been clinically depressed for months at a time. Who caused my sickness? Jesus clearly tells me that I caused my own sickness. In paragraph 7 he specifically tells us that we get sick because we are afraid to give up this world for the truth: "Sickness is a decision. It is not a thing that happens to you, quite unsought, which makes you weak and brings you suffering. It is a choice you make, a plan you lay, when for an instant truth arises in your own deluded mind, and all your world appears to totter and prepare to fall. Now are you sick, that truth may go away and threaten your establishments no more." (W-136.7:1-4)

For me, this lesson becomes easy to accept as I learn and experience that the world comes from me and not at me. This entire physical world, along with time, is simply a dream I made up. It is not real! Therefore, everything that has ever happened here stems from my mind. This is only good (or great) news. First, all of the bad things I thought happened, including the holocaust orchestrated by Hitler, never happened. Second, God has guaranteed that all people in this dream, those who previously died, the 7 billion of us alive today and those yet to be born in the future, will all eventually wake up from our dreams and be fully awake in Heaven. God sent the Holy Spirit as His Agent for this "waking up" process.

Lesson 338 states "I am affected only by my thoughts." When I've been sick, it's not my body that had anything to do with it – I "thought" myself sick. This is why, in this Lesson 136, Jesus gives us the following simple healing prayer which only makes reference to a healed mind: "Sickness is a defense against the truth. I will accept the truth of what I am, and let my mind be wholly healed today." (W-136.15:6,7) It is only our minds which can be healed because everything else is a dream and is not real. The physical body gets healed when our minds are healed. Jesus states this specifically in this lesson: "Now is the body healed, because the source of sickness has been opened to relief." (W-136.17:1)

Lesson 137 – When I am healed I am not healed alone.

A part of the truth is that God has only one Son. There are no individuals in Heaven. Though we shouldn't get preoccupied with this idea while we're still here in the dream, it does establish one simple way to understand this lesson. If I am a piece of God's Son and so are you, then when I get healed it also helps you.

However, the current benefits to me of getting (mentally) healed in this life are wonderful. It's been my experience that as I get healed, I'm able to be of significant help to many other people in my life. In paragraph 10 of this lesson, Jesus states: "And as you let yourself be healed, you see all those around you, or those who cross your mind, or whom you touch or those who seem to have no contact with you, healed along with you. Perhaps you will not recognize them all, nor realize how great your offering to all the world, when you let healing come to you. But you are never healed alone. And legions upon legions will receive the gift that you receive when you are healed." (W-137.10:1-4) It's clear to me that as I get healed, I keep getting happier which, as I indicated earlier in this book, is a primary motive for studying ACIM. I also have a very outgoing personality and when I'm in a store, such as Wal-Mart, I often brighten the day with many of the people I encounter there. My happiness is contagious.

Lesson 138 – Heaven is the decision I must make.

Nobody in their right mind, given the choice, would decide for something other than Heaven. The problem is that there are very few people in their right mind.

We all get here (in this dream world) by thinking that we actually have separated from God. This is an absurd idea because when God created us, He did so as an eternal part of Himself, sharing His Will and all He is with us. This truth and this reality, which is Heaven, continues now and forever.

When we're born into the world, we all believe this world is real and we learn the laws of the world. We certainly all see ourselves as separate from everyone else. Even for very fortunate people, the world's laws are quite harsh, always requiring some sacrifice, sadness, disharmony and, of course, always ending in death.

The first individual who understood the unreality of the world, the physical universe and time itself was Jesus. He was also able to disregard the world's voice in his mind (the ego) and be guided only by the Holy Spirit. To the best of my knowledge, there haven't been too many others in the past 2,000 years who have fully followed in his footsteps. With the publication of his ACIM book in 1976, we can certainly hope for an acceleration in the number of individuals who wake up from this dream world in the future. As Jesus indicates many times in ACIM, ultimately everyone will wake up.

Why is the decision for Heaven that difficult? One major reason is that we have to give up everything that we think this world offers us. Lesson 128 reads: "The world I see holds nothing that I want." (underscore mine) Clearly, this lesson has to be taken very literally. What makes this difficult for me, and I don't believe I'm alone here, is the paradox that as I learn and experience the principals of ACIM on an increasing basis, the world becomes a real happy place to be in for me. All I can say to you readers on this point is that my Inner Voice (Jesus/Holy Spirit) assures me that I'm on the right path.

Lesson 139 – I will accept Atonement for myself.

When God created us in Heaven, before we fell asleep dreaming up this insane world with its beginnings and endings, its good and bad times, its suffering, and its death, we were totally in God's Will. There is only One Mind in Heaven which is God's Mind which He fully shares with Us, His Son and all His Creation. In Heaven, we are happy, joyous and free without a care or concern forever and ever. This is our natural state. This is who we are. We have and are everything that our Creator has and is. We are effectively God, the only difference between God and us is that God created us and we did not create Him.

The previous paragraph describes how God created us and who we continue to be. Can I accept this? It sounds really good to me. I like the following combination of Lessons 199 and 94: "I am not a body. I am free. For I am still as God created me." When "I accept Atonement for myself", I accept that this is my reality and I also accept that this world is but a dream that I made up with the sick part of my mind which has been guided by the ego. Neither the ego nor the world are real because God did not create them and only what God created is real.

Common sense tells me, as does Jesus time and again throughout ACIM, that I can't be an eternal part of the God Mind and think that anyone else in the world is any different than me. Clearly, you too were created by God just as I was and it matters not in the slightest what good or bad things you've done here in this dream world. In Paragraph 9 of this lesson, Jesus tells us that he (Jesus) and we have a wonderful task here: "We have a mission here. We did not come to reinforce the madness that we once believed in. Let us not forget the goal that we accepted. It is more than just our happiness alone we came to gain. What we accept as what we are proclaims what everyone must be, along with us. Fail not your brothers, or you fail yourself. Look lovingly on them, that they may know that they are part of you, and you of them." (W-139.9:1-7)

Lesson 140 – Only salvation can be said to cure.

Jesus defines the word cure differently than does the world. A person with cancer is given chemotherapy and his cancer disappears. He is "cured" of cancer. All that has really happened is that both the patient and the doctor have turned a sick body into a healthy body. This is a far cry from a permanent solution because later on in life the patient still dies. (I've assumed that neither the doctor nor patient are ACIM students in this hypothetical situation.)

Salvation, on the other hand, is a cure for all eternity and the great news is that it is available in this life through studying ACIM. This has been my own experience. With the mind training of ACIM, which automatically causes our minds to progressively listen more to the Holy Spirit/Jesus and less to the ego, we can get cured forever. Please note that elsewhere in the Course, Jesus tells us that salvation and forgiveness mean the same thing as he defines them in ACIM. Therefore, this lesson could also be written as "Only forgiveness can be said to cure."

In paragraph 3 of this lesson, Jesus does a good job of describing my 15 years of studying and experiencing ACIM: "The happy dreams the Holy Spirit brings are different from the dreaming of the world, where one can merely dream he is awake. The dreams forgiveness lets the mind perceive do not induce another form of sleep, so that the dreamer dreams another dream. His happy dreams are heralds of the dawn of truth upon the mind. They lead from sleep to gentle waking, so that dreams are gone. And thus <u>they cure for all eternity</u>." (W-140.3:1-5; underscore mine)

Lessons 141-150 – Review IV (review of Lessons 121-140)

Each of these lessons, 141 through 150, reviews two previous lessons so, at the end of these 10 days, the student has reviewed the 20 lessons, 121 through 140.

Each of these ten lessons begins with the same meditative statement which can be considered another lesson because it is the truth. It is "My mind holds only what I think with God." Please note that we can hold on to ego thoughts (i.e., thoughts not from God) for a very long time but not forever. In other words, we can't wake up in Heaven with any ego thoughts. As an example, an individual can have a resentment against a spouse they divorced many years earlier but any such resentment thoughts are not from God. However, before such an individual can fully wake up from this dream world, any such unloving thoughts must be gone from his or her mind.

Lesson 151 – All things are echoes of the Voice for God.

The "Voice for God" is the Holy Spirit. The other voice in our mind is the ego.

We all start out in this life by believing the ego. What Jesus tells us is to stop listening to the ego. In this lesson, regarding the ego's voice, Jesus says specifically: "Hear not its voice. The witnesses it sends to prove to you its evil is your own are false, and speak with certainty of what they do not know. Your faith in them is blind because you would not share the doubts their lord [the ego] can not completely vanquish. You believe to doubt his [the ego's] vassals is to doubt yourself." (W-151.6:1-4)

The "Voice for God", or the Holy Spirit, is the Great Corrector. Although He knows the truth (the unified Mind of God and His Creation or Heaven), He also is able to help us in every aspect of our dream world. He can help us to take everything and every situation in this dream world and perceive it positively when we let Him direct our minds and stop listening to the ego. When we are listening only to the Holy Spirit, we are in our right mind. And when we are listening only to the Holy Spirit, "All things are echoes of the Voice for God."

Specifically in this lesson, Jesus tells us to doubt the evidence we witness in the world and let the Holy Spirit help us believe the truth of who we and our brothers are. "Yet you must learn to doubt their evidence [i.e., the ego's vassals] will clear the way to recognize yourself, and let the Voice for God alone be Judge of what is worthy of your own belief. He will not tell you that your brother should be judged by what your eyes behold in him, nor what his body's mouth says to your ears, nor what your fingers' touch reports of him. He [the Holy Spirit] passes by such idle witnesses, which merely bear false witness to God's Son. He recognizes only what God loves, and in the holy light of what He sees do all the ego's dreams of what you are vanish before the splendor He beholds." (W-151.7:1-4)

Lesson 152 – The power of decision is my own.

I can identify with Jesus because, like me, he was stuck in this dream world. And while he was here, he learned from the Holy Spirit how to wake up from this place. As a matter of fact, he was the first person to ever accomplish this and he remains to help the rest of us do the same – not in body, of course, but in spirit.

I can't readily identify with the Holy Spirit because He's never been stuck in the dream. Often, in this book, I refer to the Holy Spirit/ Jesus. What I have learned is that the thoughts I receive from the Holy Spirit and those I receive from Jesus are exactly the same which is why I often combine their names. I have also sometimes referred to their thoughts as my Inner Voice. Personally, like many other Course students, I usually think of my Inner Voice as Jesus speaking to me rather than the Holy Spirit. I love that gospel song, *What a friend we have in Jesus.*

For anyone who clings to the belief that this world is real and was created by God rather than some man made dream, paragraph 6 of this lesson really suggests you reconsider: "Is it not strange that you believe to think you made the world you see is arrogance? God made it not. Of this you can be sure. What can he know of the ephemeral, the sinful and the guilty, the afraid, the suffering and the lonely, and the mind that lives within a body that must die? You but accuse Him of insanity, to think He made a world where such things seem to have reality. He is not mad. Yet only madness makes a world like this." (W-152.6:1-7)

One of the most important facts underlying ACIM is that this world is but a dream you are in. Your job is to wake up from the dream and you can't do this by listening to the ego's voice, although the ego will do its best to convince you that his is the voice of reason because the ego's survival depends on us continuing to believe its lies. You must learn to listen to the Voice of Jesus/Holy Spirit. The power of decision is yours – you can keep listening to the ego or you can learn how to listen to the Voice for God, the Voice of Jesus/Holy Spirit. For me, the continued study of ACIM has allowed me to listen on an increasing basis to Jesus/Holy Spirit which means I'm getting ever more happy, more joyous and more free.

Lesson 153 – In my defenselessness my safety lies.

The vast majority of people in the world today believe it is real. Let's consider such a person who has lived a good life, has retired and is enjoying his retirement years in Southern California. His wife passed away a few years ago and he's accepted that. He gets to go fishing regularly which he really enjoys and has good relations with everyone. His three children are married and he's blessed with 7 grandchildren and is able to visit them on a regular basis. Financially he is well off. He goes for regular checkups with his doctor and his health is good. In general, life is good. However, he's still going to die which he's not looking forward to. In order to prolong his life, he always takes the advice of his doctor and takes some blood pressure medication and carefully monitors his diet and exercises regularly as recommended by his doctor. So this man, being "normal", is doing a lot to defend himself against his inevitable death.

By contrast, I am not at all afraid of dying because I know there is no such thing as death. I know, without a doubt, that "I am not a body. I am free. For I am still as God created me." I know, without a doubt, that this world is not at all real but a dream that I made up. God would have to be very mean, even evil, to have made a world where there is so much pain, suffering, sacrifice, anguish, hate and death. The fact is God had nothing to do with the making of this world but He did create the Holy Spirit to wake us all up from this dream world we think we're in. All we have to do to start waking up is to learn how to listen to the Holy Spirit/Jesus and stop listening to the world's voice which is the ego.

In ACIM, Jesus points out that God has no favorites among all his children (i.e., all human beings). His Voice, the Holy Spirit, is available to all of us. What Jesus says is: " 'Many are called but few are chosen' should be, 'All are called but few choose to listen.' " (T-3.IV.7:12) With the mind training guide of ACIM, I am one who is choosing to listen and I am a real happy guy today. If you believe ACIM is for you, my suggestion is keep studying it as this is what I've been doing and my life and attitude keep getting better.

Lesson 154 – I am among the ministers of God.

I, Jimmy Laws, am among the ministers of God.

Jesus states in paragraph 5 of this lesson: "A messenger is not the one who writes the message he delivers. Nor does he question the right of him who does, nor ask why he has chosen those who will receive the message that he brings. It is enough that he accept it, give it to the ones for whom it was intended, and fulfill his role in its delivery. If he determines what the messages should be, or what their purpose is, or where they should be carried, he is failing to perform his proper part as bringer of the Word." (W-154.5:1-4)

I have been learning, and more importantly experiencing, the truth underlying Jesus teachings from ACIM. In a nutshell, the world is nothing and Heaven is everything. Obviously, this book is a message from me to other ACIM students. It may also be helpful to those who are considering whether or not to dig into ACIM on a disciplined basis. The thoughts I express in this book are honest and are guided by the Voice of Jesus/Holy Spirit.

By writing this book and putting so many of the spiritual ideas into my own words, I have gained immensely in my own spiritual growth. Even if this book were read by no one else but me, it has been of tremendous value to me. This is consistent with the point Jesus makes in paragraph 6 of this lesson: "There is one major difference in the role of Heaven's messengers, which sets them off from those the world appoints. The messages that they deliver are intended first for them. And it is only as they can accept them for themselves that they become able to bring them further, and to give them everywhere that they were meant to be. Like earthly messengers, they did not write the messages they bear, but they become their first receivers in the truest sense, receiving to prepare themselves to give." (W-154.6:1-4)

Lesson 155 – I will step back and let Him lead the way.

The text of this lesson is full of the gifts received by those of us who allow ourselves to be led by God's Voice (Jesus/Holy Spirit). The world becomes a crazy dream movie made up by the ego and, using Christ's vision, we see right through it to Heaven which is the truth. While still in the movie, we play our part accordingly and become a beacon to other people. This is why Lesson 61 states: "I am the light of the world."

Listen to the promises in the 1st paragraph of this Lesson 155: "There is a way of living in the world that is not here, although it seems to be. You do not change appearance, though you smile more frequently. Your forehead is serene; your eyes are quiet. And the ones who walk the world as you do recognize their own. Yet those who have not yet perceived the way will recognize you also, and believe that you are like them, as you were before." (W-155.1:1-5)

Personally, I am not aware of anyone in my life, other than myself and my friend, Ken Wapnick, who studies ACIM on an ongoing basis, year after year. Of my many friends, only a few know I study this wonderful guide towards awakening from this world of tragedy and death. Based on my own experience, it takes a lot of dedication to even give ACIM a fair chance and, while I've suggested to a few friends to consider its study, I know of none that have pursued it. However, all my friends know me as a very happy guy with a wonderful wife, a beautiful 6-year old little girl and another baby on the way. I take care of my responsibilities, I don't fret and I really enjoy life.

You folks who have read this far in this book, God bless you. I truly hope you're enjoying it. This book is clearly no substitute for the wonderful guide that Jesus gave us and, if you want a real happy life which gets happier all the time, I suggest you study ACIM and then keep studying it. In my own experience, not only have I studied the Text continuously for 15 years but I also did the 365 lessons about 10 times during the first 12 years I studied the Course; during the past three years, I study the lessons after I study the Text but I study them as I study the Text rather than "doing" them as described in the Workbook. I do believe that I've followed my Inner Voice (Jesus/Holy Spirit) in this regard and His instructions to someone else could be a lot different.

Lesson 156 – I walk with God in perfect holiness.

Paragraph 7 of this lesson really describes my current walk in this world: "Yet you have wasted many, many years on just this foolish thought [referring to the thought of sin with all that goes with it – guilt, fear, punishment and death]. The past is gone, with all its fantasies. They keep you bound no longer. The approach to God is near. And in the little interval of doubt that still remains, you may perhaps lose sight of your Companion, and mistake Him for the senseless, ancient dream that now is past." (W-156.7:1-5)

The "senseless, ancient dream that now is past" is the world. It is not real and never was. It is just a smokescreen to keep us from seeing what is real which is Heaven. And Heaven has always been real. These thoughts combine to bring us to peace of mind which is not available from the world. Remember how ACIM begins:

> "Nothing real can be threatened [Heaven].
> "Nothing unreal exists [the world].
> "Herein lies the peace of God." (T-Introduction.2:2-4)

Lesson 157 – Into His Presence would I enter now.

At the end of this lesson, Jesus indicates that it is into Christ's Presence we enter. Specifically, he states: "Into Christ's Presence will we enter now, serenely unaware of everything except His shining face and perfect Love." (W-157.9:1) Christ, as defined in ACIM, is not Jesus but rather all that God created so Christ includes all people in the dream as well as the rest of God's Creation (including all animal and plant life). Christ therefore includes Jesus, me, you and everyone who ever lived and will live in this dream world. And Heaven can be thought of as the sum of the Creator (or Father), His Creation (Christ) and the Holy Spirit.

In Heaven, all 3 of Us share the same Mind. While here in the dream, I indicated earlier in this book that the voice or thoughts that Jesus offers us are the same as those coming from the Holy Spirit. In this lesson, Jesus indicates that Christ can also guide us: "He will direct your practicing today, for what you ask for now is what He wills." (W-157.4:1) Clearly, any guidance (words or thoughts) from Christ will be no different than those from Jesus or the Holy Spirit. I can therefore think of my Inner Voice as the Holy Spirit, Jesus or Christ communicating with me. This is consistent with what Jesus tells us in the Text of ACIM: "The Holy Spirit is the Christ Mind which is aware of the knowledge that lies beyond perception." (T-5.I.5:1)

If you are doing this lesson correctly, you will find yourself in total peace, literally without a care in the world because the whole purpose is to enter into the presence of God, or Heaven, which has nothing to do with this crazy world. It has been my experience that the ability for me to experience such peace has increased over the years though my earthly life continues to get busier.

Lesson 158 – Today I learn to give as I receive.

Paragraph 5 of this lesson is: "A teacher does not give experience, because he did not learn it. It revealed itself to him at its appointed time. But vision is his gift. This he can give directly, for Christ's knowledge is not lost, because He has a vision He can give to anyone who asks. The Father's Will and His are joined in knowledge. Yet there is a vision which the Holy Spirit sees because the Mind of Christ beholds it too." (W-158.5:1-6)

Based on the spiritual principles of ACIM, there is a powerful simple mental tool I say many times a day which I suggest you try. It is my gift to you:

> "Don't judge but use Christ's vision instead. We are all eternal, innocent, spiritual parts of Christ Himself."

It does not matter if you are the most evil person in the world. The truth of who you are was established when God created you in Heaven - eternal, joyful and innocent. In this regard, I like the combination of Lesson 199 – "I am not a body. I am free." and Lesson 94 (Lessons 110 and 162 are identical) – "I am as God created me."

Remember, once again, that this world is but a dream and is not real. Sin, of course, does appear to happen here but with the help of Jesus and the Holy Spirit, we learn to see right through the dream to the truth of who we are, along with everyone else. The preceding sentence does a good job of defining the meaning of Christ's vision.

Lesson 351 tells us why we want to see our brothers as innocent (i.e., sinless): "My sinless [innocent] brother is my guide to peace. My sinful [guilty] brother is my guide to pain. And which I choose to see I will behold."

As we become better at using Christ's vision, the benefit to us is incredibly good. This world becomes a joyful place to be in. And it matters little whether good or bad things appear to be happening in the world because we are waking up from all its illusions.

Lesson 159 – I give the miracles I have received.

In this lesson, Jesus emphasizes the gift of Christ's vision as he did in Lesson 158. Christ's vision allows me to see all people as they are in truth - eternal and innocent (i.e., sinless) spiritual children of our Creator.

Paragraph 3 of this lesson really links the miracle to Christ's vision: "Christ's vision is a miracle. It comes from far beyond itself, for it reflects eternal love and the rebirth of love which never dies, but has been kept obscure. Christ's vision pictures Heaven, for it sees a world so like to Heaven that what God created perfect can be mirrored there. The darkened glass the world presents can show but twisted images in broken parts. The real world pictures Heaven's innocence." (W-159.3:1-5) In the last sentence of this excerpt, Jesus uses the term "real world." The "real world", as defined in ACIM, is a beautiful place to be. It is when we're seeing with Christ's vision and guided by God's Voice (Jesus/Holy Spirit) but we're still a human being in this dream world.

In this lesson, Jesus points out how important Christ's vision is – "Christ's vision is the miracle in which all [other] miracles are born. It is their source, remaining with each miracle you give, and yet remaining yours." (W-159.4:1,2)

In paragraph 10, Jesus says: "Judge not God's Son, but follow in the way He has established." (W-159.10:3) Some of you will ask: "How can I stop judging all the people in my life?" Admittedly, when first commencing the study of ACIM, this was not easy for me to do simply because the world consistently teaches that to judge others is exactly what we should do. After 15 years of working ACIM, it has gotten so much easier to not get caught in that trap. Once again, following is my simple meditation tool which I use many times a day to help me stay away from judging others:

> "Don't judge but use Christ's vision instead. We are all eternal, innocent, spiritual parts of Christ Himself."

Lesson 160 – I am at home. Fear is the stranger here.

Twice a day, I mentally review a long series of memorized meditative thoughts most of which come directly from ACIM. Two consecutive sentences I include are: "My present happiness is all I see. All fear is past and only love is here." These are Lessons 290 and 293 from ACIM's Workbook. You might note that they also state pretty much what this Lesson 160 states.

When alone, I can easily think of my mind as a room with 3 people in it – myself, Jesus and Mr. Ego. So when I read paragraph 2 of this lesson, Jesus is saying to me that he and I are here in my mind but there is also this insane stranger, Mr. Ego. This paragraph says, in part: "There is a stranger in our midst [the ego], who comes from an idea so foreign to the truth [Heaven] he speaks a different language, looks upon a world truth does not know [this physical world], and understands what truth regards as senseless. (W-160.2:1)

Jesus points out in this lesson that fear and love cannot coexist. He states: "There is no home can shelter love and fear. They cannot coexist." (W-160.4:5,6) For me, I've added that they can't coexist "at the same time." Like most (perhaps all) good students of spirituality, I can be smooth sailing in this dream world for a while, basically letting Jesus/ Holy Spirit lead the way, and then get disturbed and react to some curve ball the world throws my way. Some ego temptation, usually in my personal life, has entrapped me and I get upset or angry or impatient or …. whatever. Because of my spiritual progress, I am happy to report that such disturbances are happening less frequently over time.

In paragraph 7 Jesus asks us: "Who is the stranger?" (W-160.7:1) Clearly the answer is "the ego." The mind training of ACIM teaches us to stop listening to this insane entity and only listen to the Voice of the Holy Spirit/Jesus. The ego has not left my mind but I'm not too likely to even get caught up in its lies anymore, never mind hold on to them for very long when they have caught my interest.

Please note that in the last two paragraphs of this lesson (9 and 10) Jesus brings Christ's vision into the forefront once again. Those of us who use Christ's vision still use our eyes to "see" the world but we know it's just an illusion and not true; we do our best to look on everyone we meet as eternal innocent individuals while we are still here in the dream world.

Lesson 161 – Give me your blessing, holy Son of God.

This lesson is quite different from the earlier lessons. It asks us to choose a specific person in our life and first see him as we always have with our eyes. Jesus says seeing him this way (as a body) is effectively a block to Christ's vision and a block to seeing him as your savior. Specifically, Jesus says: "Then think of this: What you are seeing now conceals from you the sight of one who can forgive you all your sins; whose sacred hands can take away the nails which pierce your own, and lift the crown of thorns which you have placed upon your bleeding head. Ask this of him, that he may set you free:

> *"Give me your blessing, holy Son of God. I would behold you with the eyes of Christ* [Christ's vision], *and see my perfect sinlessness in you."* (W-161.11:5-8)

When I see someone with Christ's vision, I see them as an eternal, innocent, joyous spirit. Thus, when I'm right-minded, this is how I conceive of myself and all other people and we're all the same.

Jesus essentially says we should be sure to use today's idea when we're about to express anger at someone. So instead of getting angry, we should say mentally "Give me your blessing, holy Son of God." When we do this, Jesus gives us this promise: "And you will see him suddenly transformed from enemy to savior; from the devil into Christ." (W-161.12:6)

In the first paragraph of this lesson, Jesus tells us: "Here is salvation in the simple words in which we practice with today's idea." (W-161.1:2) The simplicity of salvation is stated by Jesus in the Text of ACIM as follows:

> "How simple is salvation! All it says is what was never true is not true now, and will never be. [The world's a dream and never happened.] The impossible has not occurred, and can have no

> effects. And that is all. Can this be hard to learn by anyone who wants it to be true?" (T-31.I.1:1-5)

In this lesson, Jesus nicely defines Christ, God's one Son, as follows: "One brother is all brothers. Every mind contains all minds, for every mind is one. Such is the truth." (W-161.4:1-3)

As I've indicated earlier in this book, I can still get angry once in a while but such episodes are decreasing in quantity and magnitude. What's clearly been happening for me is that on an increasing basis my decisions are being guided by Jesus and the ego is losing its hold on my mind.

An important point I want to make is that Jesus/Holy Spirit allows me to make such mistakes (getting angry, annoyed, intolerant, impatient, etc.) and helps me to correct my mind after the fact. Also, where warranted and given the opportunity, I can get back to the person I got angry at and make my apologies if my Inner Voice tells me it's appropriate.

Lesson 162 – I am as God created me.

This is the third time Jesus gives us this exact lesson – Lessons 94 and 110 are the others.

This lesson is simple and powerful. God and His Creations, Who share God's One Mind, have never changed although We keep extending forever. I am part of His Creation and so are you and We continue to be as He created Us. This is our only reality. Heaven is real.

This world we think is real for a while is not. It's but an insane dream from which we will all wake up. In truth, the world is nothing.

In reality, or in Heaven, we share God's Will and are co-creators with Him. Because we share His Will, we are effectively part of God. Here's one of the many places in ACIM where Jesus explicitly states this truth:

"We accept Your [our Father's] Thoughts as ours, and our will is one with Yours eternally." (W-163.9:7) Therefore, we can summarize this lesson by saying: "God is and nothing else is." Alternatively, we can say: "God is and the world is not." We can really simplify this to just: "God is."

Lesson 163 – There is no death. The Son of God is free.

Follow this simple logic please. God is eternal and He only creates like Himself so He only creates the eternal and His Creation is happy, joyous and free like Himself. Nothing in this world is eternal so God could not have created it.

The world is but our dream and the world itself will disappear (as do all dreams) when the last person wakes up from his individual dreams.

Personally, I am not afraid of death because I know that I can't die. I'm not afraid of anyone in my life dying because I know that they can't die either although very few people in the world understand this. Of course I know that my body will stop functioning like everyone else's so within the world's dream, I (i.e., my illusionary body) will die like everyone else.

By the way, I have been to a number of funerals and am able to act appropriately and be helpful to people saddened by the loss of loved ones.

Lesson 164 – Now are we one with Him Who is our Source.

If you can experience this lesson even a little, you will begin to appreciate the gifts that God has always held for you.

An important point Jesus makes in this lesson is that the gifts of God are available to us now, in this life. By contrast, the vast majority of "believers" in the world today believe that the gifts of God will be obtained following the death of their body. Through the mind training of ACIM, the student learns that these gifts will be received in the here and now, even though Heaven is still a step away.

In the first paragraph, Jesus says, regarding Christ: "He looks past time, and sees eternity as represented there. He hears the sounds the senseless, busy world engenders, yet He hears them faintly. For beyond them all He hears the song of Heaven, and the Voice for God more clear, more meaningful, more near." (W-164.1:4-6)

We are all a part of Christ and as our mind becomes one with His, His experience becomes our experience if we are doing the lessons correctly. Consider the first two sentences of paragraph 2: "The world fades easily away before His sight [Christ's vision]. Its sounds grow dim." (W-164.2:1,2) As we learn and experience that we are one with Christ, we understand that this is where our mind should be going also, especially as we practice this lesson.

Believing the world is just a dream, you can also believe that the world is simply a huge number of "vain imaginings." This thinking may give added meaning to what Jesus tells us in paragraph 5: "This is the day when vain imaginings [the world] part like a curtain, to reveal what lies beyond them [i.e., Heaven]. Now is what is really there made visible [not to the eyes but to the mind], while all the shadows which appeared to hide it merely sink away. Now is the balance righted, and the scale of judgment left to Him Who judges true. And in His judgment will a world unfold in perfect innocence before your eyes. Now will you see it with the eyes of Christ [Christ's vision]. Now is its transformation clear to you." (W-164.5:1-6)

Lesson 165 – Let not my mind deny the Thought of God.

"What makes the world seem real except your own denial of the truth that lies beyond? What but your thoughts of misery and death obscure the perfect happiness and the eternal life your Father wills for you? And what could hide what cannot be concealed except illusion? What could keep from you what you already have except your choice to see it not, denying it is there?" (W-165.1:1-4)

The beginning of an individual's happiness is when he or she thinks, as is so often stated in ACIM: "Okay, I'm willing to consider this new idea that this world I have always considered real is, in fact, just a dream." Continue studying the Course and other ideas from the Course become believed and experienced on an increasing basis. Much of the text of this Lesson 165 is summarized by the idea from Lesson 129: "Beyond this world there is a world I want."

For those stuck on the old idea that this world is real and was made by God, please use some common sense. This world is one where its participants are striving to be happy without any permanent success. Everyone has had relationship problems, financial issues, health concerns for themselves and/or others and we all end up dead, often preceded by suffering. On a social basis, every community has to deal with crime, courts, punishment, community welfare, schools, etc. And on an international basis, we're now dealing with terrorists, drug smuggling and "wars and rumors of wars" as Jesus so succinctly stated it some 2,000 years ago. If God is good, how could He have anything to do with putting this world on the map? If God were mean and punishing, then the world could be His plan. What ACIM tells us is that God is really perfectly good and He didn't create the world; that we made it up in our minds when we thought we separated from Him; and that, although we think it real, it's only a dream from which we will all wake up. ACIM, of course, goes much further in teaching us how to wake up.

Lesson 166 – I am entrusted with the gifts of God.

Like everyone else born into this world, there was no question in my mind that this world was real. I was 49 years old before I started studying ACIM in 1999. At this time in my life, I was divorced twice with two children from my first marriage and I had been fired from a company I had worked for nearly 20 years. In other words, I had been through some tough times and my life was a mess.

Jesus describes my 1999 condition very well in paragraph 6 of this lesson: "He seems a sorry figure; weary, worn, in threadbare clothing, and with feet that bleed a little from the rocky road he walks [this is a metaphor - my feet weren't bleeding]. No one but has identified with him, for everyone who comes here has pursued the path he follows, and has felt defeat and helplessness as he is feeling them." (W-166.6:1,2)

The first 8 paragraphs of this lesson do a wonderful job of describing everyone in the world who believes the world to be real. It's my understanding that there aren't too many of us who believe otherwise. This world is really a brutal place and I say: "Thank God it's not real!"

Paragraphs 9 through 15 give us the solution which leads to the gifts of God. Jesus also tells those of us who have been entrusted with God's gifts to learn to give these gifts to others.

Our Father has no knowledge of this dream. However, when He saw that we "fell asleep" in Heaven, He instantly created the Holy Spirit for the purpose of guaranteeing that we would all wake up. And so we will. This is summarized in paragraph 10 of this lesson: "God's Will does not oppose. It merely is. It is not God you have imprisoned in your plan to lose your Self. He does not know about a plan so alien to His Will. There was a need He did not understand, to which He gave an Answer. That is all. And you who have this Answer given you have need no more of anything but this." (W-166.10:1-7;underscore mine) And the Answer God gave was the Holy Spirit. Our solution to all our problems forever is simple but not easy – Within our minds, we must stop using advice from the ego and only use advice from the Holy Spirit (or Jesus, who speaks with the same Voice).

Lesson 167 – There is one life, and that I share with God.

Among other things, this lesson tells us that we live forever in the mind of God. Although we think we're here on earth, we are but dreaming a senseless dream from which we will wake up.

Life, in the mind of God, is one of constant joy and therefore there is no discomfort whatsoever. In paragraph 2, Jesus defines death for purposes of ACIM as any feeling other than one of constant joy: "Yet we have learned that the idea of death takes many forms. It is the one idea which underlies all feelings that are not supremely happy. It is the alarm to which you give response of any kind that is not perfect joy. All sorrow, loss, anxiety and suffering and pain, even a little sigh of weariness, a slight discomfort or the merest frown, acknowledge death. And thus deny you live." (W-167.3:3-7)

We were created by God in Heaven and one with Him and this is where we remain and live in truth. The fact remains, however, that we think we are here on earth and Jesus talks a lot about this in this lesson: "The mind can think it sleeps, but that is all. It cannot change what is its waking state. It cannot make a body, nor abide within a body. What is alien to the mind does not exist, because it has no source. For mind creates all things that are, and cannot give them attributes it lacks, nor change its own eternal, mindful state. It cannot make the physical. What seems to die is but the sign of mind asleep." (W-167.6:1-7) "What seems to be the opposite of life is merely sleeping." (W-167.9:1) "When the mind awakes, it but continues as it always was [eternally joyful]." (W-167.9:4)

Lesson 168 – Your grace is given me. I claim it now.

One of the key points of this lesson is that God has never delayed His Love from us. It is we who have delayed receiving it.

"God loves His Son. Request Him now to give the means by which this world will disappear, and vision first will come, with knowledge but an instant later. For in grace you see a light that covers all the world in love, and watch fear disappear from every face as hearts rise up and claim the light as theirs. What now remains that Heaven be delayed an instant longer? What is still undone when your forgiveness rests on everything?" (W-168.4:1-4)

Are there one or more people in the world you don't like and hold some resentment against? If so, then you're not seeing him or her with Christ's vision. This could very well be why you can't let this world disappear. Jesus, in the above quoted paragraph 4 tells us what we need to do – Ask God (i.e., Jesus/Holy Spirit) for the means to overcome any such angry thoughts.

There can be other reasons why we have difficulty in letting this world totally disappear including guilt associated with harms to yourself or others, all kinds of fears and your sexual behavior and thinking. We will also see tempting good things the world will use to entice us. In all cases, the answer is the same – Ask God for help.

In the Text, Jesus tells us that God will sometimes take the final step with us which allows us to have the experience of revelation. It is a temporary experience of Heaven. A revelationary experience is what Jesus means by God's grace. In paragraph 3 of this lesson, Jesus spells this out for us: "Today we ask of God the gift He has most carefully preserved within our hearts, waiting to be acknowledged. This the gift by which God leans to us and lifts us up, taking salvation's final step Himself. All steps but this we learn, instructed by His Voice [i.e., Jesus/ Holy Spirit]. But finally He comes Himself, and takes us in His Arms and sweeps away the cobwebs of our sleep. His gift of grace is more than just an answer. It restores all memories the sleeping mind forgot; all certainty of what Love's meaning is." (W-168.3:1-6) In other words, we get to experience the full impact of Heaven during a revelationary experience.

Lesson 169 – By grace I live. By grace I am released.

This lesson, like the previous one, talks of God's grace which I have called a revelationary experience. It can also be thought of as a temporary step into Heaven. As of this writing, I have not had such an experience. However, my current spiritual state is well defined in paragraph 3: "Grace is not learned. Grace is not the goal this course aspires to attain. Yet we prepare for grace in that an open mind can hear the Call to waken. It is not shut tight against God's Voice. It has become aware that there are things it does not know, and thus is ready to accept a state completely different from experience with which it is familiarly at home." (W-169.3:1-6)

This lesson also describes the Oneness of God and His Creation (i.e., Heaven): "Oneness is simply the idea God is. And in His Being, He encompasses all things. No mind holds anything but Him. We say 'God is,' and then we cease to speak, for in that knowledge words are meaningless. There are no lips to speak them, and no part of mind sufficiently distinct to feel that it is now aware of something not itself. It has united with its Source. And like its Source Itself, it merely is." (W-169.5:1-7)

In paragraph 10, Jesus tells us that when we have a revelationary experience, we will know it: "There is no need to further clarify what no one in the world can understand. When revelation of your Oneness comes, it will be known and fully understood. Now we have work to do, for those in time can speak of things beyond, and listen to words which explain what is to come is past already. Yet what meaning can the words convey to those who count the hours still, and rise and work and go to sleep by them?" (W-169.10:1-4)

Paragraph 11 speaks to me especially, as well as other ACIM students I'm sure. It says: "Suffice it, then, that you have work to do to play your part. The ending must remain obscure to you until your part is done. It does not matter. For your part is still what all the rest depends on. As you take the role assigned to you, salvation comes a little nearer each uncertain heart that does not beat as yet in tune with God."

Regarding this book which clearly represents work I'm doing to play my part, I naturally hope a lot of other people read it, enjoy it and benefit from it. However, even if no one else reads it, I have really enjoyed writing it. More importantly, I have benefitted tremendously in my understanding of ACIM as a result of writing this book.

Lesson 170 – There is no cruelty in God and none in me.

Throughout the Course, Jesus helps us learn how not to attack others and ourselves. Clearly, attack separates me from other people and reduces or destroys my own peace of mind. Attack takes many forms. Certainly, anger and rage are attack. But so are resentments, impatience, intolerance and bad gossip. All of these are part of the "blame game" and none of these are in God. Then, of course, we have guilt, where we attack ourselves but God never does. By the way, although there may be a few exceptions, when ACIM makes reference to guilt which it does a whole lot, I've learned that its intent is to include "blame" as well. In other words, whether I think I'm guilty or someone else is guilty makes no difference – I'm way off base because the truth is that we are all innocent.

In paragraph 2 of this lesson, Jesus gives us the following important suggestion:

> *"You make what you defend against, and by your own defense against it is it real and inescapable. Lay down your arms, and only then do you perceive it false."* (W-170.2:6,7)

Lesson 153 adds to this: "In my defenselessness my safety lies." "Surrender to win" also says the same thing in a nutshell. The ego based need to be right is a very common cause for attack thoughts. Therefore, consider the following question: "Would I rather be happy or right?" (For everyone's sake, happy is the correct answer.)

In paragraph 10, Jesus asks us the question: "Where does the totally insane belief in gods of vengeance come from?" One obvious answer is from the Bible. While the Bible contains many beautiful and accurate passages concerning God, many times it tells us that God is vengeful. For example, the Bible tells us that after Adam and Eve "sinned" in the Garden of Eden, God came down and spoke to them as follows: "To the woman He said, 'I will greatly increase your pains in child bearing; with pain you will give birth to your children. Your desire will be for your husband, and he will rule over you.' To Adam He said, 'Because you listened to your wife and ate from the tree about which I commanded you, 'You must not eat of it,' cursed is the ground because of you; through painful toil you will eat of it all the days of your life. It will produce thorns and thistles for you, and you will eat the plants of the field. By the sweat of your brow you will eat your food until you return to the ground, since from it you were taken; for dust you are and to dust you will return.' " (Genesis 3:16-19)

If God actually metes out punishment like this, I would be running away from Him as fast as I could. Thank God the punishing God concept contained in the Bible is 100% myth.

Lessons 171-180 – Review V (review of Lessons 151-170)

Each of these lessons, 171 through 180, reviews two previous lessons so, at the end of these 10 days, the student has reviewed the 20 lessons, 151 through 170.

Each of these ten lessons begins and ends with the same meditative statement which can be considered another lesson because it is the truth. It is "God is but Love, and therefore so am I." Remember: "I am as God created me." (Lessons 94, 110 and 162) These 3 identical lessons include this same wonderful idea that "God is but Love, and therefore so am I." And I'll add "and so is everyone else including you who are reading these words."

I always find it very reassuring when Jesus tells us that he is always with us on every step of our journey. He does this very frequently throughout ACIM and he does so in the Introduction to the Review V lessons: "I take the journey with you. For I share your doubts and fears a little while, that you may come to recognize the road by which all fears and doubts are overcome. We walk together. I must understand uncertainty and pain, although I know they have no meaning. Yet a savior must remain with those he teaches, seeing what they see, but still retaining in his mind the way that led him out, and now will lead you out with him. God's Son is crucified until you walk the road with me." (W-Review V.Introduction.6:1-6)

Lesson 181 – I trust my brothers, who are one with me.

This lesson can be easily misunderstood. Suppose there is a person in your life who you know to have "slippery fingers." In other words, cash and jewelry seem to disappear when he visits people's homes. This lesson does not mean that you should start trusting him to be left by himself in your house.

Who is my brother? He is the same as me, an eternal innocent part of God. When I see anyone with Christ's vision, this is who I see. He is one with me and we are one with God. This is Who we are in truth and this is the brother I trust.

As Jesus instructs us in this lesson: "We enter in the time of practicing with one intent; to look upon the sinlessness within." (W-181.5:7)

Lesson 182 – I will be still an instant and go home.

As so often stated in ACIM, our home is Heaven. This is where we are in truth but we are asleep dreaming this earthly dream. The words of this lesson are clear. We try and still all our worldly thoughts for an instant and during this time try to remember our home in Heaven.

Everyone born into this world is initially convinced that this world is their home. Jesus certainly thought this in his younger years. And, of course, so did I. And I assure you that you'll not find many people in the world today who would agree that this world is but a wispy dream. However, this is exactly what Jesus tells us in ACIM. And please be real happy that this is so. I certainly am.

Paragraph 3 of this lesson tells us how the vast majority of people go about their lives: "We speak today for everyone who walks the world, for he is not at home. He goes uncertainly about in endless search, seeking in darkness what he cannot find; not recognizing what it is he seeks. A thousand homes he makes, yet none contents his restless mind. He does not understand he builds in vain. The home he seeks can not be made by him. There is no substitute for Heaven [our only home]. All he ever made was hell." (W-182.3:1-7)

A good summary of this lesson is: "Take periodic breaks during the day, leave all earthly concerns behind and rest in God (or rest in Heaven which is your home)." If we form this habit, we can be certain that our days will be much easier than they were prior to doing this.

Lesson 183 – I call upon God's Name and on my own.

You and I are God's Son and God withholds nothing from His Son. This is why Jesus says in the first paragraph of this lesson: "To call upon His Name is but to call upon your own." (W-183.1:2) For purposes of this lesson, God plus all His Creation is also God. Thus, God is Love,

God is Heaven and God is Everything. When I call upon God's Name, I am Love, I am Heaven and I am Everything. This is the essence of this lesson.

The two pages of this lesson all support what I've briefly stated in the preceding paragraph. For example: "Repeat God's Name, and you acknowledge Him as sole Creator of reality. And you acknowledge also that His Son is part of Him, creating in His Name." (W-183.8:1,2)

Lesson 184 – The Name of God is my inheritance.

God is Oneness. God is Love and so Love is Oneness. We are part of God so we, too, are Oneness. God and His Creation are Heaven so Heaven, too, is Oneness. There is no separation in God and, of course, none in Heaven.

By contrast, this world, including all stars and planets beyond earth, is one of separation. And the more we study it, whether it be with electron microscopes or powerful telescopes, the more separate parts we see.

"This is the way [the world's] reality is made by partial vision, purposefully set against the given truth [Heaven]. Its [The world's] enemy is wholeness [another name for Oneness]. It conceives of little things and looks upon them. And a lack of space, a sense of unity or vision that sees differently, become the threats which it must overcome, conflict with and deny." (W-184.4:1-4) What Jesus says here is that if you are stuck on the reality of the world, then you must deny Heaven.

Jesus also tells us that we all initially believe this world is real. He says: "Such is the teaching of the world. It is a phase of learning everyone who comes must go through." (W-184.7:1,2)

This lesson makes reference to God's inheritance. What is God's inheritance for all of us? "To be happy, joyous and free forever and ever" is a good summary. Clearly, the world will never be able to offer anyone this. Yet it's ours for the thinking – remember, Jesus describes his Course as a course in mind training. And it's clear to me that as the years roll by with ACIM as my study guide, I keep becoming more happy, joyous and free. So it is possible to unlearn the world's thinking and literally "think our way out of hell into Heaven."

The previous lesson tells us that we are One with God. Jesus tells us elsewhere that we summarize all Creation when we say "God is." Nothing else need be said. "The name of God is my inheritance." He says that simply saying "God" should allow our mind to leave all earthly thoughts behind and "be happy, joyous and free" even if its just for a few seconds. Such mental turns into the "truth" are defined as "holy instants" elsewhere in ACIM.

Lesson 185 – I want the peace of God.

In Heaven, the peace of God is always and forever. Absolute peace of mind is not a little gift and this is what "the peace of God gives us."

To receive the peace of God means you stop thinking the world has anything to offer you. "To mean you want the peace of God is to renounce all dreams [renounce all the world's temptations]. For no one means these words who wants illusions, and who therefore seeks the means which bring illusions. He has looked on them, and found them wanting. Now he seeks to go beyond them, recognizing that another dream would offer nothing more than all the others. Dreams are one to him [a dream is a dream is a .... etc.]. And he has learned their only difference is one of form, for one will bring the same despair and misery as do the rest." (W-185.5:1-6)

Jesus tells us to ask ourselves a simple question regarding any part of our life which we think, if changed, would add to our happiness. He effectively says all such plans are one and states: "And being one, one question should be asked of all of them, 'Is this what I would have, in place of Heaven and the peace of God?' " (W-185.8:8)

The world will never be able to offer anyone "the peace of God." Therefore, Lessons 128 and 129 go hand in hand with this one. Lesson 128 says: "The world I see holds nothing that I want." And Lesson 129 says: "Beyond this world there is a world I want [Heaven and the peace of God]."

Lesson 186 – Salvation of the world depends on me.

Although not discussed by Jesus in this lesson, the thinking I'll share with you in this paragraph helped me overcome many of my egotistical thoughts associated with this lesson. The complete salvation of the world occurs when the last person on earth is saved. Therefore, "Salvation of the world depends on each and every one of us." Salvation of the world depends on every one I meet in my daily activities. I am not special. Jesus says there is, in truth, no difference between him and us. In Heaven, which is truth, we are all the same and united in Oneness to our Father. Only in time and here on earth are there differences. And both time and earth are just part of a dream fabricated by the ego from which we will all wake up. Time and earth are nothing.

Throughout this lesson, Jesus talks about our function here. In the last two sentences of the lesson, he tells us specifically what our function is: "Salvation of the world depends on you who can forgive. Such is your function here." (W-186.14:5,6) If you're a student of ACIM, I remind you that the word "forgive" to you should mean that this whole world and universe is a crazy dream coming from your mind from which you will wake up at home in Heaven. You should not take the world seriously and you certainly shouldn't blame anyone (including yourself) for the so called bad parts of your dream.

I use the following meditative words every day which help keep me mindful of who I am and what the world is. If they help you, please feel free to use them with or without modification.

> *"Use the power of the light of the Atonement – I am effectively God; everything else I made up."*
>
> Explanation: In truth, I am one with God's Mind and have everything He has. Although I am not God, I have all that he has and so I say "I am effectively God." The earth, the stars, my body, your bodies, etc., are all part of a crazy dream which my ego-guided mind made up or conjured up. None of it is real.

Lesson 187 – I bless the world because I bless myself.

Included in this lesson are many of the blessings we receive as our mind gets trained to reduce and ultimately eliminate the world's thinking and replace it with God's thinking.

The lesson starts out with the idea of giving. Although you are free to give, say, a nice birthday gift to someone, ACIM is not at all referring to this type of giving. "Having had and given, then the world asserts that you have lost what you possessed. The truth maintains that giving will increase what you possessed." (W-187.1:7,8)

"Protect all things you value by the act of giving them away, and you are sure that you will never lose them." (W-187.1:1) So in general, "To have (more) love, give love." And do your best to stop valuing anything the world appears to offer you because as Lesson 128 says: "The world I see holds nothing that I want."

This lesson talks about the end of sacrifice. Fairly early on in my ACIM studies, I could appreciate that it meant the end of sacrifice for me. Since "sacrifice" to me meant doing something for another that I didn't want to do, this gift which I've accepted into my life has made me a much happier person.

The fear of people, which I carried with me most of my life has virtually disappeared as a result of my ACIM studies. When I apply Christ's vision (we are all eternal innocent joyous spiritual beings), I can't fear anyone. In this lesson, Jesus talks of this gift as well as the elimination of our fear of God (often subconscious). In this regard, who can honestly say they have no fear of God but they fear one or more of his children?

Paragraph 11 summarizes this lesson: "Now are we blessed, and now we bless the world. What we have looked upon we would extend, for we would see it everywhere. We would behold it shining with the grace of God in everyone. We would not have it be withheld from anything we look upon. And to ensure this holy sight is ours, we offer it to everything we see. For where we see it, it will be returned to us in form of lilies we can lay upon our altar, making it a home for Innocence Itself, Who dwells in us and offers us His Holiness as ours." (W-187.11:1-6)

Lesson 188 – The peace of God is shining in me now.

As we learn from ACIM, the world you see is all coming from your mind. And all your problems are coming from this world you made up. Therefore, all your problems are coming from your own mind; they are within you. And the Holy Spirit, the Wonderful Corrector, and your right mind are also within you. ACIM is a mind training course and, as you train your mind to think with the Holy Spirit (i.e., with God) and stop thinking with the world (i.e., with the ego), you become saved.

Jesus tells us in this lesson that we need not and should not delay our happiness. The "peace of God" is ours for the asking but, in general, it does take a lot of mind training to receive all the gifts available. All of our "old ideas" about the world need to get replaced with God ideas (i.e., with "the truth that sets us free.")

I like what Jesus says here about the progressive gifts God gives us: "To you, the giver of the gift, does God Himself give thanks. And in His blessing does the light in you shine brighter, adding to the gifts you have to offer to the world." (W-188.4:3,4) My increasing happiness and peace of mind as I continue my ACIM mind training work attests to increased spiritual gifts.

Lesson 189 – I feel the Love of God within me now.

This is a very important lesson. In essence, in this lesson's exercises, Jesus tells us to "feel" Heaven. In Heaven, there is no thinking because there is nothing to be learned. There are no words; in the text Jesus tells us that "words are but symbols of symbols." We simply "are." We feel happy, joyous and free in the never ending now.

In paragraph 7, Jesus gives us these specific instructions: "Simply do this: Be still, and lay aside all thoughts of what you are and what God is; all concepts you have learned about the world; all images you hold about yourself. Empty your mind of everything it thinks is either true or false, or good or bad, of every thought it judges worthy, and all the ideas of which it is ashamed. Hold onto nothing. Do not bring with you the one thought the past has taught, nor one belief you ever learned before from anything. Forget this world, forget this course, and come with wholly empty hands unto your God." (W-189.7:1-5)

The phrase "forget this course" in this quote has special meaning to me. Because of my zeal for ACIM, it took me many years to appreciate that this book is not the only path for individuals to awaken from the dream. Jesus tells us this specifically in the Course. He tells us there are thousands of other paths and everyone will, of course, awaken and find their way home. Two or three years ago, I was at a Course teaching session by Ken Wapnick who pointed this out. This is when my mind opened to this simple but important fact. (Thank you, Ken.)

Lesson 190 – I choose the joy of God instead of pain.

Among other things, this lesson tells me that I am still "a work in progress." You see yesterday, as I was mowing our lawn, I was bit by about 20 fire ants and I was in some real pain as a result; even today, I'm feeling some pain from those bites. Though I told myself a number of times yesterday as well as today that the pain I'm feeling is not real and is just a part of my dream, it still feels real to me. Jesus tells us in this lesson: "Pain is a wrong perspective. When it is experienced in any form, it is a proof of self-deception. It is not a fact at all. There is no form it takes that will not disappear if seen aright." (W-190.1:1-4)

It is my belief that sometime before Jesus was baptized by John the Baptist, he was fully in his right mind so the Holy Spirit was his only guide (i.e., the ego had stopped influencing him altogether). This means that when Jesus had those spikes nailed into him and he was hanging on the cross, he felt no pain. Although it appeared to the many witnesses that he suffered, in fact he did not suffer at all. This lesson tells me this.

Elsewhere in the Course Jesus tells us that all of our physical senses are but illusions to aid us in thinking that the world is real and, of course, that our bodies are real. In many of the lessons in the Course, including this one, he tells us to leave all our illusions behind us so we can remember and experience the joy of Heaven. I suppose if I were in excruciating pain for a time, my Inner Voice (Jesus/Holy Spirit) would direct my thinking into Heaven during that time. It would then be up to me as to whether I heeded Their Voice.

Lesson 191 – I am the holy Son of God Himself.

While Jesus doesn't say this in this particular lesson, I can't know that I am the holy son of God Himself without also knowing that you are also the holy Son of God Himself. In truth, we all share the same Mind as God. This is why I can say that "I and the Father are one", just as

Jesus said this 2,000 years ago. I can also say that "You and the Father are one", whoever you are.

For the mass of people who believe this world is real, Jesus says: "What have you done that this should be your world? What have you done that this is what you see? Deny your own Identity [the holy Son of God Himself], and this is what remains. You look on chaos and proclaim it is yourself. There is no sight that fails to witness this to you. There is no sound that does not speak of frailty within you and without; no breath you draw that does not seem to bring you nearer death; no hope you should hold but will dissolve in tears." (W-191.2:1-6)

Jesus continues: "Deny your own Identity [the holy Son of God Himself], and you will not escape the madness which induced this weird, unnatural and ghostly thought that mocks creation and that laughs at God [i.e., the world]. Deny your own Identity, and you assail the universe alone, without a friend, a tiny particle of dust against the legions of your enemies. Deny your own Identity, and look on evil, sin and death, and watch despair snatch from your fingers every scrap of hope, leaving you nothing but the wish to die." (W-191.3:1-3)

The world we think we live in has <u>nothing</u> to do with Who we are. We are the holy Son of God Himself. And God only created One Son so Our Identity is shared with everyone else including Jesus as well as people we don't like or even hate.

In this lesson, Jesus says: "For he who can accept his true Identity is truly saved." (W-191.5:3) Personally, I fully accept that I am the holy Son of God Himself and so is everyone else. Therefore, I am "truly saved." This does not mean, however, that I do not make mistakes. While I'm doing a good job of letting Jesus/Holy Spirit be my guide, the ego still gets my attention sometimes. I know this because I can still be somewhat impatient or intolerant of others and once in a while I'll even express anger at someone. These feelings are all from the ego. I'm very happy to report that such negative feelings are happening less often than ever before so my happiness continues to increase.

Lesson 192 – I have a function God would have me fill.

In the first two paragraphs of this lesson, Jesus tells us our function in Heaven is to create with God and our function here on earth is to forgive.

In paragraph 3, Jesus tells us that we need the help of the Holy Spirit. We cannot accomplish our function here without His help. In general, common sense tells us that an insane mind can't fix itself without some outside help.

The rest of the lesson largely tells us to use Christ's vision which is really a necessary part of forgiveness. And what is Christ's vision? It is seeing all people as the Holy Spirit wants us to see them, as eternal innocent spiritual beings, all beautiful, all identical to each other and all identical to our self. I can't see anyone this way with my eyes but I can do so with my mind. When I use Christ's vision, it matters not at all whether an individual is one of the most evil of all human beings or one of the most loving of all human beings; both of these people are seen as eternal innocent Creations of God. This is not difficult to do so long as we remember that this world is but a dream with many nightmare parts which we made up with our ego (insane) minds but we will all eventually wake up at home in Heaven.

There is another aspect to Christ's vision which is very important. Jesus tells us in Lesson 30 that before we see through this illusory world to truth (Heaven), we should picture all things in the world as one with us rather than as separate from us. This ties in with Jesus' famous Lord's prayer where he says to do God's Will on earth as it is in Heaven. In Heaven there is only Oneness and that's how we want to see this world also. Following are Jesus' instructions on this from Lesson 30: "Today we are trying to use a new kind of 'projection.' We are not attempting to get rid of what we do not like by seeing it outside. Instead, we are trying to see in the world what is in our minds, and what we want to recognize is there. Thus, we are trying to join with what we see [or think], rather than keeping it apart from us. That is the fundamental difference between vision and the way you see." (W-30.2:1-5)

Lesson 193 – All things are lessons God would have me learn.

The first two paragraphs of this lesson can be summarized as follows. Jesus tells us many times in ACIM that our Father God does not come into our dreams. He is not following our worldly lives at all. However, as soon as we decided to separate from Him and "fell asleep in Heaven", He created the Holy Spirit to guarantee that we would all wake up (awaken). The Holy Spirit is the Great Teacher Who teaches us how to wake up from this world we think we are in. Ever since Jesus ascended into Heaven about 2,000 years ago, he's also here to help us. So Jesus and the Holy Spirit will teach us all the lessons we need to learn.

Forgiveness, as defined by ACIM, is a word that summarizes everything we need to learn. Here's a simple definition of this all important idea: "You fell asleep in Heaven and are dreaming you're in this world but don't worry about it because you will wake up."

Jesus gives us two important meditative thoughts in this lesson to help us wake up sooner rather than later:

> *"Forgive, and you will see this differently."* (W-193.3:7)
>
> and
>
> *"I will forgive, and this will disappear."* (W-193.13:3)

For me today, I know that when my mind turns to any kind of negative thinking, I have effectively fallen into the trap of making the world real and so, with the help of my Inner Voice, I need only remember this world's but a dream and I should not take it seriously at all. With few exceptions, I become happy again within a short period of time.

I really enjoy laughter and, in this lesson, Jesus tells us that God does too. Regarding all negative acts, emotions, etc., Jesus says: "For God has willed that laughter should replace each one, and that His Son be free again." (W-193.9:5)

Lesson 194 – I place the future in the Hands of God.

This is a very important lesson which, as we approach its goal, the promises contained throughout this lesson become true.

In paragraph 1, Jesus says: "Today's idea takes another step toward quick salvation, and a giant stride it is indeed! So great the distance it encompasses, it sets you down just short of Heaven, with the goal in sight and obstacles behind. Your foot has reached the lawns that welcome you to Heaven's gate; the quiet place of peace, where you await with certainty the final step of God. How far are we progressing now from earth! How close are we approaching to our goal! How short the journey still to be pursued!" (W-194.1:1-6)

And in paragraph 2, he adds: "Accept today's idea, and you have passed all anxiety, all pits of hell, all blackness of depression, thoughts of sin, and devastation brought about by guilt. Accept today's idea, and you have released the world from all imprisonment by loosening the heavy chains that locked the door to freedom on it. You are saved, and your salvation thus becomes the gift you give the world, because you have received." (W-194.2:1-3)

Later on in this lesson, Jesus tells us our thinking doesn't have to be always accurate in order for us to accept this lesson and really benefit from it. In paragraph 7, he describes a person like me whose perception is not always accurate: "He is sure that his perception may be faulty, but will never lack correction. He is free to choose again when he has been deceived; to change his mind when he has made mistakes." (W-194.7:7,8)

There is another lesson which I use daily and which includes much of the thinking of this lesson. It is Lesson 155 which reads: "I will step back and let Him lead the way." For me, I've modified this lesson slightly in my mind because I really like having Jesus with me at all times so I say: "I will step back and let you lead the way, Jesus."

Lesson 195 – Love is the way I walk in gratitude.

What is Love? God is Love. God plus His Creation share one Mind; another name for this one Mind is Heaven. Therefore, Heaven is Love.

There are no negative thoughts in Heaven whatsoever. There is only gratitude and joy forever and ever.

In this lesson Jesus says: "Love makes no comparisons." (W-195.4:2) When we use Christ's vision to see others there is no comparison. We are all eternal innocent spiritual beings; happy, joyous and free forever. Naturally, this type of seeing has nothing to do with an individual's lot in this world and this is as it should be since this world is but a crazy dream. Truth, Love, Heaven .... or whatever other term you might like for our Real Self is so much better than who we think we are in this worldly dream.

In paragraph 6 Jesus talks about the one Mind of our Father and His Creation as follows: "We thank our Father for one thing alone; that we are separate from no living thing, and therefore one with Him. And we rejoice that no exceptions ever can be made which would reduce our wholeness, nor impair or change our function to complete the One Who is Himself completion [our Father]. We give thanks for every living thing, for otherwise we offer thanks for nothing, and we fail to recognize the gifts of God to us." (W-195.6:1-3)

Keeping this lesson simple for me, I know: "Whenever I have any negative thinking in my mind whatsoever, even if everyone in the world tells me it is appropriate, I am definitely outside of God's Will." And I sometimes have negative thinking which simply means I still make mistakes.

I remember Ken Wapnick teaching that we all make mistakes but that we shouldn't hold onto guilt as a result. Rather, forgive yourself and move on. Our mistakes become our teachers for better tomorrows because we're less likely to make the same mistake again. By the way, when you hold onto guilt as a result of a mistake, the ego is real happy; he's got you where he wants you.

Lesson 196 – It can be but myself I crucify.

After studying and experiencing ACIM for so many years, this idea is very simple for me to understand. The world I see and think about is my dream. The world is not real. It does not come at me; rather it comes from my mind. If I attack anything in the world, I am therefore attacking my own dream and I am attacking myself. The word attack, as used in ACIM, includes a host of different feelings and emotions – anger, rage, intolerance, impatience, guilt (anger at oneself), resentment, dislike, crucify, etc. This lesson, of course, uses the word crucify.

Please note that everyone on earth is dreaming their own individual dream. While we may share some common parts such as planet earth, the sun, husband and wife living under the same roof, etc., all of us meet different people in our dreams, have different conversations and our individual opinions about everything vary all over the place.

Truth, on the other hand, sees right through our dreams and acknowledges them for what they are – a temporary nothing. "And you will see within today's idea the light of resurrection, looking past all thoughts of crucifixion and of death [and past all worldly thoughts], to thoughts of liberation and [eternal] life." (W-196.3:4)

Lesson 197 – It can be but my gratitude I earn.

Let's keep this discussion real simple. God's Will for me is to be happy so whenever I'm not happy, I am not in God's Will.

Many people make sacrifices for others and expect at least a pat on the back for their work. When they don't get their just rewards, they get angry and resentful. Jesus talks about this in the first paragraph of this lesson: "You make attempts at kindness and forgiveness. Yet you turn them to attack again, unless you find external gratitude and lavish thanks." (W-197.1:2,3)

If you feel you are making a sacrifice for another, you are outside of God's Will right there. Jesus tells us repeatedly that sacrifice is never a God thing; it is always an ego thing. God knows not of sacrifice. There is no sacrifice in Love.

This does not mean I don't do things for other people. I often do but I do it because I want to and I enjoy doing it. I am happy while I'm doing it and the doing of it is its own reward. If the person thanks me for the favor, that's okay. If the person doesn't or criticizes me for not doing it "his way", that's okay too.

Lesson 198 – Only my condemnation injures me.

Another word for condemnation is judgment. So when I judge another person, this lesson tells me that I injure myself. Using Christ's vision, wherein we see in everybody an eternal innocent happy spiritual being, means we are not judging them at all. They are the same as you and me, the same as everyone else and, of course, the same as Jesus.

The world doesn't teach the lesson of non-judgment described in the preceding paragraph. For example, if someone ridicules us in a public setting, the world tells us to defend ourselves and it's not a bad idea to point the finger back at the person judging us for his wrong doing. After all, as the saying goes, "The best defense is a good offense." Consider political debates as a wonderful example of this worldly tradition.

Jesus tells us in ACIM that we need not defend ourselves (in this crazy dream of our own making). Lesson 135 says: "If I defend myself I am attacked." And Lesson 153 says: "In my defenselessness my safety lies."

I am overcoming what, for me, had been very difficult. It's where someone judged/condemned me (publicly or privately; it mattered not) and historically I'd get angry and both wanted to defend myself and make accusations against my "enemy" and that was often my recourse. The ego loved this approach because it really helps make the separation deeper between us.

With his help and the help of the Holy Spirit, Jesus says we should neither defend ourselves nor judge others. Jesus explains in ACIM that when someone loves us, the appropriate response is love. This is real easy. When someone attacks us, the appropriate response is love which is not that easy. Love never attacks or defends itself. You can think of it this way probably – Whatever your concept of Heaven is, does Heaven ever have to defend itself or accuse anyone? For the large majority of us the answer is "no." As we really start experiencing and living ACIM, see how easy it gets because Jesus points out that, regardless of the situation we find ourselves in, the only response is love. Intellectually, Jesus makes this idea real simple because he tells us that when someone gets angry he or she is "always asking for love", although the angry person will generally not agree with this.

As you study this lesson from the 3 pages of ACIM, Jesus once again tells us that forgiveness is our answer here in our dream world. And what is forgiveness? It is the realization that the world is but a dream coming from my mind while I sleep in Heaven. "There is no world! This is the central thought the Course attempts to teach." (W-132.6:2,3) The world you think you are living in is actually this massive insane hallucination your mind has concocted. If you attack or condemn anything in the world, therefore, you're attacking or condemning yourself. This largely explains the meaning of this lesson.

My suggestion is to stop taking your dream world so seriously since it's not real. You can't, as far as I know, be real serious and real joyful at the same time.

Lesson 199 – I am not a body. I am free.

This lesson goes hand in hand with Lessons 94, 110 and 162 which all read: "I am as God created me." And God created me as an eternal spirit, not restricted in any way with man made laws which control me at virtually every level of my life on earth; God created me as a totally free spirit.

It's important for me to remember that, in truth, I'm not any different than anyone else. Therefore, "You, too, are not a body and you, too, are free." The following thinking really helps me with this idea: Regardless of what's going on in my dream world and your positive or negative part in it, we are all innocent eternal spiritual beings created by God, Himself. Once again, here, I've used Christ's vision to see all people in the world.

At the end of this lesson, Jesus tells us:

> "And God Himself extends His Love and happiness each time you say:
>
> > *"I am not a body. I am free. I hear the Voice that God has given me, and it is only this my mind obeys."* (W-199.8:6-9)

The "Voice that God has given us" is, of course, that of the Holy Spirit/Jesus. We have another voice in our mind which is of our own making and has nothing to do with God. This is the voice of the ego. To only obey God's Voice and never obey the ego's voice is the goal towards which we strive. To make progress in ACIM means we're obeying God's Voice more and, therefore, we're obeying the ego's voice less. To date, I have not reached the ultimate goal, although I'm making good progress – I still obey the ego's voice sometimes. You see the ego is a cunning, deceitful and powerful thing and sometimes I think I'm totally in line with God's Mind when, in fact, the ego's tricked me again which I discover by a disturbance to my spirit and, with the help of my Inner Voice, I can usually see what mistake I made.

Lesson 200 – There is no peace except the peace of God.

Many of the baby boomers are retiring today and many of them are thinking along the following lines: "Once I retire, I'll have my winter home in Florida and my summer home on that nice lake up in New Hampshire. Life will be wonderful!" This type of plan has nothing to do with the *peace of God* because all you're doing is substituting one earthly illusion for another.

The *peace of God* can be obtained while we're in this world but we don't get it from the world. The best way I can describe the *peace of God* is that I'm wide awake and fully alert and my mind is just floating; I am totally at peace without a care in the world because I'm not thinking about anything in the world.

The *peace of God* is, of course, an ongoing attribute forever when we awaken at home in Heaven. We can get a real good taste of it while we're here on earth if we follow the directions Jesus has laid out in ACIM. Leastwise, this has been my experience. In paragraph 4, Jesus tells us to "Come home" and he's asking us to do this now as we practice this lesson. Following is this paragraph in its entirety: "Come home. You have not found your happiness in foreign places and in alien forms that have no meaning to you, though you sought to make them meaningful. This world is not where you belong. You are a stranger here. But it is given you to find the means whereby the world no longer seems to be a prison house or jail for anyone." (W-200.4:1-5)

You can remember that Jesus also tells us to "go home" to Heaven in Lesson 182 which is: "I will be still an instant and go home." There is a lot of repetition in ACIM which is necessary because of our initial conviction that this world is real and we must unlearn this lie which is "simple but not easy."

Lessons 201-220 – Review VI (review of Lessons 181-200)

In the Introduction to these review lessons, Jesus makes the point that any one of these 20 lessons, all by itself, is sufficient for our salvation. He then explains why there are 20 we need to study, rather than just one. Here's what he says: "Each of these ideas alone would be sufficient for salvation, if it were learned truly." (W-Review VI.Introduction.1:3) "Each contains the whole curriculum if understood, practiced, accepted, and applied to all seeming happenings throughout the day. One is enough. But from that one, there must be no exceptions made. And so we need to use them all and let them blend as one, as each contributes to the whole we learn." (W-Review VI.Introduction.2:2-5)

Please note from ACIM that each review lesson begins and ends with these very important ideas which tell us who we are in truth:

"I am not a body. I am free.
For I am still as God created me."
(W-Review VI.Introduction.3:3-5)

Lesson 221 – Peace to my mind. Let all my thoughts be still.

I mentally say this idea during my long meditative sessions which usually take me about 8 minutes to complete. Generally I do these sessions twice a day, once shortly after I wake up and once towards the end of the day.

This particular idea I use when I've completely left all my worldly thinking behind and my mind is just floating. This represents the peace of God which passes all "worldly" understanding. The world can't possibly understand this level of peace because the whole purpose of the world is to separate us from God and His peace.

In paragraph 2 of this lesson, Jesus lets us know that he is with us as we find God's peace: "Now do we wait in quiet. God is here, because we wait together. I am sure that He will speak to you, and you will hear. Accept my confidence, for it is yours. Our minds are joined. We wait with one intent; to hear our Father's answer to our call, to let our thoughts be still and find His peace, to hear Him speak to us of what we are, and to reveal Himself unto His Son." (W-221.2:1-6)

Lesson 222 – God is with me. I live and move in Him.

In the first paragraph of this lesson, Jesus says: "He [God] is my Source of life, the life within, the air I breathe, the food by which I am sustained, the water which renews and cleanses me." (W-222.1:2)

The first part of this sentence is clear – God the Father is clearly our Source and has given us our eternal life. While in the world, we learn from ACIM that this eternal life in Heaven is our only reality. This world we think we are in is only a dream; it is not real.

The rest of the sentence, which says God is the air we breathe, the food we eat and the water we drink and wash with, requires some explanation to understand. First, note that in ACIM Jesus often uses God to mean the Holy Spirit/Jesus; sometimes it means God the Father and the Holy Spirit/Jesus. Second, remember that God the Father knows nothing of this world; He created the Holy Spirit for purposes of waking us all up from this dream of separation so the Holy Spirit is fully aware of the dream. Finally, Jesus explains in ACIM that the Holy Spirit takes everything the ego made (for the purpose of keeping us separate and asleep) and uses it to help us awaken from the dream.

In truth, then, although the air, food and water are, like our bodies, not real, we still use them while we're in the dream not just so our dream is a better one but also to help other people in our lives awaken from their dreams. And it is the Voice of God (Jesus/Holy Spirit) Who helps us accomplish this.

Lesson 223 – God is my life. I have no life but His.

In the first paragraph of this lesson, Jesus tells us in a couple of sentences that there is literally no separation between us and God. As I like to say, we are effectively God which is far better than being an individual named Jimmy Laws. Following are the two sentences I'm referring to: "Now I know my life is God's, I have no other home, and I do not exist apart from Him. He has no Thoughts that are not part of me, and I have none but those which are of Him." (W-223.1:2,3) This can only have meaning when we understand that all our worldly thinking is just a part of our dream which is not real; this world does not exist and so our thinking about it does not really exist either.

The second paragraph effectively includes a request to God asking Him to help us to see with Christ's vision rather than "see" and judge with our eyes. When I use Christ's vision, we all become eternal, innocent, happy, joyous and free spiritual beings and 100% equal to each other. There should be no exceptions even with someone who has done me serious harm in my life here. This paragraph, in its entirety, reads as follows: "*Our Father, let us see the face of Christ instead of our mistakes. For we who are Your holy Son are sinless. We would look upon our sinlessness, for guilt* [or blame] *proclaims that we are not Your Son. And we would not forget You longer. We are lonely here, and long for Heaven, where we are at home. Today we would return. Our name is Yours, and we acknowledge that we are Your Son.*" (W-223.2:1-7)

Lesson 224 – God is my Father, and He loves His Son.

The first paragraph tells me that when I'm in God's Will (I'm allowing Jesus/Holy Spirit to direct my mind), I am one happy guy and I share this happy spirit with the people I meet. This is very much the norm for me in recent years. This paragraph reads: "My true Identity is so secure, so lofty, sinless, glorious and great, wholly beneficent and free from guilt, that Heaven looks to It to give it light. It lights the world as well. It is the gift My Father gave to me; the one as well I give the world. There is no gift but this that can be either given or received. This is reality, and only this. This is illusion's end. It is the truth." (W-224.1:1-7)

The second paragraph, on the other hand, effectively says that when I'm not happy, it means I'm not in God's Will (I'm allowing the ego to direct my mind) and I should ask God for help. This second paragraph is such a request. It reads: "*My Name, O Father, still is known to You. I have forgotten It, and do not know where I am going, who I am, or what it is I do. Remind me, Father, now, for I am weary of the world I see. Reveal what You would have me see instead.*" (W-224.2:1-4)

Lesson 225 – God is my Father, and His Son Loves Him.

The first paragraph is addressed to our Father but does not make any requests of Him. Rather, it tells Him what we must do. It reads: "*Father, I must return Your Love for me, for giving and receiving are the same, and You have given all Your Love to me. I must return it, for I want it mine in full awareness, blazing in my mind and keeping it within its kindly light, inviolate beloved, with fear behind and only peace ahead. How still the way Your loving Son is led along to You!*" (W-225.1:1-3)

As Jesus points out in this first paragraph, giving and receiving are the same. The world certainly doesn't operate this way. The way the world works, when I give something to somebody, I no longer have it and somebody else does. In Heaven, which is our Reality, there are no "things" whatsoever. There is no form whatsoever. It is a place of pure Spirit and It is Love. In Heaven, there is only "One" – God and His Creation are One Perfect Mind. Therefore, when we're in Heaven and we give (and we give Love for Love is who we are and it is Love we extend forever), we are also the recipients of our giving.

In the last two sentences of the first paragraph, we are telling God that we feel peace in our future (not fear) and we feel we're being led peacefully to God, Himself. It is Jesus/Holy Spirit Who is leading us. If you've done all the lessons prior to this one as instructed, these words to God can be said with conviction because they will be coming true for you.

In the second paragraph, Jesus is talking to us. He follows up on what we've said in the first paragraph and lets us know he's with us and one with us for the rest of our life's journey. I'll take this opportunity to thank you, Jesus, for doing this for me and so many others. Here's what Jesus tells us: "Brother, we find that stillness now. The way is open. Now we follow it in peace together. You have reached your hand to me, and I will never leave you. We are one, and it is but this Oneness that we seek, as we accomplish these few final steps which end a journey that was not begun." (W-225.2:1-5)

Lesson 226 – My home awaits me. I will hasten there.

In this lesson, Jesus tells us we can get to Heaven anytime we want. We can do this in an instant. The technical term Jesus uses in ACIM for accomplishing this is the "holy instant." Jesus gives a lot of instruction for going into a holy instant in the Text and this gets reinforced as the student proceeds through the Workbook lessons. Personally, I don't linger in holy instants but I do go there frequently.

The first paragraph of this lesson reads: "If I so choose, I can depart this world entirely. It is not death which makes this possible, but it is change of mind about the purpose of the world. If I believe it has a value as I see it now, so will it remain for me. But if I see no value in the world as I behold it, nothing that I want to keep as mine or search for as a goal, it will depart from me. For I have not sought for illusions to replace the truth." (W-226.1:1-5)

At the time you enter a holy instant, you must be in the mindset that there is nothing in this world worth pursuing. A holy instant for me brings me to a place which I've previously described in this book – my mind is alert but it's at total peace without a care in the world because I'm not thinking any worldly thoughts during these instants. There is no dialogue with Jesus or the Holy Spirit. My mind simply floats in total peace for a few seconds.

You might notice that the instructions from the first paragraph are summed up in Lesson 128: "The world I see holds nothing that I want."

Lesson 227 – This is my holy instant of release.

This lesson reinforces the previous lesson and expressly uses the technical term, "holy instant."

If you have not yet experienced peace of mind, without the use of mind altering substances, where you are fully alert yet not thinking about anything in the world for 30 seconds or more, you won't be able to appreciate what a gift these holy instants are.

Lesson 228 – God has condemned me not. No more do I.

The first paragraph of this lesson begins with: "My Father knows my holiness." (W-228.1:1) The rest of the paragraph then has us ask ourselves 3 important questions. I will now look at each of these questions individually.

"Shall I deny His knowledge, and believe in what His knowledge makes impossible?" (W-228.1:2) The world is a place of judgment, condemnation, sacrifice, and suffering, inter-mixed with some happy times, yet always ending in death. The world is a man made dream and has nothing to do with God. Heaven is a place of eternal joy and freedom. Our home and our reality is Heaven which is also God's home and God's reality. If I believe the world is real, I deny God's knowledge. If I believe God's knowledge is real, I deny the world.

"Shall I accept as true what He proclaims as false?" (W-228.1:3) If you continue to believe the world is true (i.e.,real) then, among other things, you will not benefit from ACIM. The first sentence in this lesson's idea is: "God has condemned me not." There is no condemnation in love and there is no condemnation in God. There never was and there never will be. This world, on the other hand, is full of condemnation. Thank God this world is false! It is just an insane dream.

"Or shall I take His Word for what I am, since He is my Creator, and the One Who knows the true condition of His Son?" (W-228.1:4) The second paragraph of this lesson tells me who I am and who you are, whoever you may be. It reads as follows: "*Father, I was mistaken in myself, because I failed to realize the Source from which I came. I have not left that Source to enter in a body and to die. My holiness remains a part of me, as I am part of You. And my mistakes about myself are dreams. I let them go today. And I stand ready to receive Your Word alone for what I really am.*" (W-228.2:1-6)

Lesson 229 – Love, which created me, is what I am.

And, of course, we can add to this as follows: "Love, which created you, is what you are."

And what is Love? Love is God or, for the more common and also accurate way of saying the same thing, we can reverse this to say: God is Love.

Therefore, I am God and so are you. When we are back home in Heaven and this world is a distant dream, if we remember it at all, we have everything that God has without exception. All His joy, love, power, peace …. forever and ever … belong to us also.

As Jesus states in ACIM, the only difference between God and us is that He created us and we did not create Him. It is only for this reason that I like to say "We are (or 'I am') effectively God" rather than simply "We are (or 'I am') God."

Lesson 230 – Now will I seek and find the peace of God.

One of the attributes of God is absolute peace forever and ever. Since we are, as Lesson 229 tells us, effectively God, peace is our attribute also forever and ever once we awaken in Heaven. Clearly, it is not an attribute of life on planet earth.

As we grow in understanding, we learn that all we need do is mentally say the word "God" and we can enter His peace. This is stated in the second paragraph of this lesson: "*I need but call on You to find the peace You gave.*" (W-230.2:5) We can be in the midst of some earthly emotional controversy, take a few seconds, and find perfect peace; this should allow us to weather that controversy. The technical term ACIM uses to define such sojourns into God's peace is that they are "holy instants."

The second paragraph of this lesson are words to God, letting Him know that we are understanding what we've learned from ACIM. The words summarize much of the entire Course. Here is that paragraph: "*Father, I seek the peace You gave as mine in my creation. What was given then must be here now, for my creation was apart from time, and still remains beyond all change. The peace in which Your Son was born into Your Mind is shining there unchanged. I am as You created me. I need but call on You to find the peace You gave. It is Your Will that gave it to Your Son.*" (W-230.2:1-6)

Lesson 231 – Father, I will but to remember You.

This lesson starts out with: "What can I seek for, Father, but Your Love?" (W-231.1:1) As a teenager and in my early twenties, my plan for my life included the following: I'd get a professional job making a lot of money, marry a pretty gal who would be my best friend and we would have 6 children and live happily until our death. I didn't think about the hereafter. This is what I sought and, from an earthly standpoint, it was a reasonable though very naïve plan. Suffice it to say that my life did not unfold as I had planned.

ACIM tells us to stop seeking the illusions of the world altogether because "The world I see holds nothing that I want." (W-128.title) This does not mean that you won't have many of the temporary illusionary worldly "gifts". However, no matter what's going on in your physical life, if you remember God better over time, you will be getting happier and have more peace of mind.

Understand that "Beyond this world there is a world I want." (W-129.title) This other world has many names: Heaven, truth, knowledge, God and His Creation (or just God since We are one), Eternal Oneness, and more. This lesson can be stated: "Father, I will only to remember You because I will only to remember Heaven."

Also, understand that deep down within every individual is the memory of God. Why is it so difficult to remember Him? Simply put, we think this world is real and we seek happiness from the world. Even when some worldly happiness is found, it must end. Remember the line from a country song: "No one gets out of this world alive?"

The world is full of temptations which tell us how we can be more happy: a new home, a Caribbean cruise, retire to a warm climate, more money, getting married, getting divorced, a college degree, living in the country, living in the city, less work, more work… one can add to this list ad infinitum.

Persons in physical or emotional pain will naturally be happier when their pain is alleviated. Many persons actually look forward to death so they won't have to put up with their miserable life any longer.

In ACIM, Jesus tells us that the world's pleasures and the world's pains are just two sides of the same coin. Why? Since the whole world is but an illusion (i.e., it's not real), its pleasures and pains are also not real.

In the second paragraph, Jesus is talking to us: "This is your will, my brother [i.e., to remember our Father]. And you share this will with me, and with the One as well Who is our Father. To remember Him is Heaven. This we seek. And only this is what it will be given us to find." (W-231.2:1-5)

Lesson 232 – Be in my mind, my Father, through the day.

A very simple but accurate way to think about the goal contained in this lesson is to understand that we all have two voices, or two directors, in our mind. One is the ego's voice and the other is God's Voice (or the Voice of the Holy Spirit/Jesus). The goal of ACIM is for us to listen to God's Voice increasingly and the ego's voice less. The ultimate goal is to only listen to God's Voice just as Jesus did in the last years of his earthly life.

ACIM tells us the ego's voice always speaks first. It never wants what's best for us. It's insane. It convinces us that our bodies are real as is the world. It requires our continued conviction that we are separated from each other in order for its continued survival.

God's Voice always wants the best for everyone. ACIM tells us that the Holy Spirit never asks any questions but He does answer them. He (the Holy Spirit) tells us that we're stuck in a dream but if we learn to listen to Him we will awaken again in Heaven where we "fell asleep". He tells us that only in this dream does it appear we are separated; in truth (or in Heaven), we are one with Him, one with each other and one with our Father.

In my experience, one can accomplish the goal of this lesson by the ongoing study of ACIM. I suggest you don't get side tracked into many different spiritual or religious endeavors. Let ACIM become your "way of life" and, if your experience is the same as mine, you will find yourself becoming happier, more tolerant, more joyful and less fearful. The world becomes a happy playground and you will find yourself in a position to be of help to virtually everyone you meet.

Lesson 233 – I give my life to God to guide today.

Lesson 338 reads: "I am affected only by my thoughts." This is just common sense. Everything anyone says or does originates from their thoughts. Jesus says in ACIM that it is a mind training course. And this Lesson 233 begins with: "*Father, I give You all my thoughts today.*" (W-233.1:1)

The first paragraph, in its entirety, with some explanatory comments by me, reads: "*Father, I give You all my thoughts today. I would have none of mine. In place of them, give me Your Own.* [In place of the ideas from my ego, please help me listen only to the ideas from You (i.e., those from the Holy Spirit/Jesus).] *I give you all my acts as well, that I may do Your Will instead of seeking goals which cannot be obtained, and wasting time in vain imaginings.* [Help me from thinking that worldly goals such as fame, fortune, prestige, and romance have any meaning whatsoever – They're all but illusions or vain imaginings.] *Today I come to You. I will step back and merely follow You. Be You the Guide, and I the follower who questions not the wisdom of the Infinite, nor Love whose tenderness I cannot comprehend, but which is yet Your perfect gift to me."* (W-233.1:1-7)

The second paragraph, in its entirety, reads: "Today we have one Guide [the Holy Spirit] to lead us on. And as we walk together [Jesus and I], we will give this day to Him with no reserve at all. This is His day. And so it is a day of countless gifts and mercies unto us." (W-233.2:1-4)

As I reflect on my life, in my younger years my guide was the ego. If any real God thoughts came to my attention, I don't remember them. In recent years, my mind is being led, on an increasing basis, by the Holy Spirit/Jesus. I can't prove this to anyone scientifically. With all honesty, however, I can tell you that I'm becoming ever more happy, more joyous and more free and this is proof enough for me.

Lesson 234 – Father, today I am Your Son again.

This lesson begins with: "Today we will anticipate the time when dreams of sin and guilt are gone, and we have reached the holy peace we never left." (W-234.1:1)

First, let me clarify the word "guilt" as used by Jesus in ACIM. In the world, it is very common to hear the following argument: "I'm not guilty. He's to blame." Jesus nearly always uses the word guilt to include blame as well. In other words, guilt includes guilt in one self or guilt in another person.

In truth, we are all 100% innocent, so if in our thinking we see our self or someone else is guilty at any level then we have made a mistake which needs correcting. If you stay on the path of ACIM, you can anticipate first a reduction in such mistakes and, as stated in the first sentence of this lesson, the elimination of these mistakes altogether.

Consider the last two sentences of the first paragraph of this Lesson 234: "Nothing has ever happened to disturb the peace of God the Father and the Son. This we accept as wholly true today." (W-234.1:4,5) It is accurate to think of this world as just a dream. It is also accurate to think of this world as "nothing" so that these two sentences could read: "The world has never happened to disturb Heaven. This we accept as wholly true today." Recall what Jesus says earlier in the Workbook: "There is no world! This is the central thought the course attempts to teach." (W-132.6:2,3)

The second paragraph of this Lesson 234 reads: "*We* [Jesus and I] *thank You, Father, that we cannot lose the memory of You and of Your Love. We recognize our safety, and give thanks for all the gifts You have bestowed on us, for all the loving help we have received, for Your eternal patience, and the Word* [the Holy Spirit] *which You have given us that we are saved.* (W-234.2:1,2)

Lesson 235 – God in His mercy wills that I be saved.

God also wills that I be happy all the time in this life. Consider the second sentence in the first paragraph of this lesson: "I need but keep in mind my Father's Will for me is only happiness, to find that only happiness has come to me." (W-235.1:2) Does this mean that whenever I'm not happy, I am outside of God's Will? The answer to this question is "yes."

Something in the world has made you unhappy. It could be something relatively minor like a broken shoe lace or something major like the unexpected death of a friend. It could be an ongoing resentment against someone even if you don't think about it too much. Jesus tells us many times in ACIM that it really doesn't matter whether the disturbing thoughts are minor or major. Either way, in our mind we are thinking that the world is real rather than just a dream or, as I talked about in Lesson 234, a "nothing."

Be well aware that if the ego is guiding your thoughts, he will give you many opportunities to think happy thoughts. Therefore, happy thoughts can be the result of letting the "good guide" direct your thinking (Jesus/Holy Spirit) or letting the "bad guide" direct your thinking (the ego). You can be sure, however, that if you are having negative thinking, then the ego has become your guide at least some of the time.

If my experience is typical, and there's no reason to believe it's not, continued study of ACIM over a long period of years automatically reduces and will eliminate negative thinking to nearly nothing. Perhaps in a few more years, I'll be able to change "nearly nothing" in the previous sentence to "nothing".

Lesson 236 – I rule my mind, which I alone must rule.

This lesson begins: "I have a kingdom I must rule." (W-236.1:1) All of us have a mind and this is the kingdom Jesus is referring to in this lesson.

Now, let's do some make believe in order to explain what literally happens within our minds. Make believe you're the king of some area back in the days when there were kings and queens and the king ruled his own area. Suppose further that you have two advisors, Joseph and Edward. As it turns out, Joseph was always thinking what was best for all the people in the kingdom so his advice was always very solid. Edward, on the other hand, was always thinking what was best for him, not for you (the king) or for the people. However, he disguised his selfish motive so you were not aware of it. If you fully realized what was going on, you would stop listening to Edward altogether and only listen to Joseph.

Literally, within the kingdom of our minds, we have two advisors – Jesus/Holy Spirit and the ego. In the preceding paragraph, Joseph would be analogous to Jesus/Holy Spirit and Edward would be analogous to the ego. The ultimate goal of studying ACIM is to only listen to the advice of Jesus/Holy Spirit, just as Jesus only listened to the advice of the Holy Spirit in the last years of his earthly dream. The choice is ours which is why the lesson includes the phrase "which I alone must rule."

While the concept is simple, Jesus often suggests that this can only be accomplished with a lot of mind training and practice. We shouldn't under estimate the ego. Remember, it is the ego part of our mind that has made up the entire physical world as well as time itself and convinced us it is all real. The ego is cunning, baffling and powerful. Fortunately, God created the Holy Spirit so that all of us will eventually stop taking any advice from the ego and awaken at home in Heaven.

Lesson 237 – Now would I be as God created me.

Lessons 94, 110 and 162 all read: "I am as God created me." This lesson 237 is very similar but we have advanced in our mind training quite a lot since those earlier lessons. Therefore, Jesus asks us to do our best to hold on to this idea as we move through the day in all our activities. To the extent we do this, we will be happy.

In the first paragraph, Jesus says: "I bring the world the tidings of salvation which I hear as God my Father speaks to me." (W-237.1:3) In my life today, I make friends very easily largely because I take an interest in what they are telling me – I've learned to listen to other people. I seldom talk about God or religion or ACIM. I am nearly always happy and, for me, my happiness is what I bring to others. Absolutely knowing that I and everyone I meet will all wake up in Heaven some day is a real happy thought.

The second paragraph reads: "*Christ is my eyes today, and He the ears that listen to the Voice for God today. Father, I come to You through Him Who is Your Son, and my true self as well. Amen.*" (W-237.2:1-3) In ACIM, Jesus tells us that God only created one Son and uses the term Christ as God's one Son (whereas in most, if not all, Christian religions Christ means only Jesus). When the idea of separation was accepted into the Christ mind and He fell asleep in Heaven, God immediately created the Holy Spirit to wake up His Son. Christ is therefore everything that God created, other than the Holy Spirit.

In truth, or in Heaven, we all share Christ's mind. Where Jesus says "Christ is my eyes today", he is referring to Christ's vision whereby everyone is seen as an eternal innocent spiritual being, regardless of what their earthly life looks like. Also, everything we see with our physical eyes is envisioned as joined to us just as there is no separation in Heaven. Where Jesus says "He [Christ] the ears that listen to the Voice for God today", he is referring to our ability to listen to only what the Holy Spirit/Jesus Voice is saying, regardless of what the ego tells us or what our physical ears are hearing. When Jesus says "Father, I come to You through Him [Christ] Who is Your Son, and my true Self as well", he effectively states that each of us, individually, is Christ – We all share the same Christ Mind and so we are one.

Does this mean that we have to give up our individuality before we can wake up in Heaven? The answer is "yes." The ego wants us to think this is a major obstacle but with Jesus and the Holy Spirit leading the way, we find it's not. Also, while we're still in this dream world, we obviously can't give up our individuality.

Lesson 238 – On my decision all salvation rests.

There are two ways I look at this lesson today. The first is a common sense way to reduce or eliminate the possibility that the ego will use this to make me more important than other people. "All salvation rests" on each and every one of us being saved. Complete salvation does not occur until all people are awake in Heaven so that this statement holds true for all people, not just me.

The other way I look at this lesson is that Jesus is with me every step of the way and he will help me correct all my future mistakes. In other words, I know I'll make some mistakes but with Jesus always here with me any such mistakes will be easily corrected. For me, therefore, I can rewrite this lesson's idea as: "On our (Jesus and I) decision all salvation rests." And the first paragraph can be therefore rewritten as: "*Father, Your trust in Jesus and me has been so great, we must be worthy. You created us, and know us as we are. And so You placed Your Son's salvation in our hands, and let it rest on our decision to work together. We are beloved of You indeed. And we are steadfast in holiness as well, that You give Your Son to us in certainty that he is safe Who still is part of You, and yet is ours, because He is our Self as well. Jesus and I thank You, Father, very much.*"

Lesson 239 – The glory of my Father is my own.

This is just a simple statement of truth or Heaven. In Heaven, there is but one Mind. It is Love and there is only Love, extending Itself forever. Everything the Father has and everything We, His Son, have is fully shared with no separation whatsoever. In Heaven there is only "One." As Ken Wapnick, our great ACIM teacher and a good friend to me, has said: "In the mathematics of Jesus, 2 plus 2 equals '1'." Therefore, the glory of my Father is mine and it is yours, also.

In the first paragraph of this lesson, Jesus asks: "Can we see in those with whom He shares His glory any trace of sin and guilt?" (W-239.1:3)

If my answer to this question is "yes" with respect to any individual, then I need only use Christ's vision rather than the illusion the ego is telling me is true. This individual is an eternal innocent spiritual Creation of our Father, just as I am and just as every other person is. His mistakes in his earthly life are meaningless. I dreamt them up and they never really happened.

Lesson 240 – Fear is not justified in any form.

Love, as defined by Jesus in ACIM, has nothing to do with the word "love" as commonly used in the English language. In this book, I have already defined Love as just another word for Heaven. God and all His Creation are Heaven and We are Love and We are One (which is why "The glory of my Father is my own", as we reviewed in the previous lesson).

What Jesus tells us in ACIM is that we really have only two emotions: fear and love, and they are mutually exclusive. In other words, where there is fear, love does not exist and where there is love, fear does not exist. All fear comes from the ego and all love comes from God.

All fear also comes from the world and occurs because we think the world is real. Jesus spells this out for us in the first paragraph of this lesson: "Fear is deception. It attests that you have seen yourself as you could never be, and therefore look upon a world which is impossible. Not one thing in this world is true. It does not matter what the form in which it may appear. It witnesses but to your own illusions of yourself. Let us not be deceived today. We are the Sons of God. There is no fear in us, for we are each a part of Love Itself."

The statements made to God in the second paragraph of this lesson are very helpful if we have a fear of another person (or a resentment or we just don't like him or her). One thing they're telling God is that we will try and see such a person as who they really are and not what the world is showing us. For me, when such a situation occurs, I need to see such a person using Christ's vision so they appear the same as me, an eternal innocent spiritual being and a part of Heaven Itself.

This second paragraph reads: "*How foolish are our fears! Would You allow Your Son to suffer? Give us faith today to recognize Your Son, and set him free. Let us forgive him in Your Name, that we may understand his holiness, and feel the love for him which is Your Own as well.*" (W-240.2:1-4)

Let me share my experience with fear. It is not possible to believe the world is real and be without fear. Because we all start out in the world believing it to be real, we all start out with a lot of fear. As we advance in our ACIM mind training studies or, as I like to say, as we make spiritual progress, our fears get reduced. When we become fearful, it is because we have listened to the ego. Our ultimate goal, with Jesus as both our model and our guide, is to listen only to the Voice of the Holy Spirit/ Jesus and never to the ego's voice so that fear is fully eliminated from our mind forever.

Lesson 241 – This holy instant is salvation come.

I have mentioned before in this book that the term "holy instant" is a technical term which is fully defined in the Text of ACIM. Jesus devotes a full chapter to this powerful spiritual tool (see Chapter 15 of the Text). He also makes reference to it in many other places in ACIM.

The best way I can describe a "holy instant" is that it is a short period of time when we can mentally see right through this illusionary world and have a real sense of Heaven. Somewhere in ACIM, Jesus tells us that ultimately our dream life here should become an ongoing series of Holy Instants. This happens when we stop listening to the ego altogether and only listen to Jesus/Holy Spirit.

What I've been doing on an increasing basis as I go about my daily activities is to see everything in this world as a totally fictional movie. And the maker of this entire movie is me. All the people and all their individual soap operas, good and bad, were scripted by me. And I'm not only the maker of my movie but I get to be an actor in it as well. I take none of it seriously except when the ego catches me off guard. And I seem to be playing my part very well because the other actors in my fictional world seem to be getting along very well with me. To the best of my knowledge, I have no real enemies today in my movie.

As I move through my movie during the day, I also know and think about the fact that just on the other side of my movie screen is Heaven. My worldly life, or my movie, is just a smokescreen to try and hide the truth from me. Although I don't fully remember Heaven, I mentally know that it's just on the other side of this fictional world. In this regard, Lesson 129 comes to mind: "Beyond this world there is a world I want."

My days are very full and they're filled with happy thoughts from me. So I can really identify with the first sentence of this lesson: "What joy there is today!" (W-241.1:1)

Lesson 242 – This day is God's. It is my gift to Him.

Sometimes Jesus uses the word "God" to mean the Holy Spirit and this is true of this lesson. In other words, this lesson could be stated as "I give this day to the Holy Spirit. It is my gift to Him." Although not pointed out in this lesson, when I give the day to the Holy Spirit/Jesus it is also my gift to me because "giving and receiving are the same."

Following is the first paragraph of this lesson, along with some comments by me: "I [Jimmy Laws] will not lead my life alone today. I do not understand the world today [which is understandable because the world is insane and, by definition, it is impossible to understand insanity], and so to try to lead my life alone must be but foolishness. But there is One Who knows all that is best for me [the Holy Spirit/Jesus]. And He is glad to make no choices for me but the ones that lead to God [our Father]. I give this day to Him [the Holy Spirit/Jesus], for I would not delay my coming home [awakening in Heaven], and it is He Who knows the way to God." (W-242.1:1-5)

Please note that in the Text of ACIM Jesus devotes an entire section on "Rules for Decision". (T-30.I) It includes valuable suggestions on how to start your day with the Holy Spirit/Jesus as your Guide and how to stay there during the day. Jesus suggests that our outlook be: "*Today I will make no decisions by myself.*" (T-30.I.2:2)

Lesson 243 – Today I will judge nothing that occurs.

This lesson could be stated: "Today I will have an 'Easy Does It' day."

In the first paragraph, Jesus tells us to tell ourselves: "And so I am relieved of judgments that I cannot make." (W-243.1:5) It is actually okay to judge another if we judge him or her correctly. When we judge someone as an eternal innocent part of God Himself, regardless of what's happening in their earthly life, then we have judged them as God judges all of us which, of course, is a good thing. When we do this, we are using Christ's vision to see with. The reward to us is simply stated in the next sentence of the first paragraph: "Thus do I free myself and what I look upon, to be in peace as God created us." (W-243.1:6)

Here's a good way I can look at the world today in my own words: "The world is just my own crazy dream, not to be judged at all. I simply accept it as a crazy and totally fictional movie and enjoy playing my part."

Lesson 244 – I am in danger nowhere in the world.

In my comments here, I'll share some common sense which I had to learn the hard way. This lesson is not suggesting that you can go to the war zones of the world and think that you'll be immune from being injured or killed. It is not suggesting that you should walk through the worst parts of cities at night and think you won't be mugged.

The world we made up has some very dangerous places in it. About 6 years ago, I was living in Guyana, South America with my wife and our brand new baby. My wife is a citizen of Guyana and we were waiting for her visa to be approved so we could move back here to the U.S.A.

I was at a meeting in the Tiger Bay section of Georgetown, the capital of Guyana, on this particular night. Note that Tiger Bay is considered the most crime infested section of Georgetown. It was a fairly long meeting so I stepped outside during the meeting to smoke a cigarette and walked about a block away while I was smoking. I felt very comfortable as I had done this many times over the previous 18 months. Well, on this particular night, a man walked up to me and before I knew what was happening he had a knife on my throat and stole my cash, cell phone and car keys. As no one else was around, he could have just as easily cut my throat and killed me but he didn't. I'm happy to say it wasn't yet my time so Jimmy Laws' dream continues.

I no longer walk alone at night in bad neighborhoods so chances are I'll be able to finish this book. (Ha! Ha! Ha!)

Lesson 245 – Your peace is with me, Father. I am safe.

As we stop listening to the ego's voice and listen to the Holy Spirit/Jesus' Voice on an increasing basis, the peace of God automatically grows within us. This is a wonderful gift.

A major part of this peace comes from our ability to remember, as we go about our worldly activities, that this world is just a dream, not real and, in truth, it is nothing. This is why I like to repeat these two sentences from ACIM: "There is no world! This is the central thought the course attempts to teach." (W-132.6:2,3)

It is great news for me to know that not only am I perfectly safe but so is everyone else in the world. There is no doubt in my mind that everyone in the world will eventually wake up in Heaven.

This Lesson 245 tells us that as we receive this peace from God, we naturally bring the message of peace to everyone we meet. What I've found is that as I bring this gift to others, it benefits me. Because I spend a lot of time with emotionally sick people, I really identify with the following sentences in the first paragraph of this lesson: "I bring it [God's peace] to the desolate and lonely and afraid. I give Your peace to those who suffer pain, or grieve for loss, or think they are bereft of hope and happiness." (W-245.1:4,5)

As we grow in understanding and the ability to listen only to Jesus/ Holy Spirit, we learn that there are no real rules we need to set down. Why? It is because our friend Jesus is with us every step of the way. Lesson 49 says: *"God's Voice* [Holy Spirit/Jesus] *speaks to me all through the day."* Lesson 155 says: *"I will step back and let Him* [Holy Spirit/ Jesus] *lead the way."* Lesson 233 says: *"I give my life to God* [Holy Spirit/ Jesus] *to guide today."* Lesson 254 says: *"Let every voice but God's be still in me.* [i.e., Listen only to the Holy Spirit/Jesus and not the ego.]" Lesson 324 says: *"I merely follow, for I would not lead."* And perhaps the best part is that we need not be perfect because we find that when our peace does get disturbed, it's because the ego has entered our thoughts but Jesus is right here with us to make the necessary corrections as we ask him for help.

There aren't too many people in the world today who are convinced that this entire physical world and the cosmos and time itself is but a dream.

It would be real nice if I could just tell everyone this and they would all say okay and wake up in Heaven along with me. If it were that easy, everyone would have been awake within a generation or two after Jesus first figured it all out about 2,000 years ago. Anyway, for me, I'm real happy that I can play my part with God's help.

Lesson 246 – To love my Father is to love His Son.

Suppose you've made tremendous spiritual progress, with a wonderfully happy life, no fear of death whatsoever for yourself and everyone else but there's one individual in your life who you have a small grievance against. You can explain why you are angry at him and, since you hardly ever think of this person, it doesn't concern you. Well, this lesson tells us that you have some more work to do.

Jesus tells us elsewhere in the Course that a tiny grievance is the same as raging hatred. In this lesson, he specifically states: "*And so I choose to love Your Son.*" (W-246.2:4) Lesson 68 says "Love holds no grievances." and God's Son includes all people so if you have a small grievance against even one individual, you do not love God's entire Son.

Also, remember the world is nothing. The past is also nothing. Heaven is real and nothing else is real. A grievance of any kind therefore means you are angry at nothing.

You can also correctly look at your grievance as follows: (1) The world you think you are in was made up by your mind. It is your dream. (2) Therefore, if you have a grievance against anyone or anything in the world, you really have a grievance against yourself.

Lesson 247 – Without forgiveness I will still be blind.

In this lesson, Jesus links forgiveness to Christ's vision.

What is forgiveness? It is simply the fact that this world is but a dream I made up from my mind. The world is not real. It is nothing.

What is Christ's vision? As I've stated previously in this book, it is the simple idea that everyone in the world is an eternal, innocent and happy spiritual part of God Himself and everything I see with my eyes or think with my mind is joined to me (not separate from me). If the world were real, this could not possibly be true. This is why Jesus says in this lesson: "For forgiveness is the only means whereby Christ's vision comes to me." (W-247.1:3)

Jesus also points out in this lesson and throughout ACIM that there is no sin. Why? Because there is no world.

Lesson 248 – Whatever suffers is not part of me.

This lesson starts out: "I have disowned the truth." (W-248.1:1) Heaven is truth and I had totally replaced Heaven with this world I think I've been living in for 64 years now. What we learn from ACIM is that this world is 100% false. It's just a dream. It never happened. It is nothing.

The lesson continues: "Now let me be as faithful in disowning falsity." (W-248.1:2) This, my friends, is the challenge. I think it's not that difficult to read ACIM, understand it and totally agree with it. So we study ACIM for, say, 2 hours and we then go about our day and we're busy people. When our day goes smoothly, how easy it is to enjoy our dream but then there are days when our spouse gets fired from her job or our teenage daughter gets arrested or pregnant or, we're in a hurry, and our shoe lace breaks. When all these events are also seen as interesting action events within our dream and we're not disturbed by them is when we know we're really grabbing hold of ACIM spiritual principles.

In all simplicity, either Heaven is real or the world is real. Those individuals who think both Heaven and earth are real are quite insane. What ACIM says, time and again, is that Heaven is real and the world is not. What this lesson says we should do is try to remember this fact. It effectively says: "I'll try to remember as best I can that this world is not real." As we accomplish this, we stop taking anything that happens in the world seriously and we become very happy people.

Clearly, there is no suffering in Heaven which is real. Any suffering that occurs comes from the world, whether you're suffering or others are suffering. It is not real because the world is not real. This is what this lesson is telling us.

Lesson 249 – Forgiveness ends all suffering and loss.

The first paragraph of this lesson tells us, in no uncertain terms, why we want forgiveness. And, once again, what is forgiveness as Jesus defines it in his Course? Forgiveness is the all important idea that this world does not exist. The world is but a dream we think we're in for a time and its purpose is to keep us separate from each other and separate from God. The world is an illusion. The past never happened. History is just some crazy fictional movie we thought was real but it's not. The world is zero (-0-) since it does not exist in Heaven which is the only reality.

What happens as a result of the mind training gained by the ongoing study of ACIM? My own experience is that the promises mentioned in the first paragraph of this lesson become true. Here is that first paragraph: "Forgiveness paints a picture of a world where suffering is over, loss becomes impossible and anger makes no sense. Attack is gone and madness has an end. What suffering is now conceivable? What loss can be sustained? The world becomes a place of joy, abundance, charity and endless giving. It is now so like to Heaven that it quickly is transformed into the light that it reflects. And so the journey which the Son of God began has ended in the light from which he came. [We started in Heaven and, while still in the dream, Heaven's light is waking us up.]" (W-249.1:1-7)

Lesson 250 – Let me not see myself as limited.

This one sentence, taken literally, tells me I am part of God Himself and One with Him. Everything God has, I also have. God is unlimited forever and therefore so am I.

Reading the text of this lesson, however, there is much more to this powerful lesson. If my thinking is that anyone in the world is somehow less than or greater than me in any way, then my thinking is awry. For example, if I hold a little grievance against only one individual then I have some more inside work to do and I need to ask Jesus/Holy Spirit for help.

Obviously, if I'm unlimited and One with God then so must everyone else in the world be unlimited and One with God. Therefore, for me, I've added to this lesson as follows:

"Let me not see myself as limited.
Let me not see anyone else as limited."

Lesson 251 – I am in need of nothing but the truth.

Another name for truth is Heaven and in Heaven there is eternal peace and joy. This is also the home we all appeared to leave behind. The remembrance of Heaven is within the mind of every person in the world though very few of us know this fact.

"I sought for many things, and found despair." (W-251.1:1) This is how this lesson begins. Lesson 128 says essentially the same thing: "The world I see holds nothing that I want."

This Lesson 251 continues: "Now do I seek but one, for in that one is all I need, and only what I need." (W-251.1:2) The only thing I need and the only thing I want is Heaven and this world has nothing to do with Heaven. This is why Lesson 129 says: "Beyond this world there is a world I want."

Continuing with this Lesson 251: "All that I sought before I needed not, and did not even want. My only need I did not recognize." (W-251.1:3,4) For decades, I followed the world's rules of happiness. I sought fortune, romance, and fame. For many years, this seemed to be working quite well, but a marriage separation and divorce in 1993 followed by some heavy consumption of alcohol caused my worldly life to end in despair. Now, I seek Heaven within me by studying ACIM and practice its spiritual teachings in my daily worldly activities. My life is blossoming as a result. I have never been happier.

The rest of the first paragraph of this lesson tells me where my mind is today. My worldly life is extremely active yet the promise of peace at the end of this paragraph goes with me whatever I'm doing and wherever I go. Here is the balance of the first paragraph: "But now I see that I need only truth. In that all needs are satisfied, all cravings end, all hopes are finally fulfilled and dreams are gone. Now have I everything that I could need. Now have I everything that I could want. And now at last I find myself at peace." (W-251.1:5-9)

Lesson 252 – The Son of God is my Identity.

As I indicated in the previous lesson, I have never been happier than I am now. What the first paragraph of this lesson tells me, and which

I fully believe, is that I still only have a glimpse of Heaven – I haven't seen anything yet.

My ever increasing happiness is a direct result of my dedicated studying for over 15 years of ACIM. This is why I encourage you, who are reading this, to do the same. Some, who read this, will be able to verify what I'm saying here because they have also made ACIM a predominant part of their life.

Jesus tells us in ACIM that God created only one Son which is why this lesson tells each of us that we are in truth the "Son of God." Another term for His Son is Christ so Christ includes you, me, Mother Theresa, Hitler, Jesus, everyone you ever met, etc. All people are Christ. It is accurate to say "Jesus is the Christ." It's also accurate to say "Jimmy Laws is the Christ." And to you, my reader, it's accurate for you to say to yourself "I am the Christ."

A hurdle I think most of us must pass is the erroneous idea that to give up our individual identity is a real sacrifice. The ego really wants us to think this. It was a hurdle for me. My Inner Voice (Jesus/Holy Spirit) effectively tells me "Don't worry about it. Common sense tells you that, while you're still in the dream, you're individuality must stay intact. This is why I (Jesus) didn't spend much teaching on this so-called hurdle in ACIM."

Following is the first paragraph of this Lesson 252 but I've modified it slightly. As written in ACIM, it's meant to be read so that you are telling yourself who you really are in truth. I've modified it to read as what Jesus would tell you about yourself.

Here's what Jesus tells you about you: "Your Self [Christ] is holy beyond all the thoughts of holiness of which you now conceive. Its shimmering and perfect purity is far more brilliant than is any light that you have ever looked upon. Its love is limitless, with an intensity that holds all things within it, in the calm of quiet certainty. Its strength comes not from burning impulses which move the world, but from the boundless Love of God Himself. How far beyond this world your Self must be, and yet how near to you and close to God."

Lesson 253 – My Self is ruler of the universe.

One mistake I made with this lesson for quite some time is I interpreted "universe" as our physical universe extending beyond our solar system into the far distant cosmos.

Clearly, now, this is not what Jesus is referring to at all. First, no one in their right mind can possibly think they can rule the physical universe. Second, Jesus tells us over and over that the physical realm is but an illusion; it's a dream; it's not real; it is nothing. To be the ruler of "nothing" doesn't make sense.

The only reality is Heaven. Therefore, the only universe is Heaven. So what this lesson says is: "My Self is ruler of Heaven."

In this lesson Jesus tells us, as he often does throughout ACIM, that in reality (i.e., in Heaven) there is but one Mind which we all share with God. Therefore, just as God is ruler of Heaven, so are we ruler of Heaven.

In the second paragraph of this lesson, we are asked to tell God that we understand the Oneness of the universe [i.e., of Heaven]. Here is the second paragraph of this lesson: "*You* [Father] *are the Self Whom You created Son* [Us], *creating like Yourself and One with You. My Self, which rules the universe, is but Your Will in perfect union with my own, which can but offer glad assent to Yours, that it may be extended to Itself.*" (W-253.2:1,2)

Lesson 254 – Let every voice but God's be still in me.

As I have said in earlier lessons, we all have two directors in our minds and both are trying to guide us – (1) the ego's voice which wants only what's best for the ego and never has our best interests in mind, and (2) God's Voice which always has our best interests in mind. (In ACIM, God's Voice is referred to as the Voice of the Holy Spirit.)

Our ultimate objective is to always take direction from God's Voice and never let the ego's thoughts direct our words or actions. This is exactly what Jesus tells us to do in the first sentence of the second paragraph of this lesson: "Today we let no ego thoughts direct our words or actions." (W-254.2:1)

Today, I know when the ego has affected me because there is a disturbance to my generally very peaceful spirit. I feel a twinge of guilt or anger or intolerance, etc. So Jesus tells us what to do when the ego's thoughts have affected us. He says take corrective action as follows: "When such thoughts occur, we quietly step back and look at them, and then we let them go. We do not want what they would bring with them. And so we do not choose to keep them. They are silent now. And in the stillness, hallowed by His Love, God speaks to us [i.e., the Holy Spirit speaks to us] and tells us of our will, as we have chosen to remember Him." (W-254.2:2-6) So Jesus says get rid of any such thoughts and, with his (Jesus') help, find that total peace which is really the only way we can know that we have, in fact, gotten rid of those ego thoughts.

Lesson 255 – This day I choose to spend in perfect peace.

Although I don't remember the first time I did this lesson about 14 years ago, I'm quite sure that the first sentence in this lesson was very meaningful at the time. It reads: "It does not seem to me that I can choose to have but peace today." (W-255.1:1) My interpretation of what this sentence means is: "This world is so complicated with so much to be concerned with, how is it possible to stay peaceful here?" At that time, although I had done a good job of reading the Text and doing the previous 254 lessons, I was still quite new to ACIM and there was a lot of drama in my life. Thus, spending a day in "perfect" peace certainly wasn't yet happening. However, I had made some progress toward this goal.

I think the best thing I can tell you is that after 14 more years of studying the Course, all my days are both very active and very peaceful. When my peace does get disturbed, it means to me that I have listened to the ego's voice and it held some appeal to me. I'm also fully aware that I have made a mistake and so I seek and receive the necessary guidance from the Holy Spirit/Jesus. Over time, my mistakes are decreasing so my peace of mind is increasing.

This peace of mind that I have is an incredible gift so, if you haven't already done so, I encourage you to make time to study the Course on a daily basis. My dedication to the Course is the sole reason that I've made great strides in waking up from this dream world, filled with uncertainty, fear and death.

Lesson 256 – God is the only goal I have today.

"The way to God is through forgiveness here. There is no other way." (W-256.1:1,2) This is how this lesson begins. This first paragraph ends with the following sentences: "Here we can but dream. But we can dream we have forgiven him in whom all sin remains impossible, and it is this we choose to dream today. [Sin is impossible in all of God's Creation so it is impossible that anyone in the world ever sinned.] God is our goal; forgiveness is the means by which our minds return to Him at last." (W-256.1:7-9)

What Jesus explicitly tells us here is: "If God is our only goal, then forgiveness must be the way to attain this goal." In W-Part II-Q-1, Jesus answers the question "What Is Forgiveness?" The rest of my comments on this Lesson 256 are a summary of Jesus' answer.

"Forgiveness recognizes what you thought your brother did to you has not occurred. It does not pardon sins and make them real. It sees there was no sin." (W-Q-1.1:1-3) We can also say this as follows: "The world we've been in our whole physical life has been but a dream. It never happened. Nobody ever hurt us or anyone else."

"Forgiveness, on the other hand, is still, and quietly does nothing. It offends no aspect of reality, nor seeks to twist it to appearances it likes. It merely looks, and waits, and judges not [it uses Christ's vision instead]. He who would not forgive must judge, for he must justify his failure to forgive. But he who would forgive himself must learn to welcome truth exactly as it is." (W-Q-1.4:1-5)

"Do nothing, then, and let forgiveness show you what to do, through Him Who is your Guide [Holy Spirit/Jesus], your Savior and Protector, strong in hope, and certain of your ultimate success. He has forgiven you [and everyone else in the world] already, for such is His function, given Him by God. Now must you share His function, and forgive whom He has saved, whose sinlessness He sees, and whom He honors as the Son of God." (W-Q-1.5:1-3)

Suppose a man is an avid ACIM student and continues to make spiritual progress such that he's "happy as a lark" regardless of what's happening in his life here. He truly love's everyone he meets and everyone he thinks about, even his ex-wife. He sees all of the good that came out of his marriage with her and loves her a lot whenever he thinks about her. He just has some little grievance against her but he seldom thinks about it. Well, this man has some more work to do – The Holy Spirit has 100% forgiven his ex-wife but he has not. Therefore, his will is not fully in line with God's Will. Another way to look at this is that his little grievance means he is still holding on to the idea that the world is real.

Lesson 257 – Let me remember what my purpose is.

The second paragraph of this lesson begins: *"Father, forgiveness is Your chosen means for our salvation."* (W-257.2:1) So my purpose here on earth is forgiveness which I just summarized in Lesson 256.

For most ACIM students, it is not that difficult to remember forgiveness when we are studying the Course by ourselves. The challenge is when, say, we're on our way to a wedding in which we're in the wedding party and we hit a traffic jam which will cause us to be late. In other words, can we stop worrying about the world totally, remembering all the time that it's just a dream?

You can note that Lesson 99 reads "Salvation is my only function here." A good question might be: "What's my function – forgiveness or salvation?" The answer to this question is contained in the first sentence of Lesson 99: "Salvation and forgiveness are the same." (W-99.1:1) These are just two words that mean exactly the same thing as Jesus uses them in ACIM.

Lesson 258 – Let me remember that my goal is God.

As we start "living" ACIM and not just study ACIM, we can add to this lesson as follows: "Let me remember all the time that my goal is God and the world's just a dream." Alternatively, we can say: "Let me remember every second of every day that my goal is God and the world's just a dream."

There are two earlier lessons which truly place God's plan for us in perspective. They are Lessons 128 and 129 and read as follows: "The world I see holds nothing that I want;" and "Beyond this world there is a world I want." This world, of course, is one which can appear okay at times but, no matter how good you think it can be, you always end up dead if you believe this world is real. The world beyond this world which I want is, of course, Heaven. Today, I am at the gate of Heaven. While my body will die or stop functioning at some point (just like everyone else), I know with certainty that "I am not my body" and I'll be living forever. Whoever you may be, I am as certain of this eternal life in Heaven for you as I am for me.

The second paragraph of Lesson 258 begins: *"Our goal is but to follow in the way that leads to You. We have no goal but this."* (W-258.2:1,2) Note that these sentences begin with "Our" and "We", respectively. When I read these for myself, I interpret these words to mean "Jesus and me" for I know he's with me every step of the way and will help me when I stumble. With Jesus' help, I am learning to listen only to the Holy Spirit although I've not completely accomplished this goal yet. To obey only God's Voice, and not the ego's voice, is the way that leads to God.

Lesson 259 – Let me remember that there is no sin.

In this world, People love to hear about the "sins" of others. It continues to sell newspapers and it's why so many people watch the news on television. Granted, some people watch the news for other reasons – weather, sports, lottery numbers and the stock market update are all common. However, good crimes are pretty exciting stuff.

To put this lesson in perspective, let's use an "unforgiveable sin" which has likely been happening ever since parents had children. This is where the father has sexual relations with a daughter from the time she is, say, 3 years old. The mother usually learns of it but says nothing. Once the daughter becomes old enough to understand, her response would include anger and resentment. An "appropriate" response by the parents would be guilt and shame. What does ACIM say about this extreme "sin?"

ACIM tells us the world never happened and is not happening now. Therefore, this "sin" against the daughter never happened. It's really that simple.

Let me add to this example to bring it "down to earth." Suppose I learn of a young family in my neighborhood where this exact "sin" is occurring – the father is sexually molesting their 3-year old daughter. ACIM in no way tells me to simply ignore the situation because "it's not real." God's Voice (the Holy Spirit/Jesus) is here all the time to guide me in my dream. He will let me know what my part should be to help all 3 of the people involved.

Lesson 260 – Let me remember God created me.

This lesson reinforces one of the simplest and most important lessons in the Course. This other lesson is: "I am as God created me." The fact that Jesus repeats this lesson 3 times in the Workbook (Lessons 94, 110 and 162) tells us how important it is.

Let me remember God created only one Son who we call Christ. The Father and the Son shared the same Mind. We call this mind Heaven. We were all there, happy and joyous forever. We, God's Son, thought to leave our Father and try living on our own. Although this was impossible, we thought we had accomplished this and fell into a deep sleep and we continue in that sleep now, dreaming of this life on earth. God created the Holy Spirit to enter our dreams and wake us up. Importantly, the first person to wake up is the author of ACIM, Jesus.

So we are all still an integral part of God but we are dreaming that we are all separate from Him and, of course, separate from each other. Thank God it's all a dream and we'll all wake up some day!

One of the spiritual tools Jesus mentions in this Lesson 260 is "Christ's vision." Here's a good definition of this powerful tool: "Just as I am eternally innocent and happy, regardless of what my life is like here on earth, so is everyone else in the world eternally innocent and happy, regardless of what their life is like here on earth. Additionally, everything I see with my eyes and think with my mind is joined to me and a part of me rather than apart from me (which, of course, is how the world thinks)."

Lesson 261 – God is my refuge and security.

The last few sentences of the first paragraph of this lesson are: "I live in God. In Him I find my refuge and my strength. In Him is my Identity. In Him is everlasting peace. And only there will I remember Who I really am." (W-261.1:4-8)

The word "there" in the last sentence means "in God" so the last sentence can be written: "And only in God will I remember Who I really am." God is not in the dream world so He can't be found in the world yet he can be found while we're still in the world. It's important to recognize that there is no physical form, whether it be a temple or a quiet cabin on a lake or the city of Jerusalem, where one can find God. All physical form is a symbol of our separation from God. Once we begin to understand that Heaven is, in truth, the One Mind of God and all His Creation, it is obvious that this world of nearly infinite separation really has nothing to do with God. This world is our dream and not God's Reality.

There is a real simple answer to the question: "Where do I find God?" The answer is: "He's in your mind where He has always been." As we let go of the belief that this world is real (i.e., as we remove from our mind the obstacles between ourselves and God), God becomes clearer and clearer and our joy increases accordingly.

An important point is that this lesson does not read: "God will be my refuge and security." In other words, God is available to us now. For the millions of people who believe that their current life is difficult but they'll enter directly into Heaven after they die, Jesus tells us this thinking is erroneous. And other advanced ACIM students will tell you exactly what I'm experiencing – increasing happiness. Heaven's gifts are available to us here in this life. I'm about the happiest person I know because of ACIM.

Lesson 262 – Let me perceive no differences today.

Going right to the top which is Heaven, God and all His Creation share the same perfect Mind. Another name for this perfect Mind is Heaven.

In this lesson, Jesus emphasizes that all people combined represent God's One Son. All of us combined are Christ. Naturally, while I'm in this dream world I'll continue appearing to be an individual even though I know it's not Who I am. I am Christ. You are Christ. Everyone we meet is also Christ. This is our Identity. Once again, God only has one Son.

Sometimes, when walking through a store, I'll mentally say to many of the people I pass: "You are me." In other words, since I'm Christ and everyone I see is also Christ, we are exactly the same in truth. This practice has helped me which is why I'm sharing it here. You might want to try it.

The ego will likely tell you that to believe ACIM means you'll have to give up your individual identity and you don't want to do that! It is true that we won't have individual identities in Heaven because, by definition, Heaven is total Oneness. The idea that's helped me overcome the idea that my individuality is important is that I, along with everyone else, will have all the glory, peace, bliss, joy and power of God Himself forever and ever. As Jesus so often says in ACIM, God shares everything with His Son and hides nothing from us. So you might ask yourself the following simple question: "Would I rather be an individual or God?" My answer to this is God.

Lesson 263 – My holy vision sees all things as pure.

The first paragraph of this lesson reads: *"Father, Your Mind created all that is, Your Spirit entered into it, Your Love gave life to it. And would I look upon what You created as if it could be made sinful?* [My answer to this is 'no.'] *I would not perceive such dark and fearful images. A madman's dream is hardly fit to be my choice, instead of all the loveliness with which You blessed creation; all its purity, its joy, and its eternal, quiet home in You."* (W-263.1:1-4)

This entire physical realm and time itself represent "a madman's dream." Who is this insane individual? ACIM refers to him as the ego and, like it or not, he is in our mind. In this we have no choice. However, within our mind we also have a sane individual, namely Jesus/Holy Spirit or the Voice of God. And through the mind training of ACIM, we learn that we can choose to listen to God's Voice rather than the ego's voice and we learn through patient study and practice how to accomplish this goal.

The preceding paragraph is a good summary of ACIM. Personally, my ongoing study and practice of ACIM is leading me to the gate of Heaven. My life here in the dream continues to get happier and more productive in terms of my ability to help other people. If you have not been giving ACIM much study time and your life here is not getting happier, I encourage you to place the study of ACIM at the top of your list of things to do.

Lesson 264 – I am surrounded by the Love of God.

All of us are surrounded by the Love of God. Nearly all people, however, believe this world is real so God's Love is blocked out. God needs teachers in this dream world who can help other people understand the world is but a dream.

The first teacher who understood this was, of course, our wonderful friend, Jesus. In one short phrase in the gospel of John, Jesus gave us a summary of ACIM about 2,000 years ago. He said: "The Spirit gives life; the flesh counts for nothing." (John 6:63) As this has been explained throughout ACIM, the word "flesh" should be understood to mean this entire physical realm. In other words: "This entire physical realm counts for nothing." Why? It's because it's only a dream and, no matter how good one thinks he's doing here, it's always a dream of separation and death.

God is real and the world is not real. In all its simplicity, ACIM can be summarized as:

"God is and the world isn't."

Here is the "We" version of this Lesson 264: "We are surrounded by the Love of God." This is because "We are as God created us." He created us as eternal Spirit, one with Him, forever joyous and free. We are literally in God.

Here's a good analogy. If I have a bucket of water and then add a little additional water into the bucket, the additional water will be surrounded by and joined with the original water.

In the same way, we are surrounded by God and one with God. As I've stated before in this book, we are effectively God, the only difference is that God created us and we didn't create Him.

Lesson 265 – Creation's gentleness is all I see.

The first part of this first paragraph reads: "I have indeed misunderstood the world, because I laid my sins on it and saw them looking back at me. How fierce they seemed! And how deceived was I to think that what I feared was in the world, instead of in my mind alone." (W-265.1:1-3)

Like everyone born into this world, I thought the world made me. And I went through some pretty good years up until 1993 when I separated from my first wife, followed by some real hellish years. Thank God for ACIM and its author, Jesus! Today, I know that I made the world from my mind; the world comes from me and not at me. I still can't control the world but I can really enjoy it. It's truly like this huge comedy movie which I produced and get to play my part. When I'm right minded, my director is Jesus/Holy Spirit.

The second part of the first paragraph defines in more eloquent terms my current life in my movie. It reads as follows: "Today I see the world in the celestial gentleness with which creation shines. There is no fear in it. Let no appearance of my sins obscure the light of Heaven shining on the world. What is reflected there is in God's Mind. The images I see reflect my thoughts. Yet is my mind at one with God's. And so I can perceive creation's gentleness." (W-265.1:4-10)

Lesson 266 – My holy Self abides in you, God's Son.

In truth, or in Heaven, God has but one Son Who is called Christ by Jesus in ACIM. Christ has but one Mind which He shares with God, our Creator. This is why the last sentence of the first paragraph of this lesson makes this statement to our Creator: "Let not Your Son forget his Name is Yours." (W-266.1:5)

Since, in truth, we all have the one Mind of Christ, each of us is Christ and we all abide in Christ, God's Son. What this lesson is literally saying to anyone I meet or think about is: "Since you are Christ and I abide in Christ, I therefore abide in you. There is no separation between us."

In this dream world, we certainly appear to be many which is consistent with the world's purpose – to make us believe we are separate from each other and separate from God.

In ACIM, Jesus teaches us that everyone we meet, or think about, is our savior. This is why this lesson begins with: "*Father, You gave me all Your Sons, to be my saviors and my counselors in sight; the bearers of Your holy Voice to me.*" This does not, by any means, suggest we don't need God's Voice (the Voice of the Holy Spirit/Jesus) to help us to properly interpret and respond to the words and actions of other people and to ultimately wake us all up from this crazy dream. It is essential that we rely on Jesus/Holy Spirit because, when we don't, it means we're relying on the ego which is clearly not in our best interests.

The second paragraph of this lesson has some wonderful promises: "This day we enter into Paradise, calling upon God's Name and on our own, acknowledging our Self in each of us [Each of us is Christ, God's Son.]; united in the holy Love of God. How many saviors God has given us! [There are about 7 billion of us in the world today.] How can we lose the way to Him, when He has filled the world with those who point to Him, and given us the sight to look on them? [The "sight" is Christ's vision wherein we are all eternal innocent happy parts of God's Creation and all of us are joined with everything else in the world.]" (W-266.2:1-3)

Lesson 267 – My Heart is beating in the peace of God.

Note that the "power" of God must include "the peace of God." God's power, despite what some may think, never includes the ability to beat up your enemy, whether the enemy is a bully down the street or another country which is causing problems for your home country. By contrast, the word power in the world means just the opposite of peace. For example, the United States has more "power" than any other country because of its military strength and ability to wage war.

The peace of God does in fact "pass all understanding" from the world's perspective because no one can learn it from the world. For anyone who believes the world real, it may be possible to get glimpses of this wonderful gift, but it would not be possible to sustain it for any length of time.

For students of ACIM, however, we learn of the unreality of the world and as we learn and practice its spirituality, we should have God's peace on an increasing basis. Leastwise, this has been my experience over the 15 years I've been studying the Course.

Also, it is not at all difficult to understand God's peace. For example, let's suppose I start worrying about something so Jesus might say to me: "Hey Jimmy, don't worry about something that doesn't even exist."

By the way, this is the 11th time the word "peace" is included in the title of a lesson. The first 10 times are as follows:

1. Lesson 63 – *The light of the world brings peace to every mind through my forgiveness.*
2. Lesson 93 – *Light and joy and peace abide in me.*
3. Lesson 105 – *God's peace and joy are mine.*
4. Lesson 185 – *I want the peace of God.*
5. Lesson 188 – *The peace of God is shining in me now.*
6. Lesson 200 – *There is no peace except the peace of God.*
7. Lesson 221 – *Peace to my mind. Let all my thoughts be still.*
8. Lesson 230 – *Now will I seek and find the peace of God.*
9. Lesson245 – *Your peace is with me Father. I am safe.*
10. Lesson 255 – *This day I choose to spend in perfect peace.*

Note that the word "peace" is also included in the title of the remaining 98 lessons another 11 times. If God's gifts could be rated according to importance, I think His gift of "total peace of mind" would likely be at the top of the list.

Lesson 268 – Let all things be exactly as they are.

What Jesus might tell me is: "Hey Jimmy, let all things be, don't try and control anything, and just relax and enjoy your dream."

Following are a few common expressions which are consistent with this lesson:

"Live and let live."
"Go with the flow."
"Easy does it."
"Would I rather be right or happy?" Happy is the correct answer.
"Don't rock the boat."
"Don't worry. Be happy."
"Mind your own business."
"Let go and let God."

In the Text of ACIM Jesus gives some great advice in dealing with human relations. He says if someone asks me to do something, even if it seems crazy to me, then I should do it. The exception is if it could harm either one of us or someone else, I of course shouldn't do it. For example, if a friend of mine asks me to steal a car with him, I would not do it.

Many people have world changing ideas which sound good on the surface. These ideas can range from ways to make a lot of money (selfish) to making sure the starving people in the world get food (unselfish). These ideas and thousands more, are really meaningless. Why? As we students of ACIM know, the entire world is just one big illusion so, even if such an idea were implemented and accomplished, the only thing that would happen would be the substitution of one illusion for another.

The world will end once all people are using God's Voice rather than the ego's voice to direct their thinking. It will end because everyone will be awake back home in Heaven so the dream world will simply disappear just as our night time dreams disappear when we wake up from our sleep. Jesus does indicate that it will be a very long time before this happens. However, it is quite possible, on an individual basis, to wake up now in this lifetime.

Lesson 269 – My sight goes forth to look upon Christ's face.

Let's go back to the beginning when there was only God our Father. He was and is perfect, eternal, joyous and all good Spirit, always extending but never changing. As pure Spirit, God has no form and no face. So in the beginning, God was Heaven.

God decided He wanted a Son to share Heaven with. As I envision what happened, God created His One Son by simply expanding Himself by, say, 50% instantaneously and We were all created there in Heaven. God and We were One just as if we took 2 gallons of water and added 1 more gallon. We would have everything God had and He would have everything we had. Going forward, We (God and Christ, His Son) continued to extend Our Self but never changed. We were co-creators with God in Heaven. (As a matter of fact, we still are since this world we think we're living in never happened.) An important point I want to make here is that Christ, like Our Father, is pure Spirit and has no form and no face.

From the first paragraph of this lesson, I've made the following request to God: "*I ask Your blessing on my* [spiritual] *sight today. It is the means which You have chosen to become the way to show me my mistakes, and look beyond them. It is given me to find a new perception through the Guide* [Holy Spirit/Jesus] *You gave to me, and through His lessons to surpass perception and return to truth. I ask for the illusion which transcends all those I made. Today I choose to see a world forgiven in which everyone shows me the face of Christ, and teaches me that what I look upon belongs to me; that nothing is, except Your holy Son.*" (W-269.1:1-5)

I have, in many places in this book, defined Christ's vision as seeing everyone I meet as an eternal, innocent and joyous spirit and no different than me regardless of what their life on earth looks like. Thinking of Christ, God's one Son, as a radiant light, we would all be rays coming from that light. That radiant light is my perception of the face of Christ.

Lesson 270 – I will not use the body's eyes today.

I think of Christ's vision as having two parts to it – (1) Seeing everyone I meet or think about as an eternal, innocent and joyous spirit and no different than me regardless of what their life on earth looks like, and (2) Joining with everything and everyone in the world rather than seeing everything and everyone as separate from me.

You can note that this is consistent with the first paragraph of this Lesson 270 which reads: *"Father, Christ's vision is Your gift to me, and it has power to translate all that the body's eyes behold into the sight of a forgiven world. How glorious and gracious is this world! Yet how much more will I perceive in it than sight can give. The world forgiven signifies Your Son acknowledges his Father, lets his dreams be brought to truth, and waits expectantly the one remaining instant more of time which ends forever, as Your memory returns to him.* [Personally, I'm waiting expectantly for God to take this final step for me.] *And now his will is one with Yours. His function now is but Your Own, and every thought except Your Own is gone."* (W-270.1:1-6)

Lesson 271 – Christ's is the vision I will use today.

In this lesson, Jesus once again reinforces the use of Christ's vision as we travel through our dream. For newcomers to ACIM, it might seem that as we mature spiritually, the world should become more distant and we would be less attentive to other people. A wonderful paradox for me is that the world has become a much more peaceful and happier place and I have become much more attentive to all the people I meet.

The first paragraph of this lesson is: "Each day, each hour, every instant, I am choosing what I want to look upon, the sounds I want to hear, the witnesses to what I want to be the truth for me. Today I choose to look upon what Christ would have me see, to listen to God's Voice, and seek the witnesses to what is true in God's creation. In Christ's sight, the world and God's creation meet, and as they come together all perception disappears. His [Christ's] kindly sight redeems the world from death, for nothing that He looks on but must live [forever], remembering the Father and the Son; Creator and creation unified." (W-271.1:1-4)

And the second paragraph is: *"Father, Christ's vision is the way to You. What He* [Christ] *beholds invites Your memory to be restored to me. And this I choose to be what I would look upon today."* (W-271.2:1-3)

Lesson 272 – How can illusions satisfy God's Son?

About 2,000 years ago, Jesus said "The Kingdom of God is within you." In ACIM, he has shortened this to "The Kingdom of God is you" because God has given us everything He has so there is no difference between us and everything. And everything is Heaven (i.e., the Kingdom of God) whereas the world is nothing.

A common expression often heard today is "Happiness is an inside job." This is absolutely correct because it's inside our minds where God is and where true happiness can be found.

In Chapter 31, Section IV of the Text of ACIM, Jesus talks about the futility of searching for happiness in the world. Following are some excerpts from this easy to read section:

> "Real choice is no illusion. But the world has none to offer. All its roads but lead to disappointment, nothingness and death. There is no choice in its alternatives. Seek not escape from problems here. The world was made that problems could not

be escaped. Be not deceived by all the different names its roads are given. They have but one end [death]." (T-31.IV.2:1-8) "On some you travel gaily for a while, before the bleakness enters. And on some the thorns are felt at once. The choice is not what will the ending be but when it comes." (T-31.IV.2:12-14)

"There is no choice where every end is sure [death]. Perhaps you would prefer to try them all, before you really learn they are but one. The roads this world can offer seem to be quite large in number, but the time must come when everyone begins to see how like they are to one another. Men have died on seeing this, because they saw no way except the pathways offered by the world. And learning they led nowhere, lost their hope. And yet this was the time they could have learned their greatest lesson. All must reach this point, and go beyond it. It is true indeed there is no choice at all within the world. But this is not the lesson in itself. The lesson has a purpose, and in this you come to understand what it is for." (T-31.IV.3:1-10) Learning the world offers no hope is a very important lesson. Where does hope lie? In your own mind because that's where God resides. And the greatest teacher who ever lived, Jesus, has given us this ACIM book as a step by step approach to training our minds to be in communion with God. As a good student of ACIM, I can tell you it really works!

"Think not that happiness is ever found by following a road away from it. This makes no sense, and cannot be the way. To you who seem to find this course to be too difficult to learn, let me repeat that to achieve a goal you must proceed in its direction, not away from it. And every road that leads the other way will not advance the purpose to be found. If this be difficult to understand, then is this course impossible to learn. But only then. For otherwise, it is a simple teaching in the obvious." (T-31.IV.7:1-7)

The study of ACIM can be called an inner study leading to eternal life. By contrast, all paths offered by the world lead to death.

This current lesson, of course, is consistent with Lesson 128: "The world I see holds nothing that I want."

Lesson 273 – The stillness of the peace of God is mine.

The world is a very chaotic place. This lesson might suggest to a new ACIM student that their lives will become less active and they will become meditative gurus so they can simply enjoy the "peace of God". While this may be true of some Course students, it has certainly not been true in my case nor the few other dedicated ACIM students I have met.

When I first started studying the Course 15 years ago, I was a single guy living by myself. Today, I'm happily married with a wonderful 6-year old girl and another baby on the way. One constant over this 15 year period is my ongoing study of ACIM. Although I'm much more active now, my peace of mind has increased miraculously.

Although I'm, of course, conscious of this world, I seldom react to anything that goes on. What is clear to me is that "I'm stepping back and letting God lead the way" on an increasing basis. Based on my experience, this just happens if you are consistent in studying ACIM.

In the first paragraph of this lesson, Jesus says: "If we give way to a disturbance, let us learn to dismiss it and return to peace." I can still get disturbed occasionally and when I do I know I've allowed the ego to catch me off guard. With the help of Jesus/Holy Spirit, I generally figure out where I went wrong. Over time, disturbances are becoming less frequent and less severe. My peace of mind and happiness are increasing. What a deal! I plan on continuing my study of ACIM for the rest of my life.

Lesson 274 – Today belongs to love. Let me not fear.

If I judge people the way the world tells me I'm supposed to, I know I will not have peace of mind and I will have fear. Additionally, I will be far removed from God's love.

The first paragraph of this lesson reads: "*Father, today I would let all things be as You created them, and give Your Son the honor due his sinlessness; the love of brother to his brother and his Friend. Through this I am redeemed. Through this as well the truth will enter where illusions were, light will replace all darkness, and Your Son will know he is as You created him.*" (W-274.1:1-3)

In my words, here's what I'm telling our Creator or Father: "Dear God, no matter what any individual has said or done to me or anyone else in the world, I'll see him or her as the eternal, innocent and joyous spirit as You created us all in Heaven. In his ACIM book, Your Son Jesus uses the term Christ's vision to define this type of seeing. Thank you Jesus, Holy Spirit and Father for all Your gifts and for Your patience with me."

Lesson 275 – God's healing Voice protects all things today.

"God's healing Voice" is the Holy Spirit. I really like the fact that Jesus lets us know frequently that he's with us also because I can identify a lot more with him, who like me was a person at one point in time, than I can with the Holy Spirit. In the first paragraph of this lesson, for instance, Jesus tells us: "Join me in hearing." (W-275.1:3)

In the next sentence, Jesus tells us: "For the Voice for God tells us of things we cannot understand alone, nor learn apart." (W-275.1:4) Jesus repeatedly tells us the world is insane and we absolutely need God's help to restore us to sanity. For any readers who haven't yet acknowledged the insanity of the world, consider the fact that under the world's rules, everyone must die. By contrast, God created us to live eternally just as

He lives eternally. This is common sense and it is sane thinking. There can be no reconciling the world's thinking with God's because the world is insane. Thank God the world is but a dream we're stuck in for a while! We'll all wake up at some point. By the way, there's no eternal hell for anyone so you can forget that idea even for your worst enemy.

The second paragraph of this lesson tells us to tell God: "*Your healing Voice protects all things today, and so I leave all things to You. I need be anxious over nothing. For Your Voice will tell me what to do and where to go; to whom to speak and what to say to him, what thoughts to think, what words to give the world. The safety that I bring is given me. Father, Your Voice protects all things through me.*" (W-275.2:1-5) The title of Lesson 155 says this in a nutshell: "*I will step back and let Him lead the way.*"

Lesson 276 – The word of God is given me to speak.

In this lesson, Jesus defines in one simple sentence the definition of "the Word of God." The definition is: " 'My Son is pure and holy as Myself.' " (W-276.1:2) This is how we were created and this is what we are now because as Lessons 94, 110 and 162 say: "I am as God created me." Therefore, "You, too, are as God created you."

Although we can think this world is real, thank God we are only asleep in Heaven dreaming this insane impossible dream. Through the Holy Spirit, God has guaranteed that we will all wake up at the end of our time.

The second paragraph of this lesson tells us to tell God: "*Father, Your Word is mine. And it is this that I would speak to all my brothers, who are given me to cherish as my own, as I am loved and blessed and saved by You.*" (W-276.2:1,2) I can see all people as eternal, innocent and joyous spiritual beings, the same as me. There is no fixed formula as to exactly what I say to any one of them. The Holy Spirit and Jesus are always with me to guide me in everything I say and everything I do. When I make a mistake, They're here to help me correct my mistakes.

Lesson 277 – Let me not bind Your Son with laws I made.

The second paragraph of this lesson reads: "Let us not worship idols, nor believe in any law idolatry would make to hide the freedom of the Son of God. He is not bound except by his beliefs. Yet what he is, is far beyond his faith in slavery or freedom. He is free because he is his Father's Son. And he cannot be bound unless God's truth can lie, and God can will that He deceive Himself." Rest assured, God's truth can't lie and God can't deceive Himself.

In Section VIII of Chapter 29 of the Text of ACIM, Jesus talks about idols and their purpose. Following are the last two paragraphs of this section in their entirety. To a large extent, these summarize the entire Course.

> "What purpose has an idol, then? What is it for? This is the only question that has many answers, each depending on the one of whom the question has been asked. The [illusionary] world believes in idols. No one comes [here] unless he worshipped them, and still attempts to seek for one that yet might offer him a gift reality [Heaven] does not contain. Each worshipper of idols harbors hope his special deities [idols] will give him more than other men possess. It must be more. It does not really matter more of what; more beauty, more intelligence, more wealth, or even more affliction and more pain. But more of something is an idol for. And when one fails another takes its place, with hope of finding more of something else. Be not deceived by forms the 'something' takes. An idol is a means for getting more. And it is this that is against God's Will." (T-29.VIII.8:1-13) Why is "getting more" against God's Will? The next paragraph answers this question.

> "God has not many Sons, but only One. Who can have more, and who be given less? [Since there's but One, this is a rhetorical question.] In Heaven would the Son of God but laugh, if idols could intrude upon his peace. It is for him the Holy Spirit speaks, and tells you idols have no purpose here. For more than Heaven can you never have. If Heaven is within [and it is], why would you seek [outside] for idols that would make of Heaven less, to give you more than God bestowed upon your brother and on you, as one with Him? God gave you all there is. And to be sure you could not lose it, did He also give the same to every living thing as well. And thus is every living thing a part of you, as of Himself. No idol can establish you as more than God. But you will never be content with being less than God." (T-29.VIII.9:1-11)

I really like the way Jesus ends the last paragraph – We shouldn't be content until we have all that God has because in Our Creation He gave this to us and "We are as God created us."

Lesson 278 – If I am bound, my Father is not free.

The word "free" in this lesson really means "eternally free." Those who believe this world is real, rather than just a temporary dream, must also believe they and everyone else must die. And death is not freedom. For me, the knowledge that death is not real was one of the earliest gifts I received in my studying of ACIM.

The last 3 sentences of the first paragraph read: "If I am bound in any way, I do not know my Father nor my Self. And I am lost to all reality [Heaven]. For truth is free, and what is bound is not a part of truth." (W-278.1:3-5) The gift of freedom which, of course, is part of Heaven gets transferred to our lives here on earth as we study the Course. Leastwise, this has been my experience.

This world is but a dream and as I learn to listen only to my Inner Voice (Jesus/Holy Spirit) which means I will think appropriately, then I am able to act and speak appropriately also which in turn allows me to really enjoy my dream and help many others along the way. The increasing freedom that has occurred in my life over the past 15 years can be described as ever decreasing fear and an ever increasing freedom to love. Ever increasing happiness is the wonderful byproduct.

Lesson 279 – Creation's freedom promises my own.

The second paragraph of this lesson is where I say to our Father: *"I will accept Your promises today, and give my faith to them. My Father loves the Son Whom He created as His Own. Would You withhold the gifts You gave to me?"* (W-279.2:1-3) This, like many of the questions Jesus asks in the Course, is a rhetorical question. God's Voice answers us along the following lines: "Of course not! The gifts of Heaven are available to you while you're still in your dream. These gifts materialize as you allow Us (Jesus and the Holy Spirit) to gently wake you up from your earthly dream over time."

Lesson 280 – What limits can I lay upon God's Son?

This question is answered in Lesson 250 whose title is: *"Let me not see myself as limited."* In the discussion of Lesson 250, Jesus also tells us: "Let me not see anyone else as limited."

So the answer to the question raised here in Lesson 280 is: "I can't place any limits on anyone." It's really quite simple in that in our Creation, God gave to us everything He has and God is unlimited. Therefore, we are unlimited also.

This is clearly not true in this world we think we're in......until we learn that we're not in this world. This world is nothing but an insane dream. It is not real. It is nothing. And we say: "Thank God there is no world!"

Using Christ's vision, we are able to see all people as eternal, innocent and joyous spirits, the same as we see our self. And we give honor to all people who are part of Christ and one with us. This is why in the second paragraph of this Lesson 280 we tell our Father: "*Today let me give honor to Your Son, for thus alone I find the way to You. Father, I lay no limits on the Son You love and You created limitless. The honor that I give to him is Yours, and what is Yours belongs to me as well.*" (W-280.2:1-3)

Lesson 281 – I can be hurt by nothing but my thoughts.

The first 3 sentences of the first paragraph of this lesson read: "*Father, Your Son is perfect. When I think I am hurt in any way, it is because I have forgotten who I am, and that I am as You created me. Your thoughts can only bring me happiness.*" (W-281.1:1-3)

Today, when I feel hurt in any way, whether emotionally or physically, I know that I've made this dream world real. I have forgotten who I am which is an eternal, innocent and joyous part of God Himself; I am not a body in my own dream. For the fully mature spiritual person, I am convinced that even severe physical torture will not affect them because they can place their mind totally outside this world. At this point in time, I can't identify with this level of spiritual maturity.

This ability to overcome physical torture is consistent with the balance of the first paragraph which reads: "*If ever I am sad or hurt or ill, I have forgotten what You think, and put my little meaningless ideas in place of where Your Thoughts belong, and where they are. I can be hurt by nothing but my thoughts. The Thoughts I think with You can only bless. The Thoughts I think with You alone are true.*" (W-281.1:4-7)

Lesson 282 – I will not be afraid of love today.

God and His Creation share One Mind. This Oneness is all there is. Nothing else exists. This Oneness has many names within the terminology of ACIM. This Oneness is called Love, Heaven, truth, knowledge, reality, etc. Therefore, this lesson might also read: "I will not be afraid of Heaven today."

The first sentence of this lesson reads: "If I could realize but this today, salvation would be reached for all the world." (W-282.1:1) All this means I think is that I understand that the whole world is saved and I've mentioned this many times in this book. Specifically, I've said all people will eventually wake up back home in Heaven regardless of what their earthly life had been like at times.

However, the decision to wake up must be made by each individual. God won't do it for them (He doesn't threaten or force) but His Voice is certainly necessary in the waking up process. I certainly can't do it for anyone but myself although I can serve as a power of example to others to follow my lead just as I'm following the lead of Jesus/Holy Spirit. Jesus couldn't do it for others 2,000 years ago but he sure was a great example as he followed the Holy Spirit's lead.

The whole world is saved! I know this even though very few other people know it for themselves. So long as the world is believed to be reality by the vast majority of people, the knowledge of salvation will remain hidden.

Lesson 283 – My true Identity abides in You.

This lesson begins: "*Father, I made an image of myself, and it is this I call the Son of God.*" (W-283.1:1) Like every other person here, I had a dream and in my dream I made my body thinking this was who I was. And, like everyone here, I thought this dream was real and I thought my dream (i.e., the world) made me. Now I know that the world is not real and that I am still as God created me – an eternal, innocent, happy part of God Himself. In a nutshell, I now know that the world didn't make me but, in my dreaming, I made the world and everything in it.

As we wake up from our dream, the rest of this lesson makes perfect sense. The rest of the first paragraph reads: "*Yet is creation as it always was, for Your creation is unchangeable. Let me not worship idols. I am he my Father loves. My holiness remains the light of Heaven and the Love of God. Is not what is beloved of You secure? Is not the light of Heaven infinite? Is not Your Son my true Identity, when You created everything that is?*" (W-283.1:2-8) In my ACIM book, I wrote in the margin "Of course" to the 3 questions in this paragraph.

The second paragraph of this lesson is: "Now are we [Jesus and me] one in shared Identity, with God our Father as our only Source, and everything created part of us. And so we offer blessing to all things, uniting lovingly with all the world, which our forgiveness has made one with us." (W-283.2:1,2)

Lesson 284 – I can elect to change all thoughts that hurt.

This is really a continuation of Lesson 281 whose title is: "*I can be hurt by nothing but my thoughts.*" In my discussion of Lesson 281, above, I wrote: "For the fully mature spiritual person, I am convinced that even severe physical torture will not affect them because they can place their mind totally outside this world." This current Lesson 284 says this explicitly.

As I've matured spiritually over the past 15 years as a direct result of my ongoing study of ACIM, I can really identify with the progressive nature of this lesson as Jesus describes it in the first paragraph. The first paragraph reads: "Loss is not loss when properly perceived. Pain is impossible. There is no grief with any cause at all. And suffering of any kind is nothing but a dream. This is the truth, at first to be but said and then repeated many times; and next to be accepted as but partly true, with many reservations. Then to be considered seriously more and more, and finally accepted as the truth. I can elect to change all thoughts that hurt. And I would go beyond these words today, and past all reservations, and arrive at full acceptance of the truth in them." (W-284.1:1-8)

One thing is very clear from this lesson. Jesus did not suffer and he felt no pain when they nailed him to the cross.

Lesson 285 – My holiness shines bright and clear today.

Early in the Text of ACIM, Jesus includes a paragraph which defines the word "holiness". This paragraph also assures us we'll all return to Heaven and gives a good definition of a miracle. Here it is: "Ultimately, every member of the family of God must return. The miracle calls him to return because it blesses and honors him, even though he may be absent in spirit. 'God is not mocked' is not a warning but a reassurance. God *would* be mocked if any of His creations lacked holiness. The creation [i.e., Christ] is whole, and the mark of wholeness is holiness. Miracles are affirmations of Sonship, which is a state of completion and abundance." (T-1.V.4:1-6)

So holiness is a term to define the wholeness or Oneness of all of God's Creation. And we are holy just as God is holy because that's how God created us and "We are still as God created us."

Instead of waking up and saying "*My holiness shines bright and clear today*", I can wake up and say "I've decided I'm going to have a real happy day today." When you read the lesson, you can see this is what the lesson is saying. For example, the first line of the text of this lesson reads: "Today I wake with joy, expecting but the happy things of God to come to me." (W-285.1:1)

My suggestion is to go about your business but don't take it seriously. Just play your part. Try to remember it's only a dream and not real no matter what happens.

Also, for my holiness to shine bright and clear, I try to see everyone else's holiness shining bright and clear. The only way I can do this for many of the people I encounter is to see them with Christ's vision rather than with my eyes and ears. In other words, I must see the truth in them despite their anger and complaints and hurts and grievances. They are eternal, innocent and joyous parts of God's Creation just as I am. If I don't use Christ's vision, I know I will not be able to have a real happy day.

Lesson 286 – The hush of Heaven holds my heart today.

There is God's peace which does in fact pass all worldly understanding. Neither the world nor the ego knows anything of this peace.

However, "We are still as God created us." In our natural state, in Heaven, the peace of God is ours now and forever more. By practicing ACIM, we can attain this peace here "on earth as it is in Heaven." God is both the means (by listening only to Jesus/Holy Spirit and not the ego) and the end which is Heaven.

If you have been practicing the holy instant, you should be learning that this peace is attainable at least during such practice periods. Jesus tells us that our life here on earth can become a continuous series of holy instants wherein all our days can be peaceful although we may be quite active within our dream world. This is the essence of this lesson.

Lesson 287 – You are my goal, my Father, Only You.

This lesson starts out: "Where would I go but Heaven?" (L-287.1:1) One of the best descriptions of what Heaven is like is contained in two paragraphs from Lesson 107. These two paragraphs are copied here.

"Can you imagine what a state of mind without illusions is? How it would feel? Try to remember when there was a time, - perhaps a minute, maybe even less – when nothing came to interrupt your peace; when you were certain you were loved and safe. Then try to picture what it would be like to have that moment be extended to the end of time and to eternity. Then let the sense of quiet you felt be multiplied a hundred times, and then be multiplied another hundred more [100 times 100 is 10,000]." (W-107.2:1-5)

"And now you have a hint, not more than just the faintest intimation of the state your mind will rest in when the truth has come. Without illusions there could be no fear, no doubt and no attack. When truth has come all pain is over, for there is no room for transitory thoughts and dead ideas to linger in your mind. Truth occupies your mind completely, liberating you from all beliefs in the ephemeral [i.e., the temporary]. They have no place because the truth has come, and they are nowhere. They can not be found, for truth is everywhere forever, now." (W-107.3:1-6)

Lesson 288 – Let me forget my brother's past today.

I, Jimmy Laws, have done some dastardly things in my life. The worst part of my life started when I separated from my first wife in 1993. We had been married for 17 years. I immediately started drinking "like a fish." As a result, I was fired from my professional executive position at the end of 1995. I had been with that company for 20 years at the time. I had become a falling down drunk, better off dead than alive. I hurt me and everyone I met. My family wanted no part of me. I had "burnt all my bridges." Thank God I quit drinking in 1997. Also, thank God I took to ACIM like "a fish takes to water" beginning in 1999.

What have I learned? My past history that I've summarized above never happened. It was just part of my dream. How simple it is to forgive myself for something that never happened. And, as I make spiritual progress, how much simpler is it becoming for me to forgive others because what I thought they did also never happened. Remember, as I've quoted a number of times before in this book: "There is no world! This is the central thought the course attempts to teach." (W-132.6:2,3)

In the first paragraph of this lesson, Jesus tells us to tell God that we understand all people are our saviors: "*My brother is my savior. Let me not attack the savior You have given me. But let me honor him who bears Your Name, and so remember that It is my own.*" (W-288.1:7-9)

In the second paragraph, Jesus says: "Forgive me [i.e., Jesus, who is speaking to us], then, today. And you will know you have forgiven me if you behold your brother in the light of holiness. He cannot be less holy than I [Jesus], and you can not be holier than he." (W-288.2:1-3) What Jesus is really saying here is that if I'm holding even a small resentment against just one person in my life, then I haven't forgiven God's Son. Since Jesus, like all of us, is a part of God's Son this means I haven't forgiven Jesus.

When I use Christ's vision, rather than my eyes and ears, all of God's children .... You, me, Jesus, Mother Theresa, Hitler, etc. .... are seen as eternal, innocent and joyous equal parts of God's Creation, and I can have no resentments.

Lesson 289 – The past is over. It can touch me not.

This lesson begins: "Unless the past is over in my mind, the real world must escape my sight." (W-289.1:1;underscore mine) The "real world" is a term Jesus uses frequently in ACIM to describe the ultimate goal we strive for while we're still in our dream world.

On the page following Lesson 290, Jesus answers the question: "What is the Real World?" (W-Q 8.title)

In the first paragraph of the answer, Jesus says: "The real world cannot be perceived except through eyes forgiveness blesses, so they see a world where terror is impossible, and witnesses to fear can not be found." (W-Q 8.1:4) And, in all its simplicity, what is forgiveness? It is the fact that this world never happened so there is nothing to forgive. The terror and fear that others seem to experience because they think the world is real should have no effect on me because I know such things never happened, they're not happening now, and they can't happen in the future.

I'll use the analogy that my earthly life is a movie that I produced even though I don't have the slightest idea what the rest of my movie looks like. In other words, I can't foretell my future. I'm enjoying playing my part and doing my best to let Jesus/Holy Spirit direct me as my script unfolds which turns out to be a real good thing for me and for all the other cast members (i.e., everyone else in my life). (When the ego was my director, my life at times appeared okay but it led me ultimately to a miserable lonely hell on earth.) My mind is my movie projector so I can see with my eyes and hear with my ears like other people. But I know my earthly life is not real; it's like a fictional movie I'm watching and it's very enjoyable today. Just on the other side of my movie is the gate of Heaven and I simply "know" this. (This is actually true for everyone in the world but the vast majority don't know it because they think this world is real and so is death and suffering and pain and so they, of course, take this world seriously.) My understanding is that to be in the real world means the ongoing knowledge that this world is not real and ongoing reliance on God's Voice (i.e., Jesus/Holy Spirit) for direction in this fictional movie the world calls life.

Lesson 290 – My present happiness is all I see.

What a wonderful lesson. Through the mind training from ACIM and the ongoing internal help I receive from Jesus/Holy Spirit, I can nearly always honestly say "My present happiness is all I see."

Following is the first paragraph of this lesson with some comments by me: "Unless I look upon what is not there [So long as I remember the world is just a big smokescreen and not real], my present happiness is all I see. Eyes that begin to open [by using Christ's vision] see at last. And I would have Christ's vision come to me this very day. What I perceive without God's Own Correction for the sight I made is frightening and painful to behold. [God's Own Correction is the ongoing help I need from Jesus/Holy Spirit.] Yet I would not allow my mind to be deceived by the belief the dream I made is real an instant longer. [The world I see, hear, feel, taste and smell is not at all real. It is just a dream I've been in for a long time and I'm ready to wake up back home in Heaven.] This the day I seek my present happiness, and look on nothing else except the thing I seek." (W-290.1:1-6)

Lesson 291 – This is a day of stillness and of peace.

If I use Christ's vision to see, then the promises of this lesson will hold true. If I fall back to my old way of thinking, using the ego as my guide, these promises will not come true.

The promises I'm talking about are contained in the first paragraph which reads: "Christ's vision looks through me today. His sight shows me all things forgiven and at peace, and offers this same vision to the world. And I accept this vision in its name, both for myself and for the world as well. What loveliness we look upon today! What holiness we see surrounding us! And it is given us to recognize it is a holiness in which we share; it is the Holiness of God Himself." (W-291.1:1-6)

Lesson 292 – A happy outcome to all things is sure.

Before this world existed, we were all in Heaven, one with God and all His Creation. Our peace and joy and the extension of this was all we knew. Following is my understanding of the "Separation" and our return to Heaven.

Then we (God's Creation) made a stupid decision. We thought we could separate from God and elected to do so. The result was that we fell into a deep sleep in Heaven and started dreaming this dream we call the world. At that point, God created the Holy Spirit to reach us in our dream and make sure we all wake up back home in Heaven. So from the beginning of time (which can be thought of as the opposite of eternity) "God made sure that a happy outcome to all things was certain."

Jesus points out in ACIM that we don't die and then wake up in Heaven. We wake up at the gate of Heaven while we're still in our body. At some point while we're still in our body, God Himself takes the final step. It's His call, not ours.

Although Jesus doesn't discuss this issue at length in ACIM, it's my understanding that I have had many past earthly lives. I don't remember any of them. In all of them, I'm sure I pursued many different worldly ways of achieving lasting happiness; I had been trying to find something in the world that couldn't be found in the world. In all those previous lives, I died and was born as a baby into a new life. In those previous lives, my mind was still listening to the ego and therefore I had not achieved what I like to call "the Jesus level of spirituality". I think there's a reasonable chance that the ACIM path I'm on now will get me into Heaven in this lifetime.

Whether I awaken in Heaven in this lifetime or later on is not nearly as important as my conviction that we will all ultimately wake up in Heaven. It is our Inheritance and it is guaranteed by God through the Holy Spirit.

Jesus says in the first paragraph of this lesson that when we wake up is up to us. Although God takes the final step, He won't do this until we have made ourselves ready. So it's in our control, not God's. Specifically, he says: "God's promises make no exceptions. And He guarantees that only joy can be the final outcome for everything. [I'll add some clarity here by saying the eternal joy of Heaven is the final outcome.] Yet it is up to us when this is reached; how long we let an alien will [i.e., the ego] appear to be opposing His. And while we think this will is real [which also means we think the world is real], we will not find the end He has appointed [Heaven] as the outcome of all problems we perceive, all trials we see, and every situation that we meet. Yet is the ending certain. For God's Will is done in earth and Heaven. We will seek and we will find according to His Will, which guarantees that our will is done." (W-292.1:1-7)

Lesson 293 – All fear is past and only love is here.

If one believes the world is real then fear will also be real. Following is an excerpt from ACIM's *Manual for Teachers*: "Awareness of dreaming is the real function of God's teachers. They watch the dream figures come and go, shift and change, suffer and die. Yet they are not deceived by what they see. They recognize that to behold a dream figure as sick and separate is no more real than to regard it as healthy and beautiful. Unity alone is not a thing of dreams. And it is this God's teachers acknowledge as behind the dream, beyond all seeming and yet surely theirs." (M-12.6:6-11)

This world was made by our belief in separation which in turn caused us to make up this world of separation. However, we can't separate what God created as One. So this world is a make believe world and it is not real. As a teacher of God, I fully acknowledge that just beyond this make believe world is Heaven and Unity (or Oneness). Heaven is not make believe; it is Reality. Heaven is also called Love.

The preceding two paragraphs help to clarify this Lesson 293. The first paragraph of Lesson 293 reads: "All fear is past, because its source is gone, and all its thoughts gone with it. Love remains the only present state, whose Source is here forever and forever. Can the world seem bright and clear and safe and welcoming, with all my past mistakes oppressing it, and showing me distorted forms of fear? [Answer - Of course not!] Yet in the present love is obvious, and its effects apparent. All the world shines in reflection of its holy light, and I perceive a world forgiven at last." (W-293.1:1-5)

Lesson 294 – My body is a wholly neutral thing.

Today, I think of my body as simply a vehicle to communicate to other people in my life. In a sense, my body is really no different than the car I drive to get from one place to another.

Within this dream world, I have an invisible pilot who instructs me on the communication He wants me to give and to whom. This pilot is Jesus/Holy Spirit. I am simply the copilot doing my best to follow the instructions from this perfect pilot.

In the first paragraph of this Lesson 294, Jesus asks: "Did God create the mortal and corruptible?" (W-294.1:3) The body is both mortal, in that it dies, and often does very corrupt things. God only creates like Himself which means He only creates purely eternal good things. The point is that God did not create our bodies just as God did not create the world.

A number of times in ACIM, Jesus tells us that the Holy Spirit can take everything in the world (made by the ego) and use it for good purpose. He also tells us that the sole purpose of the body, when under the direction of the Holy Spirit, is to communicate to other people in the dream world.

Lesson 295 – The Holy Spirit looks through me today.

I am so much more comfortable knowing that Jesus is with me every split second of every day. When I'm in God's Will, it means I'm taking direction only from Jesus (or the Holy Spirit since Jesus and the Holy Spirit are always one), and ignoring the ego. When I'm in God's Will, it also means Jesus and I are one. In the Introduction to Review V of the Workbook (just after Lesson 170) Jesus tells us "Let this review be then your gift to me. For this alone I need; that you will hear the words I speak, and give them to the world. You are my voice, my eyes, my feet, my hands through which I save the world." (W-Review V.Introduction.9:1-3)

Because of my ongoing need for Jesus and the comfort I get, I have mentally modified this Lesson 295 as follows: "The Holy Spirit looks through us today." The us, of course, means Jesus and me. Although, we (Jesus and I) can use my eyes to see the world like everyone else, we use Christ's vision to see the world in truth. Using Christ's vision, everyone is seen as an eternal, innocent and joyous spirit, the same as Jesus and me. Even the most corrupt murderer is seen in this light because, in truth, that is who they are.

Lesson 296 – The Holy Spirit speaks through me today.

As I discussed in the previous lesson, my need for Jesus and the comfort I get knowing he is always with me has caused me to mentally modify this lesson to: "The Holy Spirit speaks through us today." The us reflects Jesus and me, together.

When I am in God's Will (and therefore not the ego's will), I am in fact the voice, the eyes, the feet, and the hands of Jesus through which he saves the world. I just play my part in this incredible fictional movie we call the world.

I can really identify with the last sentence of this lesson which reads: "How gladly does the Holy Spirit come to rescue us from hell, when we allow His teaching to persuade the world, through us, to seek and find the easy path to God." (W-296.2:3)

Lesson 297 – Forgiveness is the only gift I give.

In Lesson 293, above, I quoted an excerpt from the *Manual for Teachers.* I am repeating it here because it does a great job of defining forgiveness, although it never uses the term: "Awareness of dreaming is the real function of God's teachers. They watch the dream figures come and go, shift and change, suffer and die. Yet they are not deceived by what they see. They recognize that to behold a dream figure as sick and separate is no more real than to regard it as healthy and beautiful. Unity alone is not a thing of dreams. And it is this God's teachers acknowledge as behind the dream, beyond all seeming and yet surely theirs." (M-12.6:6-11)

What is forgiveness? It is the realization that this world never happened, is not happening now and won't be happening in the future. It is but a dream. Nothing bad ever happened here either for the simple reason that the world never happened.

In order for me to remember that the world is a dream on an ongoing basis (i.e., to continue forgiving) and to help others who don't even have a clue that this world is but a dream, I need to stay in constant contact with Jesus. But this is great both for me and other people in my life because I've found that his direction in my life brings more happiness to me and other people in my life. Prior to my years of study of ACIM, I didn't know how to communicate with Jesus and my life went to "hell in a hand basket."

Lesson 298 – I love You, Father, and I love Your Son.

In ACIM, Jesus tells us that to love our Father means to love all His Sons as well, without exception. So we can't say, for example, I love God but I can do without that no good boss of mine.

During my 15 years of studying ACIM, I've had some grievances against certain individuals. I also knew this was my problem. These individuals have been my greatest teachers because they caused me to look more at me so I could fully understand what Christ's vision truly means. It simply means to see everyone as God created them, as eternal, innocent and joyous parts of God's Creation, the same as me. It matters not what an individual does in this dream world. The truth of who they are was established by God before this world was dreamed up and it has never changed.

The first paragraph of this Lesson 298 reads: "My gratitude permits my love to be accepted without fear. And thus am I restored to my reality at last. All that intruded on my holy sight forgiveness takes away. And I draw near the end of senseless journeys, mad careers and artificial values. I accept instead what God establishes as mine, sure that in that alone I will be saved; sure that I go through fear to meet my Love." (W-298.1:1-5)

Lesson 299 – Eternal holiness abides in me.

Here's a very common earthly cliché: "God works in mysterious ways." While this works for most people, students of ACIM learn that this is not at all true. We learn that God wants to be understood and hides nothing from His Sons.

An analogy would be to consider an insane individual who spent 10 years in a mental asylum during which time he needed assistance at every level of living. His only real friend was his psychiatrist who visited him every day. To the patient, whose entire world was limited to the insane asylum, the psychiatrist worked in mysterious ways. The patient would see this friend come into his world (i.e., the insane asylum) but knew he left every day and would wonder where he was going. This was a real mystery to him. After 10 years, the patient got better and left the asylum and, after a few years with a lot of professional help, started living a normal life. Now that he was no longer insane, he was able to reflect back to his asylum days and understand why his psychiatrist friend left the asylum every day. His friend's life was no longer considered mysterious.

What's insanity got to do with God and ACIM? Everything! Jesus often uses the term in ACIM. Anyone who thinks the world is real must either be insane or think God is mean and cruel. As we start understanding God's world (Heaven), we see that it is planet earth which is mysterious. It is planet earth which is insane and therefore not understandable. I have learned that God is not mean and cruel and, for all those years I thought the world real, I was absolutely insane. But I fit in well because everybody I knew thought the same thing.

Now after many years of studying, understanding and living ACIM, I've found that God is not mysterious nor is He complicated. It's this separated world with its billions of people and trillions of separate components that is complicated and impossible to understand. Why? Because it represents this massive insane asylum with very few able psychiatrists. The world can't be understood for the simple fact that it is insane. Using the terminology of ACIM, there really is only one Great Psychiatrist, called the Holy Spirit and He is ably and perfectly assisted by our good friend, Jesus. The job of the Holy Spirit and Jesus is to heal our minds so we can all go back home to Heaven.

Since "eternal holiness abides in all of us" and since the Holy Spirit's job isn't done until we've all become sane again, it's God's guarantee that all of us will be awake in Heaven at the end of time.

Lesson 300 – Only an instant does this world endure.

This lesson can be looked at in a negative way. For instance, a person might think: "Thank God I only have to endure this life of mine for a while. Death sounds pretty good to me." Jesus effectively says this in the first sentence of this lesson: "This is a thought which can be used to say that death and sorrow are the certain lot of all who come here, for their joys are gone before they are possessed, or even grasped." (W-300.1:1)

On the other hand, as the mind training of ACIM takes hold, we start thinking of the world as nothing more than a thin cloud and start realizing and appreciating the gifts of Heaven in this earthly life. Further, we come to know that there is no death. The peace and serenity of Heaven become ours. In the last two sentences of the first paragraph Jesus tells us: "Yet this is also the idea that lets no false perception keep us in its hold [i.e., The world is just one big chunk of false perception.], nor represent more than a passing cloud upon a sky eternally serene [i.e., Behind the world is the eternal serene sky of Heaven.]. And it is this serenity we seek, unclouded, obvious and sure, today." (W-300.1:2,3)

Lesson 301 – And God Himself shall wipe away all tears.

This lesson begins: "*Father, unless I judge I cannot weep.*" (W-301.1:1) In other words: "If I don't judge then I can't weep."

So then the question becomes: "How do I not judge?" As our understanding becomes clearer, the answer becomes real simple. Instead of looking at people in this dream world with my physical eyes, use Christ's vision to see them as they are in truth. Without exception, all of us are eternal, innocent and joyous parts of God's Creation.

The second paragraph of this lesson offers us the following: "God's world [Heaven] is happy. Those who look on it [by using Christ's vision] can only add their joy to it, and bless it as a cause of further joy to them.

We wept because we did not understand. But we have learned the world we saw [this dream world] was false, and we will look upon God's world today." (W-301.2:1-4)

Lesson 302 – Where darkness was I look upon the light.

The first 4 sentences of this lesson read: "*Father, our eyes are opening at last. Your holy world* [Heaven] *awaits us, as our sight* [Christ's vision] *is finally restored and we can see. We thought we suffered. But we had forgot the Son* [Christ] *whom You created.*" (W-302.1:1-4) All of us, including Jesus in his younger years, had thought to separate from our Father and made up this illusionary world to block us from God. But none of it is real and through the mind training of ACIM we learn to understand it is but a dream. Of course, when the world was real to us, we forgot Who God was and we forgot who we were.

In his early years Jesus thought the world was real like everyone else. Although he doesn't tell us in ACIM, I expect that sometime before he was baptized by John the Baptist, he was able to figure out the world was just a dream by listening only to the Holy Spirit and not the ego. He was the first person in the history of the world to do this. This is what makes him very important. He's also given us the simple tools necessary to follow in his footsteps through ACIM. Thank you very much, Jesus, for doing this for me and countless others.

In the early part of the Text, Jesus tells us about himself, including the fact that he is not separate or different from us: " 'No man cometh unto the Father but by me' does not mean that I am in any way separate or different from you except in time, and time does not really exist. The statement is more meaningful in terms of a vertical rather than a horizontal axis. You stand below me and I stand below God. In the process of 'rising up,' I am higher because without me the distance between God and man would be too great for you to encompass. I bridge the distance as an elder brother to you on the one hand, and as a Son of God on the other. My devotion to my brothers has placed me in charge of the Sonship, which I render complete because I share it. This may appear to contradict the statement 'I and my Father are one,' but there are two parts to the statement in recognition that the Father is greater." (T-1.II.4:1-7)

The balance of the first paragraph of this Lesson 302 tells ourselves and our Father what's happening within us as we start understanding the truth of Heaven which sets us free: "*Now we see that darkness is our own imagining* [The world is a dream we made up.], *and light is there for us to look upon. Christ's vision changes darkness into light, for fear must disappear when love has come. Let me forgive Your holy world today, that I may look upon its holiness and understand it but reflects my own.*" (W-302.1:5-7)

Lesson 303 – The holy Christ is born in me today.

Our Father only created One Son Who is called Christ by Jesus in ACIM. Originally, our Father and His Son, Christ, lived joyfully forever as One in Heaven. Later on when Christ thought to separate from His Father, God created the Holy Spirit to wake us all up from this earthly dream or illusion. So here you have the definition of the Trinity – Father, Son and Holy Spirit.

We are, of course, a part of Christ, God's only Son. In truth, or in Heaven, we share the same Mind. We don't have any separate thoughts and we live joyfully and eternally together as One. Because each of us shares the same Christ Mind, each of us is, in fact, Christ. Jesus says this explicitly in the second paragraph of this Lesson 303. Referring to Christ, God's One Son, Jesus has us tell our Father: "He is my Self as You created me." (W-303.2:6)

We also share the Mind of our Father because He shares everything He has with His Son.

Although we need not dwell on this while we're still in the dream, this lesson tells us that we will be giving up our individuality and our secret thoughts when we wake up in Heaven. The ego will tell us: "You don't ever want to give up this precious gift!" My answer to the ego who, by the way, is totally ignorant of the truth, is: "I would rather be one with God and His Creation and have everything God has, without any cares, happy and joyous forever, than to be stuck in this insane world with all its problems, sorrows, tragedy, wars, fears and certain death, so I'll follow Jesus and stop listening to you."

Lesson 304 – Let not my world obscure the sight of Christ.

The term "my world" in this lesson means this physical world. Although it seemed real for a long time, I now know that it is just a dream I made up. It is not real. Its whole purpose was to obscure the sight of Heaven where God and Christ, His Son, reside. Although the ego will continue to tempt me, I want to remember that: "*The world I see holds nothing that I want.*" (Lesson 128)

With the ongoing help of Jesus/Holy Spirit, I can envision at a good level what's on the other side of this dream. To put it another way, I am certain I want to wake up from this dream and once again be at home in Heaven. This is my goal and, with the help of ACIM, I'm making very good progress.

Christ's Voice is the Voice of the Holy Spirit/Jesus. Christ's sight is Christ's vision or the ability for me to see all people as eternal, innocent and joyous parts of Christ, Himself, the same as me, and to join with all I see or think rather than be separate from everyone and everything.

In general, we can break ACIM into two major components. The first is to understand that this world is only a dream and not real. The second is to understand that we want to replace this dream world with Heaven and we must do this while we're in our physical life (i.e., not after we die). Lesson 129 says: "*Beyond this* [physical] *world there is a world I want.*" The world we all want is Heaven. And of course we want it because it means we'll be happy, joyous and free now and forever more!

Lesson 305 – There is a peace that Christ bestows on us.

As this lesson says, all we need to do to receive this wonderful "peace which is beyond the world's understanding" is to simply use Christ's vision as we move about in our dream world.

There is a sentence in the first paragraph of this lesson which reads: "Comparisons are still before this peace." Using Christ's vision, there can be no comparisons and there can be no judgment because we are all the same. We are all eternal, innocent and joyous spiritual parts of Christ, God's One Son, and 100% joined with everyone and everything. This is who we are in truth and this is how we see ourselves and everyone else when we use Christ's vision.

The entire first paragraph of this lesson reads: "Who uses but Christ's vision finds a peace so deep and quiet, undisturbable and wholly changeless, that the world contains no counterpart. Comparisons are still before this peace. And all the world departs in silence as this peace envelops it, and gently carries it to truth, no more to be the home of fear. For love has come, and healed the world by giving it Christ's peace." (W-305.1:1-4)

Lesson 306 – The gift of Christ is all I seek today.

The "gift of Christ" is just another name for Christ's vision. And all Christ's vision means is to see all people as they are in truth (rather than who they think they are as they scramble around in this meaningless dream world) and be joined with them all and with every thing. I'll add that in my experience it does take a lot of practice to not get caught up in everyone's worldly soap operas. But with the help of Jesus, who is always with me, I've gotten much better at not reacting to the many soap operas all my friends seem to have and I'm enjoying life more than ever.

The first paragraph of this lesson reads: "What but Christ's vision would I use today, when it can offer me a day in which I see a world so like to Heaven that an ancient memory returns to me? Today I can forget the world I made. Today I can go past all fear, and be restored to love and holiness and peace. Today I am redeemed, and born anew into a world of mercy and of care; of loving kindness and the peace of God." (W-306.1:1-4)

Lesson 307 – Conflicting wishes cannot be my will.

Jesus asks us the following question in the Text: "Do you prefer that you be right or happy" (T-29.VII.1:9) For a long time, my fun answer to this was "both" (ha! ha! ha!) Relatively recently, my Inner Voice (Jesus/Holy Spirit) suggested I take this question seriously and I did and answered "I'd rather be happy." What a huge difference this has made in my human relations. Even where I know someone is wrong, I need not point it out to him or her. What difference does it make anyway? This world is just one massive insane asylum which isn't even real. If you want to have great relationships, forget about being right. The "need to be right" has perhaps caused more damage in relationships than anything else.

Heaven is reality. In Heaven there is, of course, no conflict. God's Will, which is our will, is eternal joy and harmony without conflict of any kind. To be in God's Will, therefore, means that "Conflicting wishes cannot be my will."

Lesson 308 – This instant is the only time there is.

In this dream world, we do need to do something. For instance, if I stopped eating and drinking my body would die in a relatively short period of time. I've found I need a certain amount of sleep or I can't think properly. The point is that while we think we're here in the dream, we must deal with time.

In Heaven which is reality, there are no bodily concerns. We are pure spirit forever. Time is a meaningless term. There are no worries, no planning and no conflicts whatsoever. In Heaven, we are happy and free every instant. We are in the eternal now.

While in this dream, the best mental tool to get a flavor of the eternal now is called the "Holy Instant." In the Text of ACIM, Jesus gives us important directions on how to get to the Holy Instant. The last 5 lessons of the Workbook for Students are devoted to this very important mental tool.

Lesson 309 – I will not fear to look within today.

The ego tells us do not look at our self. He tells us we have sinned and fall far short of the glory of God. He also tells us to look at others who are worse sinners than we are and this way we can feel good about ourselves, as defined by the ego. He has all sorts of other tricks up his sleeve to keep us from looking at ourselves.

However, as we allow ACIM to infiltrate our minds, we do look within and find that what Jesus says is true and what the ego says is false. Over the time I've studied ACIM and effectively peeled the false layers from who I am, I've discovered that I am in fact an eternal, innocent and joyous part of Christ, God's One Son and so is everyone else. We are God's Creation and we share in His glory forever.

The ego is not a part of Heaven so, like the world, it is not part of reality. Like this dream world, it doesn't exist and its purpose is to make sure we don't wake up. Ultimately, of course, we will all wake up and once the last of us wakes up in Heaven, the ego disappears just like the dream world it helped us build. The religious term for the ego, by the way, is Satan or the Devil.

Lesson 310 – In fearlessness and love I spend today.

I really find tremendous comfort in the second paragraph of this lesson. In it, Jesus is effectively telling us that he is with us every step and every instant of our earthly journey. He says: "We spend this day together, you and I [me and Jesus]. All the world joins us in our song of thankfulness and joy to Him Who [either the Holy Spirit or our Father Who created the Holy Spirit to save us from our dream] gave salvation to us, and Who set us free. We are restored to peace and holiness. There is no room in us for fear today, for we have welcomed love into our hearts [fear and love can't coexist just as darkness can't exist in light]." (W-310.2:1-4)

Lesson 311 – I judge all things as I would have them be.

In the second paragraph of this lesson Jesus tells us to tell our Father: "*Father, we wait with open mind today, to hear Your Judgment of the Son You love. We do not know him, and we cannot judge. And so we let Your Love decide what he whom You created as Your Son must be.*" (W-311.2:1-3)

If God talked to us regarding judgment, He would say something like: "I only created one Son. You and everyone else in your world are a part of my Son. You are all eternal, happy and innocent rays emanating from Him. When you wake up from your individual dreams and nightmares, you will all know this truth. And, of course, in truth there is nothing to judge against." So all I need do as I go about my worldly life being critical of some people sometimes, is to step back and use Christ's vision to see these people as exactly the same as me. In other words, to see these people in truth (eternal, innocent and joyous spiritual parts of God's Creation, the same as me) and not as they appear in my dream.

This Lesson could be written as: "Using Christ's vision, I judge all people and things as they are in truth."

Lesson 312 – I see all things as I would have them be.

My purpose and my goal today is to forgive the world I made and see through God's eyes using Christ's vision rather than what the world would have me think and see.

This is what Jesus tells us to tell God in the second paragraph of this lesson: "*I have no purpose for today except to look upon a liberated world, set free from all the judgments I have made. Father, this is Your Will for me today, and therefore it must be my goal as well.*" (W-312.2:1,2)

Lesson 313 – Now let a new perception come to me.

The new perception referred to in this lesson is "Christ's vision", although Jesus refers to it simply as "vision" in this lesson. In the first paragraph, Jesus tells us to tell our Father: "*Father, there is a vision which beholds all things as sinless, so that fear has gone, and where it was is love invited in. And love will come wherever it is asked. This vision is Your gift. The eyes of Christ look on a world forgiven. In His sight are all its sins forgiven, for He sees no sin in anything He looks upon. Now let His true perception come to me, that I may waken from the dream of sin and look within upon my sinlessness, which You have kept completely undefiled upon the altar to Your holy Son, the Self with which I would identify.*" (W-313.1:1-6)

In the second paragraph, Jesus once again lets us know he's with us always. The "us" and the "we" in this paragraph refer to Jesus and me. Here is this wonderful paragraph: "Let us today behold each other in the sight of Christ. How beautiful we are! How holy and how loving! Brother, come and join with me today. We save the world when we are joined. For in our vision it becomes as holy as the light in us." (W-313.2:1-6)

Lesson 314 – I seek a future different from the past.

In this world, many people seek a future different from the past. At a young age, a common dream is to get a good job, get married, have children and live a happy life. Later on in life, the future dream might be to divorce this miserable spouse and be free at last. As we near retirement, a common dream is to retire to a warm climate and live out our senior years comfortably.

This lesson has <u>nothing</u> to do with such plans. It has to do with how we perceive the people and the world about us, regardless of our worldly circumstances.

Following is the first paragraph of this lesson with some comments from me: "From new perception [Christ's vision] of the world there comes a future very different from the past. The future now is recognized as but extension of the present. Past mistakes can cast no shadows on it [since the world is but a dream, the past never happened], so that fear has lost its idols and its images, and being formless, it has no effects. Death will not claim the future now, for life is its goal, and all the needed means are happily provided. [Personally, I no longer have any fear of physical death though I hope to be around for quite a while in my dream.] Who can grieve or suffer when the present has been freed, extending its security and peace into a quiet future filled with joy? [And that future extends into Heaven and eternity.]" (W-314.1:1-5)

Lesson 315 – All gifts my brothers give belong to me.

I can really identify with what Jesus tells us in the first paragraph of this lesson. When I walk through a store and see people smiling and being kind and joking with one another, it warms my heart. I need not be directly involved to receive these loving gifts for myself.

So I say to God as Jesus tells us to do in the second paragraph: "*I thank You, Father, for the many gifts that come to me today and every day from every Son of God. My brothers are unlimited in all their gifts to me. Now may I offer them my thankfulness, that gratitude to them may lead me on to my Creator and His memory* [i.e., to You, Father]." (W-315.2:1-3)

Lesson 316 – All gifts I give my brothers are my own.

In a simple and broad way, both this lesson and the previous one are obvious. God has only One Son, we call Him Christ. Collectively, all mankind and all life on earth are Christ. Also, individually, I am Christ, you are Christ, Jesus is Christ, etc. because Christ has but One Mind. So in Lesson 315, above, any gift given to another in the world is a gift to Christ and I therefore benefit from it. In this Lesson 316, any gift I give to anyone is a gift to Christ and therefore I, too, am the recipient of the gift I give.

For me, personally, fear of all people has essentially disappeared. Therefore, I'm able to have friendly conversations with many strangers and give gifts of friendship and laughter to many people and I can really identify firsthand how such gifts are mine also.

Lesson 317 – I follow in the way appointed me.

When I read this lesson, there is an earlier lesson which comes directly to my mind. It is Lesson 155 which reads: "*I will step back and let Him lead the way.*" The "Him" in this lesson refers to the Voice for God within our dream which is Jesus/Holy Spirit. Personally, I've internally modified this lesson slightly to: "I will step back and let you lead the way, Jesus."

There is no doubt in my mind that the writing of this book is part of God's plan for me. The solitary benefits to me alone of looking at the lessons again and articulating them for others have helped me immensely. Naturally, I also hope that you who are reading this will also benefit.

Lesson 318 – In me salvation's means and end are one.

Any ideas the world has for my salvation will not work because all of the world's ideas are insane. Remember, the world can be thought of as one massive insane asylum. Its ideas had been embedded in my mind for a long time but over the past 15 years I've been able to clear away most of the world's thinking because of my individual studying of ACIM and practicing the spiritual principles learned in my daily activities.

Now I know that my path must be directed by God's Voice (Jesus/Holy Spirit) and I must use Christ's vision as I travel through my dream world in order to continue on this new productive and happy path.

God's Voice and Christ's vision are the means for my salvation and are within my mind. My mind is also part of Heaven where I will, like everyone else, end up. That is, the "end" referred to in this lesson is waking up in Heaven. Therefore, both the means for my salvation and my ultimate goal are both within my mind. This is, of course, true for you too.

In the second paragraph of this lesson, Jesus tells us to tell God: "*Let me today, my Father, take the role You offer me in Your request that I accept Atonement for myself. For thus does what is thereby reconciled in me become as surely reconciled to You.*" (W-318.2:1,2) To "accept Atonement for myself" simply means I accept that I am one with our Father and, since he shares all He has with His Son, I have all the power and blessings and love and goodness that our Father has. We can also say that to "accept Atonement for myself" is to fully know that the separation never happened because the world never happened.

Lesson 319 – I came for the salvation of the world.

Of course, when Jesus showed up about 2,000 years ago, he also came for the salvation of the world. Jesus, being the first person to be the "light of the world", has now documented how we can accomplish the same thing in his ACIM books. Since Jesus, there have apparently been a few people who have been able to follow in his footsteps. With ACIM now available, there should be some speed up in the number of individuals who can be the "light of the world." In Lesson 61, Jesus tells us to tell ourselves: *"I am the light of the world."* Over the years, as I've studied and practiced ACIM, this lesson becomes ever clearer to me – I am the light of the world, along with some other ACIM students. Also, I'm sure there are other people who are also "the light of the world" although they are applying a different spiritual path than ACIM.

To me, this Lesson 319 – *I came for the salvation of the world* – and Lesson 61 – *I am the light of the world* – are really the same idea.

A Course in Miracles, by the way, is only one of thousands of different paths to awaken in Heaven. Jesus says this explicitly in his Course. If you are new to ACIM and enthused about it, you might do what I did early on. First, despite what Jesus says in ACIM, you might be convinced that this is the only way to "real spirituality." Second, you might try and get your friends, as well as others you meet, to get a copy so they too can advance spiritually. My suggestion to you, if you like the Course and you're new to it, is not to be an evangelist with it, but do give it a lot of study on your own.

Lesson 320 – My Father gives all power unto me.

To summarize this lesson, each of us individually has all the power of our Father's Will.

Here's the first paragraph of this lesson: "The Son of God is limitless. There are no limits on his strength, his peace, his joy, nor any attributes his Father gave in his creation. What he wills with his Creator and Redeemer must be done. His holy will can never be denied, because his Father shines upon his mind, and lays before it all the strength and love in earth and Heaven. I [Jimmy Laws and everyone else too] am he to whom all this is given. I am he in whom the power of my Father's Will abides." (W-320.1:1-6)

In the second paragraph, I am being told that through me alone God's Will can get extended around the world. (Of course, this can be accomplished through you too since I'm really no different than anyone else.) In this paragraph, Jesus tells us to tell our Father: "*Your Will can do all things in me, and then extend to all the world as well through me. There is no limit on Your Will. And so all power has been given to Your Son.*" (W-320.2:1-3)

Lesson 321 – Father, my freedom is in You alone.

Naturally, when I "knew" the world was real, I followed the ways of the world in search of freedom and happiness. All of the roads of the world are dead ends and, of course, they all end in death. The world, we learn, is not real. It's but a dream. Thank God! Today, I know "*The world I see holds nothing that I want.*" [Lesson 128] Today, I'm also learning how to hear God's Voice [Jesus/Holy Spirit] and let His Voice direct my mind and to disregard the ego's voice. This is all I have to do. It's simple but not always easy because the ego is cunning, baffling and powerful, so I still make mistakes. These mistakes are corrected by God's Voice and

I move on. In this regard, here's a nice cliché: "I'm a work in progress. God isn't finished with me yet."

Jesus does tell us in the Text of ACIM that it is possible to only listen to God's Voice (the Voice of Jesus/Holy Spirit) and disregard the ego's voice completely. This is, of course, my ultimate goal but it hasn't been accomplished yet.

In the first paragraph, Jesus tells us to tell our Father: "*I did not understand what made me free, nor what my freedom is, nor where to look to find it. Father, I have searched in vain until I heard Your Voice directing me. Now I would guide myself no more. For I have neither made nor understood the way to find my freedom. But I trust in You. You Who endowed me with freedom as Your holy Son will not be lost to me. Your Voice directs me, and the way to You is opening and clear to me at last. Father, my freedom is in You alone. Father, it is my will that I return.*" (W-321.1:1-9)

Lesson 322 – I can give up but what was never real.

The only things God wants us to sacrifice are things that harm us. In Heaven, which is reality, there is of course no such thing as sacrifice. Illusions hurt us and all the world is merely a near infinite number of illusions. The title of this lesson effectively tells us to give up this illusionary world which was never real anyway. On the other side of our illusions is Heaven which is Reality.

Here's what Jesus tells us to tell our Father in the second paragraph of this lesson: "*Father, to You all sacrifice remains forever inconceivable. And so I cannot sacrifice except in dreams. As You created me, I can give up nothing You gave me. What You did not give has no reality. What loss can I anticipate except the loss of fear, and the return of love into my mind?*" (W-322.2:1-5)

Lesson 323 – I gladly make the "sacrifice" of fear.

Jesus tells us in ACIM that there really are only two emotions - love and fear. When my mind is being directed by Jesus, I am being directed by love and I feel total peace of mind. When my mind is being directed by the ego, I feel some form of fear which, of course, means anything but total peace of mind.

One difficulty is that our minds are extremely active and make thousands of decisions every hour, perhaps 50 or more per second. Further, to go back and forth between Jesus and the ego guiding my decisions is tantamount to having the ego in control. It's my current experience that I still do this. However, over time an ever increasing percentage of my decisions are guided by Jesus and I understand this is typical of maturing spiritual students and teachers.

When I go for a while with total peace of mind, whether it be for 10 seconds or 10 hours, I know Jesus is guiding my thoughts. Whenever I don't have total peace of mind, the ego is definitely in there directing at least some of my thoughts. This ties in with what Jesus told us 2,000 years ago: "You can't serve two masters."

Lesson 324 – I merely follow, for I would not lead.

This lesson carries the same message as Lesson 155: "*I will step back and let Him* [Jesus/Holy Spirit] *lead the way.*"

Both paragraphs of this Lesson 324 tell me it's okay if I make some mistakes, which I do sometimes, because God's Voice [Jesus/Holy Spirit] will guide me back again.

In the first paragraph, Jesus has us say to our Father: "*Father, You are the One Who gave the plan for my salvation to me. You have set the way I am to go, the role to take and every step in my appointed path. I cannot lose the way. I can but choose to wander off a while, and then return. Your loving Voice* [Jesus/Holy Spirit] *will always call me back, and guide my feet aright. My brothers all can follow in the way I lead them. Yet I merely follow in the way to You, as You direct me and would have me go."* (W-324.1:1-7)

The second paragraph reads: "So let us [Jesus and me] follow One Who [the Holy Spirit] knows the way. We need not tarry, and we cannot stray except an instant from His loving Hand. We walk together, for we follow Him. And it is He Who makes the ending sure, and guarantees a safe returning home [Heaven]." (W-324.2:1-4)

Lesson 325 – All things I think I see reflect ideas.

The essence of this lesson is that no "thing" in the world is real. Just as the world is not real, no subset of the world is real either.

Jesus explains in this lesson that all things we think are real (or thought were real) are actually thoughts or ideas projected from our mind, just like a movie projector projects images on to a screen. As we understand this better, Lesson 338 becomes much clearer also. It reads: "*I am affected only by my thoughts.*"

The first 5 sentences of this Lesson 325 are: "This is salvation's keynote: What I see reflects a process in my mind, which starts with my idea of what I want. From there, the mind makes up an image of the thing the mind desires, judges valuable, and therefore seeks to find [e.g., fortune, fame, adventure, romance, etc.]. These images are then projected outward, looked upon, esteemed as real and guarded as one's own. From insane wishes comes an insane world. From judgment comes a world condemned." (W-325.1:1-5) So Jesus has very effectively defined the problem which, of course, comes from my mind.

As the mind training of ACIM begins to take hold, so does the solution which Jesus summarizes in the last sentence of the first paragraph: "And from forgiving thoughts a gentle world comes forth, with mercy for the holy Son of God, to offer him a kindly home where he can rest a while before he journeys on, and help his brothers walk ahead with him, and find the way to Heaven and to God." (W-325.1:6)

Lesson 326 – I am forever an Effect of God.

In the first paragraph of this lesson, Jesus tells us to tell God the truth that sets us free.

For instance, the first four sentences are as follows: "*Father, I was created in Your Mind, a holy Thought that never left its home. I am forever Your Effect, and You forever and forever are my Cause. As You created me I have remained. Where You established me* [in Heaven] *I still reside.*" (W-326.1:1-4) Lessons 94, 110 and 162 say the same thing. They read: "*I am as God created me.*"

Sentences 5 and 6 read: "*And all Your attributes abide in me, because it is Your Will to have a Son so like his Cause that Cause and Its Effect are indistinguishable. Let me know that I am an Effect of God* [i.e., You], *and so I have the power to create like You.*" (W-326.1:5,6) In the Text of ACIM, Jesus tells us that in Heaven (or in truth), there is no difference between him and us. On earth, the only difference is in time – Jesus was the first to awaken in Heaven and we will all follow in due course. Jesus also said about 2,000 years ago that he and the Father were one. Here, in these two sentences, he tells me that I, Jimmy, and the Father are also one. This is, of course, true for everyone in the world though very few can perceive this yet.

The last two sentences of this paragraph tell us we can recognize these truths here on earth and we can also, based on my experience, receive the gifts of Heaven while we're still in this dream world. These sentences are: *"And as it is in Heaven, so on earth. Your plan I follow here, and at the end I know that You will gather Your effects* [all people] *into the tranquil Heaven of Your Love, where earth will vanish, and all separate thoughts unite in glory as the Son of God."* (W-326.1:7,8) At the end, we'll all be awake again in Heaven and earth will vanish since no one will be "dreaming it up" any more.

Lesson 327 – I need but call and You will answer me.

I really like the text of this message. A lot of what Jesus says in ACIM is written in absolute terms. However, this lesson clearly tells us that waking up in Heaven is a process which clearly happens over a period of time. This has certainly been my own experience over the past 15 years. I like to say: "I claim spiritual progress and not spiritual perfection." This simply means I'm not yet 100% guided by Jesus/Holy Spirit but I'm moving in that direction.

The first paragraph of this lesson reads: "I am not asked to take salvation on the basis of an unsupported faith. For God has promised He will hear my call, and answer me Himself. Let me but learn from my experience that this is true, and faith in Him must surely come to me. This is the faith that will endure, and take me farther and still farther on the road that leads to Him. For thus I will be sure that He has not abandoned me and loves me still, awaiting but my call to give me all the help I need to come to Him." (W-327.1:1-5)

Lesson 328 – I choose the second place to gain the first.

This lesson tells us simply to do our best to be guided only by God's Voice, Jesus/Holy Spirit (and not by the ego). The first sentence of the first paragraph of this lesson reads: "What seems to be the second place is first, for all things we perceive are upside down until we <u>listen to the Voice for God</u>. (emphasis added) (W-328.1:1)

Lesson 155 effectively says the same thing: "*I will step back* [I'll be second] *and let Him* [Jesus/Holy Spirit] *lead the way.*"

Lesson 254 says: "*Let every voice but God's be still in me.*" In the Text of ACIM, Jesus tells us that the ego's voice always speaks first. Our job is to do our best to ignore this voice and only listen to God's Voice.

Lesson 324 clearly says we should choose the second place. It reads: "*I merely follow, for I would not lead.*"

The last 5 lessons (361 through 365) are the same and read as follows: "*This holy instant would I give to You* [Jesus/Holy Spirit]. *Be You in charge. For I would follow You, certain that Your direction gives me peace.*" (underscore mine)

In the context of this Lesson 328, I also like the following statement Jesus tells us to tell ourselves from Lesson 199: "*I hear the Voice that God has given me, and it is only this my mind obeys.*" (W-199.8:9)

Lesson 329 – I have already chosen what You will.

To recognize the truth of this lesson, we need only to forgive but this requires a lot of mind training. For forgiveness means to acknowledge on an ongoing basis that this world is not real, is but a dream and never really happened at all. As we wake up from our dreaming, the truth of our Reality (Heaven) is ever clearer in our mind.

The acceptance of our Reality (Heaven) is emphasized in the second paragraph of this lesson. It reads: "Today we will accept our union with each other and our Source [our Father]. We have no will apart from His, and all of us are one because His Will is shared by all of us. Through it [God's Will which is our own] we recognize that we are one. Through it we find our way at last to God." (W-329.2:1-4)

Lesson 330 – I will not hurt myself again today.

This lesson could be stated: "I will forgive so I won't hurt myself again today." Alternatively, we could say: "I will remember all day today that this world is but a dream."

The first sentence of this paragraph states: "Let us this day accept forgiveness as our only function." (W-330.1:1) Why should we do this? The rest of the paragraph gives us some really great reasons: "Why should we attack our minds, and give them images of pain? Why should we teach them they are powerless, when God holds out His power and His Love, and bids them take what is already theirs? The mind that is made willing to accept God's gifts has been restored to spirit, and extends its freedom and its joy, as is the Will of God united with its own. The Self which God created cannot sin, and therefore cannot suffer. Let us choose today that He be our Identity, and thus escape forever from all things the dream of fear [i.e., the world] appears to offer us." (W-330.1:2-6) Although the world can certainly <u>appear</u> to offer us good things, remember Lesson 128: "*The world I see holds <u>nothing</u> that I want.*" (underscore mine)

Lesson 331 – There is no conflict, for my will is Yours.

Think about the following question: Who, in their right mind, could possibly think that a loving God could ever have created this world? It is true that most of us have had some happy times in our earthly lives. However, consider all the wars, the crimes, the inhumanity, the worries, the individual conflicts both in public and in our families, the pain, the fears and the injustices all around us, the prejudices, insane sexual behavior, covert government operations… and, of course, we can add to this list. Even for those individuals who have a "relatively" happy life, they of course must die. Could a loving God really be responsible for the creating of such a place. Thank God the answer is a loud "NO!" As our minds start getting restored to sanity and we realize the world is just a dream (really a nightmare when compared to Reality which is Heaven), we of course appreciate what Jesus tells us about this world: "There is no world! This is the central thought the course attempts to teach." (W-132.6:2,3)

In the first paragraph of this Lesson 331, Jesus tells us to tell our Father essentially what I have said in the preceding paragraph and a lot more: "*How foolish, Father, to believe Your Son could cause himself to suffer! Could he make a plan for his damnation, and be left without a certain way to his release? You love me, Father. You could never leave me desolate, to die within a world of pain and cruelty. How could I think that Love has left Itself? There is no will except the Will of Love. Fear is a dream, and has no will that can conflict with Yours. Conflict is sleep, and peace awakening. Death is illusion; life, eternal truth. There is no opposition to Your Will. There is no conflict, for my will is Yours.*" (W-331.1:1-11)

Lesson 332 – Fear binds the world. Forgiveness sets it free.

Jesus tells us in ACIM that there are really only two emotions. They are fear and love.

The ego is the source of all fear. God is Love and, since God and all His Creation are One (which is Heaven), Heaven is Love. Another term Jesus uses for Love or Heaven is truth, which is the term he uses in the first paragraph of this lesson.

Forgiveness, as defined in ACIM, is the awareness that this world is but a dream and has nothing whatsoever to do with Reality which is Heaven. And dreams are not real. They don't exist. Through the mind training of ACIM, this awareness increases as we wake up from the dream and we become happier over time. Leastwise, this has been my experience.

Of course, when we're fully awake in Heaven forgiveness is not at all necessary. However, forgiveness is absolutely necessary while we're still in the dream. As a matter of fact, it is the central teaching of ACIM. Here's a concise definition of forgiveness as taught by Jesus in his Course: "Forgiveness means there is no world. The world's a dream and dreams aren't real. They don't exist." And here's a quote I've used a number of times in this book: "There is no world! This is the central thought the course attempts to teach." (W-132.6:2,3) In other words, forgiveness is the central teaching of ACIM.

In the first paragraph of this Lesson 332, Jesus explains how forgiveness allows Love to shine right into this dream world: "The ego makes illusions. Truth [Love] undoes its evil dreams by shining them away. Truth never makes attack. It merely is. And by its presence is the mind recalled from fantasies, awaking to the real. Forgiveness bids this presence [Love] enter in, and take its rightful place within the mind. Without forgiveness is the mind in chains, believing in its own futility. Yet with forgiveness does the light [Love] shine through the dream of darkness, offering its hope, and giving it the means to realize the freedom that is its inheritance." (W-332.1:1-8)

Lesson 333 – Forgiveness ends the dream of conflict here.

One of Love's attributes is total peace of mind. In Heaven, there is no conflict; there is 100% peace of mind always. Conflict is an ego device for keeping the apparent separation from God and our brothers intact.

Forgiveness is God's tool for ending conflict here in the dream. As discussed in the preceding lesson, forgiveness allows God's Love to shine right into this dream world. In the second paragraph of this Lesson 333, Jesus tells us to tell God: "*Father, forgiveness is the light You chose to shine away all conflict and all doubt, and light the way for our return to You. No light but this can end our evil dream. No light but this can save the world. For this alone will never fail in anything, being Your gift to Your beloved Son.*" (W-333.2:1-4)

Lesson 334 – Today I claim the gifts forgiveness gives.

This lesson makes clear to me that God's greatest gift in this world of fear is absolute peace of mind. I say this because in both of the paragraphs of this lesson, the only specific gift that Jesus mentions is God's peace.

The first paragraph reads: "I will not wait another day to find the treasures that my Father offers me. Illusions are all vain, and dreams are gone even while they are woven out of thoughts that rest on false perceptions. Let me not accept such meager gifts again today. God's Voice is offering the peace of God to all who hear and choose to follow Him. This is my choice today. And so I go to find the treasures God has given me." (W-334.1:1-6)

And the second paragraph reads: "*I seek but the eternal. For Your Son can be content with nothing less than this. What, then, can be his solace but what You are offering to his bewildered mind and frightened heart, to give him certainty and bring him peace? Today I would behold my brother sinless* [using Christ's vision]. *This Your Will for me, for so will I behold my sinlessness.*" (W-334.2:1-5) Note that the last two sentences tell me that unless I see everyone else as sinless, I won't be able to see myself as sinless. This idea leads right into the next lesson, Lesson 335.

Lesson 335 – I choose to see my brother's sinlessness.

At the heart of this lesson is for me to use Christ's vision to see everyone. This means to see everyone as an eternal, innocent and joyous spiritual part of God's Creation which is what I know myself to be. Regardless of outward appearances here on earth, this is how I want to see everyone in the world.

Here's what Jesus tells us to tell ourselves in the first paragraph of this lesson: "Forgiveness is a choice. I never see my brother as he is, for that is far beyond perception. What I see in him is merely what I wish to see, because it stands for what I want to be the truth. It is to this alone that I respond, however much I seem to be impelled by outside happenings. I choose to see what I would look upon, and this I see, and only this. My brother's sinlessness shows me that I would look upon my own. And I will see it, having chosen to behold my brother in its holy light." (W-335.1:1-7)

Lesson 336 – Forgiveness lets me know that minds are joined.

God and all His Creation share One Mind. We and the Father are One. Heaven is in fact this "One Mind of God." Jesus says this explicitly in the Text of ACIM as follows: "Heaven is not a place nor a condition. It is merely an awareness of perfect Oneness, and the knowledge that there is nothing else; nothing outside this Oneness, and nothing else within." (T-18.VI.1:5,6) Therefore, I'll add to this lesson as follows: "Forgiveness lets me know that minds are joined <u>as one</u>."

The most wonderful gift of peace of mind is obtained through forgiveness. This is spelled out in the first paragraph of this lesson which reads: "Forgiveness is the means appointed for perception's ending. Knowledge is restored after perception first is changed, and then gives way entirely to what remains forever past its highest reach. For sights and sounds, at best, can serve but to recall the memory that lies beyond them all. Forgiveness sweeps away distortions, and opens the hidden altar to the truth. Its lilies shine into the mind, and call it to return and look within, to find what it has vainly sought without. For here [within our mind], and only here, is peace of mind restored, for this the dwelling place of God Himself." (W-336.1:1-6)

Lesson 337 – My sinlessness protects me from all harm.

The promises contained in the first paragraph of this lesson are wonderful and they are true. The little I must do to receive them is contained in the 4th sentence.

This first paragraph is: "My sinlessness ensures me perfect peace, eternal safety, everlasting love, freedom forever from all thought of loss; complete deliverance from suffering. And only happiness can be my state, for only happiness is given me. What must I do to know all this is mine? I must accept Atonement for myself, and nothing more. God has already done all things that need be done. And I must learn I need do nothing of myself, for I need but accept my Self, my sinlessness, created for me, now already mine, to feel God's Love protecting me from harm, to understand my Father loves His Son; to know I am the Son my Father loves." (W-337.1:1-6;underscore mine)

To accept Atonement for myself, I simply need to see myself as an eternal, innocent and joyous spiritual part of God's Creation. Another way to think of Atonement is to know the separation never happened because the world never happened. Meanwhile, however, we're still in this dream world (which never happened) and we have some work to do which is to continue waking up ourselves and helping others do the same with the help of Jesus/Holy Spirit.

It is not possible for me to see myself as innocent (sinless) unless I see everyone else in the same light. This is clearly stated in Lesson 335: "I choose to see my brother's sinlessness [innocence]." In other words, I simply need to use Christ's vision to see everyone in the world.

General note: As I did in the previous sentence, I use the words "simple" and "simply" quite a lot in this book. The idea is simple but to practice the idea is not easy. In my experience, with continued practice of the spiritual principles contained in ACIM, my mistakes are fewer and my life is becoming ever happier.

Lesson 338 – I am affected only by my thoughts.

I'll start my comments on this lesson by repeating the first two paragraphs on my discussion of Lesson 325: "*All things I think I see reflect ideas.*" These two paragraphs are as follows:

> The essence of this lesson is that no "thing" in the world is real. Just as the world is not real, no subset of the world is real either.
>
> Jesus explains in this lesson that all things we think are real (or thought were real) are actually thoughts or ideas projected from our mind, just like a movie projector projects images on to a screen. As we understand this better, Lesson 338 becomes much clearer also. It reads: "*I am affected only by my thoughts.*"

The first paragraph of this Lesson 338 reads: "It needs but this to let salvation come to all the world. For in this single thought is everyone released at last from fear. Now has he learned that no one frightens him, and nothing can endanger him. He has no enemies, and he is safe from all external things. His thoughts can frighten him, but since these thoughts belong to him alone, he has power to change them and exchange each fear thought for a happy thought of love. He crucified himself. Yet God has planned that His beloved Son will be redeemed." (W-338.1:1-7) In other words: "The only possible enemy I can have is me."

In the second paragraph, Jesus tells us to tell our Father: "*Your plan is sure, my Father,-only Yours. All other plans will fail. And I will have thoughts that frighten me, until I learn that You have given me the only Thought* [Jesus/Holy Spirit] *that leads me to salvation. Mine alone will fail, and lead me nowhere. But the Thought You gave me promises to lead me home* [Heaven], *because it holds Your promise to Your Son.*" (W-338.2:1-5)

Lesson 339 – I will receive whatever I request.

A literal reading of this lesson tells us that if we ask God to win the state lottery, then that will happen. The large majority of people believe a large windfall of money would bring them happiness. They think they can then use this money to purchase happiness within this world. However, Lesson 128 tells us: "The world I see holds nothing that I want." In other words, happiness cannot be obtained by chasing after things in this world and God does not give us harmful things. Thus, this lesson could be written: "I will receive whatever I request if it is good for me."

In the first paragraph of this lesson Jesus tells us: "Everyone will receive what he requests. But he can be confused indeed about the things he wants; the state he would attain. What can he then request that he would want when he receives it? [A good answer is 'happiness.'] He has asked for what will frighten him, and bring him suffering. [God won't give him this.] Let us resolve today to ask for what we really want, and only this, that we may spend this day in fearlessness, without confusing pain with joy, or fear with love." (W-339.1:5-9)

A good general request is: "Dear God, please grant me peace of mind, health and happiness." I've also found that to help me reduce or eliminate a grievance I've got against another individual, I'll call Mr. Smith, I would say: "Dear God, please let Mr. Smith have peace of mind, health and happiness like I want for myself."

The second paragraph of this lesson tells us to tell our Father: *"Father, this is Your day. It is a day in which I would do nothing by myself, but hear Your Voice in everything I do; requesting only what You offer me, accepting only Thoughts You share with me."* (W-339.2:1,2) As a rule, we absolutely do not know what's best for our self but God does. That's why this paragraph tells us not to ask God for any specifics.

It seems clear to me, however, based on my own personal experience with alcohol, that the alcoholic who knows his drinking is hurting himself and everyone else in his life can and should ask God: "God, please keep me from drinking any alcohol." Personally, I have not had a drink of alcohol in over 16 years – Thank God!

Lesson 340 – I can be free of suffering today.

Clearly, God only wants happiness for us. Therefore, all suffering is outside God's Will.

What the first paragraph of this lesson tells me is that with forgiveness, Christ's vision and the guidance of Jesus, I will be free of suffering today. Forgiveness tells me I made up the world I see from my mind and it's not real. Christ's vision tells me to see all people as eternal, innocent and joyous spiritual parts of God's Son, just as I am, and to join with everything I see (rather than being separate from everything which is what the world teaches). If I'm being guided by Jesus, I won't react negatively to anything the world throws at me today but will "Step back and let Jesus lead the way."

When I accomplish these things, the second paragraph tells me the kind of day I will have. It reads: "Be glad today! Be glad! There is no room for anything but joy and thanks today. Our Father has redeemed His Son this day. Not one of us but will be saved today. [When I see with Christ's vision, everyone in the world is saved.] Not one who will remain in fear, and none the Father will not gather to Himself, awake in Heaven in the Heart of Love." (W-339.2:1-6)

Lesson 341 – I can attack but my own sinlessness, and it is only that which keeps me safe.

The world I see comes from my mind and my mind alone. The world is my dream and it's not real. (Note that in these two sentences I have defined forgiveness.) Therefore if I attack anything in the world, I am attacking only my own mind. I am hurting myself. I am also attacking nothing since my dream is nothing.

Meanwhile, who I am is a part of Heaven Itself. I am sinless. I am innocent. God created me eternally sinless and innocent and I am still as God created me. And, of course, what's true for me is also true for everyone else in the world.

Therefore, Jesus tells us in the second paragraph of this lesson: "Let us not, then, attack our sinlessness, for it contains the Word of God to us. And in its kind reflection we are saved." (W-341.2:1,2)

Lesson 342 – I let forgiveness rest upon all things, for thus forgiveness will be given me.

In the first paragraph of this lesson, Jesus refers to the world as "the hell I made" and then says "It is not real." Although I don't personally remember Heaven, as I mature spiritually, I am convinced it is inconceivably better than the best life anyone can imagine here on earth. How can I say this? Because Jesus tells us this in ACIM and, after many years of accruing ACIM into my mindset, Jesus has never lied to me – ACIM is right on! The benefit to me has been ever increasing peace of mind and happiness (i.e., Heaven's gifts) right here in my current lifetime. Therefore, even for those who are having a wonderful life here (which, of course, must still end in death), ACIM is an incredible spiritual path to take.

Here's what Jesus tells us to tell our Father in the first paragraph: "*I thank You, Father, for Your plan to save me from the hell I made. It is not real. And You have given me the means to prove its unreality to me. The key is in my hand, and I have reached the door beyond which lies the end of dreams. I stand before the gate of Heaven, wondering if I should enter in and be at home. Let me forgive all things, and let creation be as You would have it be and as it is. Let me remember that I am Your Son, and opening the door at last, forget illusions in the blazing light of truth, as memory of You returns to me."* (W-342.1:1-8)

In the second paragraph Jesus is talking to us: "Brother, forgive me now. I come to take you home [to Heaven] with me. And as we go, the world goes with us on our way to God." (W-342.2:1-3) You might ask why would Jesus say to you: "Brother, forgive me now." Your response might be: "Of course I forgive you, Jesus. I've always loved you and never thought anything bad about you."

What Jesus is really telling us here is that if we have a grievance against anyone, then we have a grievance against Jesus. Why? Because God only has One Son. Therefore, if I have a grievance against anyone in the world, I also have a grievance against myself and the entire Sonship, which naturally includes Jesus.

Here is another way to look at this idea. If the world is not real but just a dream I'm having, then for me to be angry at any aspect of it is insane on my part. Forgiveness is not a partial thing. Either I forgive or I don't. Either the world is not real or the world is real. Thank God the world is not real and Heaven is real!

Lesson 343 – I am not asked to make a sacrifice to find the mercy and the peace of God.

Today, my days are very active yet there is a deep contentment as I go about my business. I am happy. This is because my mind has been trained to be guided by Jesus, not the ego, and it is God's Will that I be happy. (Of course, it's God's Will that all His children – all people – be happy.)

At times in past years, I was not at all happy. During the last couple of years of my drinking, I was absolutely miserable. I often had to make sacrifices which I felt were required of me even though I didn't want to.

The laws of the world have always required sacrifices. Today, I abide by the world's laws but I don't consider these things as sacrifices any more.

Lesson 344 – Today I learn the law of love; that what I give my brother is my gift to me.

The world is a dream and so it is not real. It is, in truth, nothing. However, even in this dream, God's laws are operational.

In our Creation, God only created one Son. All of us are a part of God's only Son. As a matter of fact, since we all share the same mind in truth (Heaven), each of us is God's only Son. Therefore, when I give something of value to anyone I am also giving it to myself.

Don't get confused in the physical world with the type of giving that Jesus is referring to here. Clearly, in this world, if I give someone a gift of $100, I'm $100 poorer and the recipient is $100 richer. Remember, this world is but a dream and all things in the dream are not real, including the $100. The giving of money or anything physical is <u>not at all</u> what Jesus is referring to in this lesson.

In the first paragraph of this Lesson 344 Jesus first has us tell our Father about the futility of the dream world. Then he has us tell our Father about the value to us of giving the gift of forgiveness to our brothers. We learn that this is all we need to do to fulfill the law of love. Also, as Lesson 297 tells us: "*Forgiveness is the only gift I give.*" This helps us keep "the law of love" real simple.

Here is this powerful first paragraph: "*This is Your law, my Father, not my own. I have not understood what giving means, and thought to save what I desired for myself alone. And as I looked upon the treasure that I thought I had* [such as my physical assets], *I found an empty place where nothing ever was or is or will be* [i.e., the world is nothing]. *Who can share a dream? And what can an illusion offer me? Yet he whom I forgive will give me gifts beyond the worth of anything on earth. Let my forgiven brothers fill my store with Heaven's treasures, which alone are real. Thus is the law of love fulfilled. And thus Your Son arises and returns to You."* (W-344.1:1-9)

Lesson 345 – I offer only miracles today, for I would have them be returned to me.

At the end of the first paragraph of this lesson, Jesus tells us miracles are born of true forgiveness. True forgiveness means I fully understand this world is but a dream and all people are eternally innocent and sinless. Also, beyond this world is Heaven for all of us. To be miracle minded, then, means to have a change in mind wherein this world is seen as valueless and Heaven is seen as everything. Jesus points out in the Text of ACIM that we do not have to be in this state of mind all the time to offer miracles to the people we meet. By the way, I've never performed any physical miracles. In this regard, ACIM states: "The use of miracles as spectacles to induce belief is a misunderstanding of their purpose." (T-1.I.10:1)

Personally, the miracles I see in my life are where all of my relationships with others are on a very good basis today. Many of these were virtually destroyed 16 years ago at the time I quit drinking, especially with family members. Today, as a result of my studying ACIM for many years, I can say that to the best of my knowledge I don't have an enemy in the world.

In the first paragraph of this Lesson 345, Jesus tells us the following regarding miracles: *"Father, a miracle reflects Your gifts to me, Your Son. And every one I give returns to me, reminding me the law of love is universal. Even here, it takes a form which can be recognized and seen to work. The miracles I give are given back in just the form I need to help me with the problems I perceive. Father, in Heaven it is different, for there, there are no needs. But here on earth, the miracle is closer to Your gifts than any other gift that I can give. Then let me give this gift alone today, which, born of true forgiveness, lights the way that I must travel to remember You."* (W-345.1:1-7)

Lesson 346 – Today the peace of God envelops me, and I forget all things except His Love.

What a great day I have when I stick to this lesson! In the first paragraph of this lesson Jesus tells us to tell our Father: "*Father, I wake today with miracles correcting my perception of all things.* [So I wake realizing the things of this world and worldly dreams are valueless but Heaven is staring me in the face.] *And so begins the day I share with You as I will share eternity, for time has stepped aside today. I do not seek the things of time, and so I will not look upon them. What I seek today transcends all laws of time and things perceived in time. I would forget all things except Your Love. I would abide in You, and know no laws except Your law of love. And I would find the peace which You created for Your Son, forgetting all the foolish toys I made as I behold Your glory and my own.*" (W-346.1:1-7)

Don't take this too literally. For example, we tell our Father we will not look upon the things of time but, if you're driving a car, please keep your eyes on the road.

Personally, my days are extremely active yet I can identify with the peace of God Jesus describes in the second paragraph: "And when the evening comes today, we [Jesus and me] will remember nothing but the peace of God. For we will learn today what peace is ours, when we forget all things except God's Love." (W-346.2:1,2)

Lesson 347 – Anger must come from judgment. Judgment is the weapon I would use against myself, to keep the miracle away from me.

The first paragraph of this lesson is an appeal to God to have us listen only to the Holy Spirit/Jesus. It is He Who teaches us what forgiveness means and also about Christ's vision.

When anger creeps into my life at any level, it is because I have allowed the ego to guide my thoughts again. It's really that simple.

Forgiveness tells me this world is but a dream I made up from my mind and has nothing to do with my reality which is Heaven. Therefore, whenever I get angry, I'm only getting angry at myself. I'm getting angry at this giant hallucination I'm having. I have forgotten that this world is just a dream.

Christ's vision tells me every person in the world is an eternal, sinless (innocent), and joyous part of God's Son, the same as me, and everything I see with my eyes is joined with me.

Here's my suggestion. Play your part in your dream but don't take the world seriously. It's really just one big cosmic soap opera and, as you let Jesus/Holy Spirit direct you, it becomes a lot of fun. Remember too, of course, it's just a dream from which you will wake up.

Lesson 348 – I have no cause for anger or for fear, for You surround me. And in every need that I perceive, Your grace suffices me.

As with anger, when fear creeps into my life at any level, it's because I have allowed the ego to guide my thoughts again. It's that simple.

What is God's grace? "Grace is the natural state of every Son of God." (T-7.XI.2:1) Therefore, when we are fully awake in Heaven, our natural state, we are certainly in God's grace. God's grace is also available to us here in the dream.

As I become ever more convinced that this world is truly "nothing", I become more convinced that there is "nothing" which separates me from God and I am moving ever closer to my natural state in Heaven. In other words, I'm becoming more accepting of God's grace. However,

I'm still in this dream world and I need ongoing direction from Jesus to direct my thoughts (and therefore my words and actions).

The two paragraphs of this lesson become more meaningful as we advance towards our goal (Heaven). The first paragraph reads: "*Father, let me remember You are here, and I am not alone. Surrounding me is everlasting Love. I have no cause for anything except the perfect peace and joy I share with You. What need have I for anger or for fear? Surrounding me is perfect safety. Can I be afraid, when Your eternal promise goes with me? Surrounding me is perfect sinlessness. What can I fear, when You created me in holiness as perfect as Your Own?*" (W-348.1:1-8)

The second paragraph is: "God's grace suffices us in everything that He would have us do. And only that we choose to be our will as well as His." (W-348.2:1,2)

Lesson 349 – Today I let Christ's vision look upon all things for me and judge them not, but give each one a miracle of love instead.

Here are a few things ACIM says about miracles. "The miracle establishes you dream a dream, and that its content is not true." (T-28.II.7:1) "Miracles praise God through you. They praise Him by honoring His creations, affirming their perfection. They heal because they deny body-identification and affirm spirit-identification." (T-1.I.29:1-3) "The miracle acknowledges everyone as your brother and mine. It is a way of perceiving the universal mark of God." (T-1.I.40:1,2)

What is Christ's vision? It is seeing everyone (and every living thing) as an eternal, innocent and joyous spiritual part of God's One Son, and seeing all physical things as joined with me. It totally bypasses body identification and anything anyone's ever done in the world, good or bad. Christ's vision tells me everyone in the world is the same as me. We are all brothers, uniting to form God's Son and God and His Son are One. In Heaven, there is but One Mind and this is the universal mark of God.

Seeing anyone or everyone with Christ's vision means there is no judgment and it is a miracle.

When I see using Christ's vision, the promises contained in this lesson become mine. The first paragraph tells me to tell our Father: "*So would I liberate all things I see, and give to them the freedom that I seek. For thus do I obey the law of love, and give what I would find and make my own. It will be given me, because I have chosen it as the gift I want to give. Father, Your gifts are mine. Each one that I accept gives me a miracle to give. And giving as I would receive, I learn Your healing miracles belong to me.*" (W-349.1:1-6)

The second paragraph tells us: "Our Father knows our needs. He gives us grace to meet them all. And so we trust in Him to send us miracles to bless the world, and heal our minds as we return to Him." (W-349.2:1-3)

Lesson 350 – Miracles mirror God's eternal Love. To offer them is to remember Him, and through His memory to save the world.

During the time of a miracle, I see this world as valueless and Heaven as everything. It's really that simple. There is no need for me to tell anyone I'm thinking this way, I just think it. In the Text of ACIM, Jesus tells us to let him direct any miracles. However, this goes without saying because it is essential for me to have Jesus (and not the ego) be guiding my thoughts here in the dream for me to have a wonderful dream life here.

The first paragraph of this lesson emphasizes forgiveness. The question could be asked what do miracles and forgiveness have in common?

Here again is the quote from the Text of ACIM that I included in my discussion of Lesson 349, above: "The miracle establishes you dream a dream, and that its content is not true." (T-28.II.7:1) Forgiveness means the same thing – The world's a dream I made up from my mind; it's not real and has nothing to do with who I am.

Lesson 351 – My sinless brother is my guide to peace. My sinful brother is my guide to pain. And which I choose to see I will behold.

Here's my suggestion to me and every student of ACIM – Simply use Christ's vision to see everyone in the world. By definition, when we do this, everyone is sinless (innocent).

Here's what Jesus tells us to tell our Father in this lesson: "*Who is my brother but Your holy Son? And if I see him sinful I proclaim myself a sinner, not a Son of God; alone and friendless in a fearful world. Yet this perception is a choice I make, and can relinquish. I can also see my brother sinless, as Your holy Son. And with this choice I see my sinlessness, my everlasting Comforter and Friend* [Jesus/Holy Spirit] *beside me, and my way secure and clear. Choose, then, for me, my Father, through Your Voice* [Jesus/Holy Spirit]. *For He alone gives judgment in Your Name.*" (W-351.1:1-7) And here is the judgment from Jesus/Holy Spirit: "All of you are 100% innocent which has always been the truth."

Lesson 352 – Judgment and love are opposites. From one come all the sorrows of the world. But from the other comes the peace of God Himself.

Using forgiveness, Christ's vision and obeying only God's Voice (Jesus/Holy Spirit), we won't judge and love comes streaming in from Heaven.

Here's what Jesus tells us to tell our Father in this lesson: "*Forgiveness looks on sinlessness alone, and judges not. Through this I come to You. Judgment will blind my eyes and make me blind. Yet love, reflected in forgiveness here, reminds me You have given me a way to find Your peace again. I am redeemed when I elect to follow in this way. You have not left me comfortless. I have within me both the memory of You, and One* [Jesus/Holy Spirit] *Who leads me to it. Father, I would hear Your Voice* [Jesus/Holy Spirit] *and find Your peace today. For I would love my own Identity* [Christ], *and find in It the memory of You.*" (W-352.1:1-9)

Lesson 353 – My eyes, my tongue, my hands, my feet today have but one purpose; to be given Christ to use to bless the world with miracles.

In a nutshell, when I only obey God's Voice (Jesus/Holy Spirit), my entire physical being becomes a tool to carry the message of salvation to the rest of the world. For me, this is seldom done in words but in the happy and responsible spirit that is with me. My dream world is a very happy place today.

Christ is God's only Son. I am Christ and so are you and everyone else. He is our shared Identity. There is, of course, no separation in Heaven. As I've matured spiritually here, this truth becomes a part of me while I'm here in the dream.

Here's what Jesus tells us to tell our Father in this lesson: "*Father, I give all that is mine today to Christ, to use in any way that best will serve the purpose that I share with Him. Nothing is mine alone, for He and I have joined in purpose. Thus has learning come almost to its appointed end. A while I work with Him to serve His purpose. Then I lose myself in my Identity, and recognize that Christ is but my Self.*" (W-353.1:1-5)

Lesson 354 – We stand together, Christ and I, in peace and certainty of purpose. And in Him is His Creator, as He is in me.

In this lesson, Jesus has us step totally out of this world and out of time into eternity. That is, we're home in Heaven.

Here's what Jesus tells us to tell our Father in this lesson: "*My Oneness with the Christ establishes me as Your Son, beyond the reach of time, and wholly free of every law but Yours. I have no self except the Christ in me. I have no purpose but His Own. And He is like His Father. Thus must I be one with You as well as Him. For who is Christ except Your Son as You created Him? And what am I except the Christ in me?*" (W-354.1:1-7)

Lesson 355 – There is no end to all the peace and joy, and all the miracles that I will give, when I accept God's Word. Why not today?

Inherent in this lesson is the fact that God's gifts are available to us here in the dream. We don't have to wait until our bodies stop functioning to receive them.

The point here is that we "accept God's Word" and stop listening to the ego. Here's something Jesus says about this from the Text of ACIM: "That is why you must choose to hear one of two voices within you [Jesus/Holy Spirit or the ego]. One you made yourself, and that one is not of God. But the other is given you by God, Who asks you only to listen to it. The Holy Spirit is in you in a very literal sense. His is the Voice that calls you back to where you were before and will be again. It is possible even in this world to hear only that Voice and no other. It takes effort and great willingness to learn. It is the final lesson that I [Jesus] learned, and God's Sons are as equal as learners as they are as Sons." (T-5.II.3:4-11)

The last thing Jesus tells us from the above quote is that if he did it, so can we. In my experience, the willingness and effort Jesus refers to has meant devoting a good chunk of time to studying ACIM. The payoff for me has been an increasingly happy and productive life.

I think what slows a lot of people down is they think this world offers something they want and so they devote their time to another vain pursuit rather than studying ACIM. A lot of ACIM students also split their spiritual studies between ACIM and some religion or other spiritual philosophy. This can cause confusion within the mind of the student. ACIM is a standalone pathway to the gate of Heaven.

Lesson 356 – Sickness is but another name for sin. Healing is but another name for God. The miracle is thus a call to Him.

Like everyone else, my body will get sick and die; alternatively, of course, I could die in some accident. However, my view of death is not at all bad. It is very nicely described by Jesus in The Song of Prayer supplement to ACIM as follows:

> "Yet there is a kind of seeming death that has a different source. It does not come because of hurtful thoughts and raging anger at the universe. It merely signifies the end has come for usefulness of body functioning. And so it [the body] is discarded as a choice, as one lays by a garment now outworn.
>
> "This is what death should be; a quiet choice, made joyfully and with a sense of peace, because the body has been kindly used to help the Son of God along the way he goes to God. We thank the body, then, for all the service it has given us. But we are thankful, too, the need is done to walk the world of limits, and to reach the Christ in hidden forms and clearly seen at most in lovely flashes. Now we can behold Him without blinders, in the light that we have learned to look upon again.

"We call it death, but it is liberty. It does not come in forms that seem to be thrust down in pain upon unwilling flesh, but as a gentle welcome to release. If there has been true healing, this can be the form in which death comes when it is time to rest a while from labor gladly done and gladly ended. Now we go in peace to freer air and gentler climate, where it is not hard to see the gifts we gave were saved for us. For Christ is clearer now; His vision more sustained in us; His Voice, the Word of God, more certainly our own."

(Song-3.II.1:8-11, 3.II.2:1-4, 3.II.3:1-5)

Lesson 357 – Truth answers every call we make to God, responding first with miracles, and then returning unto us to be itself.

Here's what Jesus tells us to tell our Father in this lesson: "*Forgiveness* [the world is nothing but my own mad dream], *truth's reflection* [Heaven's reflection], *tells me how to offer miracles* [seeing the world as valueless and Heaven as everything], *and thus escape the prison house* [the world] *in which I think I live. Your holy Son* [Christ] *is pointed out to me, first in my brother; then in me. Your Voice* [Jesus/Holy Spirit] *instructs me patiently to hear Your Word* ['I am as God created me' or 'We are as God created us'], *and give as I receive. And as I look upon Your Son today, I hear Your Voice instructing me to find the way to You, as You appointed that the way shall be:*

'Behold his sinlessness [see with Christ's vision], *and be you healed.'*"
(W-357.1:1-5)

Lesson 358 – No call to God can be unheard nor left unanswered. And of this I can be sure; His answer is the one I really want.

Here's what Jesus tells us to tell the Holy Spirit/Jesus and our Father in this lesson: "*You* [Jesus/Holy Spirit] *Who remember what I really am alone remember what I really want. You speak for God, and so You speak for me. And what You give me comes from God Himself. Your Voice* [Jesus/Holy Spirit's Voice], *my Father, then is mine as well, and all I want is what You offer me, in just the form You choose that it be mine. Let me remember all I do not know, and let my voice be still, remembering. But let me not forget Your Love and care, keeping Your promise to Your Son in my awareness always. Let me not forget myself is nothing, but my Self is all.* [There are no individuals in Heaven; we are all One in God's Son, Who in turn is One in God.]" (W-358.1:1-7)

Lesson 359 – God's answer is some form of peace. All pain is healed; all misery replaced with joy. All prison doors are opened. And all sin is understood as merely a mistake.

Here's what Jesus tells us to tell our Father in this lesson: "*Father, today we will forgive Your world, and let creation be Your Own. We have misunderstood all things* [because we thought the world was real]. *But we have not made sinners of the holy Sons of God. What You created sinless so abides forever and forever. Such are we* [because we are still as You created us]. *And we rejoice to learn that we have made mistakes which have no real effects on us. Sin is impossible, and on this fact forgiveness rests upon a certain base more solid than the shadow world we see. Help us forgive, for we would be redeemed. Help us forgive, for we would be at peace.*" (W-359.1:1-9)

Lesson 360 – Peace be to me, the holy Son of God. Peace to my brother, who is one with me. Let all the world be blessed with peace through us.

Here's what Jesus tells us to tell our Father in this lesson: *"Father, it is Your peace that I would give, receiving it of You. I am Your Son, forever just as You created me, for the Great Rays* [of You] *remain forever still and undisturbed within me. I would reach to them in silence and in certainty be found. Peace be to me, and peace to all the world. In holiness were we created, and in holiness do we remain. Your Son is like to You in perfect sinlessness. And with this thought we gladly say 'Amen' "* [W-360.1:1-7]

The title of this lesson is one which I have memorized and say to myself at least four times a day. However, I have modified it slightly although the meaning is the same. My modified version is as follows: "Peace be to me, the holy Son of God. Peace to my brothers (i.e., all people), who are one with me. Let all the world be blessed with peace through us."

Lessons 361 to 365 – This holy instant would I give to You. Be You in charge. For I would follow You, certain Your direction gives me peace.

Because of its importance, Jesus finishes the Workbook with these 5 identical lessons, telling us to use this most powerful spiritual tool, the <u>holy instant</u>. In all simplicity, what the holy instant allows us to do is go to Heaven for a little while.

In the Text of ACIM, Jesus devotes an entire chapter to the holy instant. Chapter 15 is titled "The Holy Instant." Following are some excerpts from this chapter along with some comments by me:

> "You will never give this holy instant to the Holy Spirit on behalf of your release while you are unwilling to give it to your brothers on behalf of theirs." (T-15.I.12:1) Included in the holy

instant are all people since all people are in Heaven and joined with God's Mind though we all dream different dreams here on earth.

"Holiness lies not in time, but in eternity." (T-15.I.15:4) The holy instant, like Heaven, is outside of time and form and space. It has nothing to do with this world. As discussed throughout ACIM, this dream world contradicts Heaven at every turn.

"Offer the miracle of the holy instant through the Holy Spirit [Jesus], and leave His giving it to you to Him." (T-15.I.15:11) I included this sentence primarily to note that a holy instant is a miracle.

In paragraphs 5 and 6 of Section II (of Chapter 15 of the Text), Jesus tells us to continue practicing the holy instant even if we have not yet experienced its full impact. Based on my own experience after many years of ACIM discipline, I've found that Jesus' comments in these paragraphs map my own experience. I have therefore included these two paragraphs in their entirety.

"The holy instant has not yet happened to you. Yet it will, and you will recognize it with perfect certainty. No gift of God is recognized in any other way. You can practice the mechanics of the holy instant, and will learn much from doing so. Yet its shining and glittering brilliance, which will literally blind you to this world by its own vision, you cannot supply. And here it is, all in this instant, complete, accomplished and given wholly." (T-15.II.5:1-6)

"Start now to practice your little part in separating out the holy instant. You will receive very specific instructions as you go along [from Jesus/Holy Spirit]. To learn to separate out this single second, and to experience it as timeless, is to begin to experience yourself as not separate. Fear not that you will not be given help in this. God's Teacher [Holy Spirit/Jesus] and His lesson will support your strength. It is only your weakness that will depart from you in this practice, for it is the practice of the power of God in you. Use it but for one instant, and you will never deny it again. Who can deny the Presence of what the universe bows to, in appreciation and gladness? Before the recognition of the universe [Heaven; not the physical universe] that witnesses to It, your doubts must disappear." (T-15.II.6:1-9)

"God is not willing that His Son be content with less than everything. For He is not content without His Son, and His Son cannot be content with less than his Father has given him." (T-15.III.4:10,11) Remember that God has given us everything He has and, in Heaven, We and God are One. As I've stated before in this book, we are "effectively God."

"The reason this course is simple is that truth is simple. Complexity is of the ego, and is nothing more than the ego's attempt to obscure the obvious. You could live forever in the holy instant, beginning now and reaching to eternity, but for a very simple reason. Do not obscure the simplicity of this reason, for if you do, it will be only because you prefer not to recognize it and not to let it go. The simple reason, simply stated, is this: The holy instant is a time in which you receive and give perfect communication. This means, however, that it is a time in which your mind is open, both to receive and give. It is the recognition that all minds are in communication. It therefore seeks to change nothing, but merely to accept everything." (T-15.IV.6:1-8)

"In time, you have been told to offer miracles as I direct, and let the Holy Spirit bring to you those who are seeking you. Yet in the holy instant you unite directly with God, and all your brothers join in Christ. Those who are joined in Christ are in no way separate. For Christ is the Self the Sonship shares, as God shares His Self with Christ." (T-15.V.10:7-10) I use Christ's vision to see all people as eternal, innocent and joyous spiritual beings, just as I am. We are all the same. Each of us is a wonderful ray emanating from Christ and, together, we are the Christ, God's One Son. We are also One with our Father and, as One, We are Heaven.

> "Fear not the holy instant will be denied you, for I [Jesus] denied it not. And through me the Holy Spirit gives it unto you as you will give it. <u>Let no need you perceive obscure your need of this</u>. For in the holy instant you will recognize the only need the Sons of God share equally, and by this recognition you will join with me in offering what is needed." (T-15.VI.6:7-10; underscore mine) The sentence that I underscored tells us the importance of practicing the holy instant.

> "The holy instant is truly the time of Christ. For in this liberating instant no guilt is laid upon the Son of God, and his unlimited power is thus restored to him. What other gift can you offer me [Jesus], when only this I choose to offer you? And to see me is to see me in everyone, and offer everyone the gift you offer me." (T-15.X.2:1-4)

In the Workbook of ACIM, these 5 final lessons are preceded by 6 paragraphs of introductory text. Following are the last 3 paragraphs which I have included in their entirety because they summarize all of ACIM very well:

> "It is our function to remember Him [God, our Father] on earth, as it is given us to be His Own completion in reality [Heaven]. So let us not forget our goal is shared, for it is that remembrance which contains the memory of God and points the way to Him and to the Heaven of His peace. And shall we not forgive our brother, who can offer this to us? [Answer – Yes, we must.] He [our brother] is the way, the truth and life that

shows the way to us. In him resides salvation, offered us through our forgiveness, given unto him. [As Jesus tells us elsewhere in ACIM, every person in the world is our savior, though we can't meet them all here.] (W-Final Lessons.Introduction.4:1-5)

"We will not end this year without the gift our Father promised to His Holy Son. We are forgiven now. And we are saved from all the wrath we thought belonged to God, and found it was a dream. [God has <u>nothing</u> to do with this dream world but He created the Holy Spirit to make sure we all wake up from it.] We are restored to sanity, in which we understand that anger is insane, attack is mad, and vengeance merely foolish fantasy. We have been saved from wrath because we learned we were mistaken. Nothing more than that. And is a father angry at his son because he failed to understand the truth?" [Answer – Not if he's a good father.] (W-Final Lessons.Introduction.5:1-7)

"We come in honesty to God and say we did not understand, and ask Him to help us learn His lessons through the Voice of His Own Teacher [Holy Spirit/Jesus]. Would He hurt His Son? [Answer – No, never!] Or would He rush to answer him, and say, 'This is my Son, and all I have is his?' [Answer – Yes, always!] Be certain He will answer thus, for these are His Own words to you. And more than that can no one ever have, for in these words is all there is, and all that there will be throughout all time and in eternity." (W-Final Lessons.Introduction.6:1-5)

One of Jesus' quotes I include above is "You could live forever in the holy instant, beginning now and reaching to eternity…" At this point in time, I am not always in a holy instant, although I've made a lot of progress towards this goal over my years of studying ACIM. This is consistent with another Jesus quote I've included above: "You can practice the mechanics of the holy instant, and will learn much from doing so." Over the years, I've received help from Jesus/Holy Spirit in refining the mechanics I use to get into the holy instant. While I'm sure other ACIM students use different mechanics, I felt it could be helpful to my readers to list my current approach wherein I say mentally to myself:

1. Forgiveness is the home of miracles. [just a fact]
2. What's a miracle?
3. Answer – I question the world and say 'I made all this up in my mind. It is not real.' I correct it or replace it with a holy instant.
4. How do I do a holy instant? [The balance of this numbered list answers this question.]
5. First I say: "I'm willing to give up all my littleness."
6. Next I say: "I'm humble before God but great in Him." [Comment: I'm great in God because I have everything He has, including all His Creation. I'm humble before Him because He is my Source and I am His effect. I acknowledge God is greater than I am.]
7. Then I say: "I forget the future."
8. Then I say: "This holy instant would I give to you, Jesus. Be you in charge. For I would follow you, certain that your direction gives me peace." [Comment: Note that I have substituted Jesus for the Holy Spirit in this lesson. The Holy Spirit's Voice and Jesus' voice are the same – As Jesus tells us in ACIM he (Jesus) is the manifestation of the Holy Spirit. Personally, I can identify readily with Jesus who was, like me, a man in this dream. I can't identify with the Holy Spirit.]
9. Now I think of Jesus and me alone in what I refer to as "the holy instant room" and say: "God grant me peace."
10. Jesus and I then jump into the Holy Spirit Who correctly perceives the whole world - He sees the whole world as an insane dream and corrects it for us.
11. Then, We step into Christ and We literally become Christ, God's Creation.
12. Then We, as Christ, dive into our Father and say: "We are surrounded by Your Love, Father. We are immersed in Your Love. We are Your Love. We are not a body. We are free. For

> We are still as You created us. Above the battleground, We are determined to see peace to Our Mind. Let all our thoughts be still." At this point in my mind, I am enjoying the peace of Heaven with no worldly thoughts at all. I am in a holy instant.

Although this might appear to be a lengthy process, it generally takes me less than 45 seconds to process all these steps in my mind.

ABOUT THE AUTHOR

James R. Laws grew up in a good family of five children learning good discipline, morals and respect for others. After high school he pursued a professional career which allowed him to earn a large salary. At the age of 26 he married and he and his wife were blessed with two children. Although Jimmy and his wife divorced in 1993, their two children (now adults) are both doing very well.

Jimmy and his first wife had been married for 17 years. In October, 1994, Jimmy got married to his second wife but she left him after only two months. This divorce gave Jimmy more reasons for drinking than he ever had and he became a daily drinker. This in turn caused him to get fired by his employer at the end of 1995. He had been with that company for nearly 20 years.

His drinking worsened after he lost his job and nearly cost him his life on more than one occasion. In August of 1997, he stopped drinking abruptly and has not had a drink since.

In 1998, a friend gave him a copy of *A Course in Miracles.* Jimmy took to the book and its program for living like a "duck takes to water." For all practical purposes, he has been studying it on a daily basis since early 1999.

In 2004, Jimmy moved to St. Martin in the Caribbean and lived there for two years. During that time, he met his third wife, Tesha Fortune who was a citizen of Guyana, South America. In May of 2006, Tesha and Jimmy moved from St. Martin to Guyana and were married on June 15, 2006.

Today, Jimmy and Tesha live in Arcadia, Florida with their wonderful 6-year old daughter, Jimesha. Tesha is, as of this writing, pregnant with their next baby who is due on March 20, 2014. Jimesha would prefer to have a baby sister (smile).

Author's Postscript: The actual writing of this book was completed on November 5, 2013. I am very pleased to say that on March 17, 2014, Tesha gave birth to a 7 lb. 11 oz. healthy and happy baby boy who we have named James Richard Laws, Jr. Even though he's not a girl, Jimesha is delighted with her little brother.

NOTES

NOTES

NOTES